POLICE OFFICER, NASSAU COUNTY
POLICE DEPARTMENT (NCPD)

DUTIES

Performs general law enforcement duties, and patrols an assigned area for the protection of lives and property, and the enforcement of laws and ordinances over which the Police Department has jurisdiction; performs related duties as required.

SCOPE OF THE EXAMINATION

The written test will cover knowledge, skills and/or abilities in such areas as:

1. Reading comprehension;
2. Reasoning ability;
3. Work, school and general life experiences that are associated with successful performance of law enforcement duties; and
4. Personality traits that are associated with successful performance of law enforcement duties.

HOW TO TAKE A TEST

I. YOU MUST PASS AN EXAMINATION

A. WHAT EVERY CANDIDATE SHOULD KNOW

Examination applicants often ask us for help in preparing for the written test. What can I study in advance? What kinds of questions will be asked? How will the test be given? How will the papers be graded?

As an applicant for a civil service examination, you may be wondering about some of these things. Our purpose here is to suggest effective methods of advance study and to describe civil service examinations.

Your chances for success on this examination can be increased if you know how to prepare. Those "pre-examination jitters" can be reduced if you know what to expect. You can even experience an adventure in good citizenship if you know why civil service exams are given.

B. WHY ARE CIVIL SERVICE EXAMINATIONS GIVEN?

Civil service examinations are important to you in two ways. As a citizen, you want public jobs filled by employees who know how to do their work. As a job seeker, you want a fair chance to compete for that job on an equal footing with other candidates. The best-known means of accomplishing this two-fold goal is the competitive examination.

Exams are widely publicized throughout the nation. They may be administered for jobs in federal, state, city, municipal, town or village governments or agencies.

Any citizen may apply, with some limitations, such as the age or residence of applicants. Your experience and education may be reviewed to see whether you meet the requirements for the particular examination. When these requirements exist, they are reasonable and applied consistently to all applicants. Thus, a competitive examination may cause you some uneasiness now, but it is your privilege and safeguard.

C. HOW ARE CIVIL SERVICE EXAMS DEVELOPED?

Examinations are carefully written by trained technicians who are specialists in the field known as "psychological measurement," in consultation with recognized authorities in the field of work that the test will cover. These experts recommend the subject matter areas or skills to be tested; only those knowledges or skills important to your success on the job are included. The most reliable books and source materials available are used as references. Together, the experts and technicians judge the difficulty level of the questions.

Test technicians know how to phrase questions so that the problem is clearly stated. Their ethics do not permit "trick" or "catch" questions. Questions may have been tried out on sample groups, or subjected to statistical analysis, to determine their usefulness.

Written tests are often used in combination with performance tests, ratings of training and experience, and oral interviews. All of these measures combine to form the best-known means of finding the right person for the right job.

II. HOW TO PASS THE WRITTEN TEST

A. NATURE OF THE EXAMINATION

To prepare intelligently for civil service examinations, you should know how they differ from school examinations you have taken. In school you were assigned certain definite pages to read or subjects to cover. The examination questions were quite detailed and usually emphasized memory. Civil service exams, on the other hand, try to discover your present ability to perform the duties of a position, plus your potentiality to learn these duties. In other words, a civil service exam attempts to predict how successful you will be. Questions cover such a broad area that they cannot be as minute and detailed as school exam questions.

In the public service similar kinds of work, or positions, are grouped together in one "class." This process is known as *position-classification*. All the positions in a class are paid according to the salary range for that class. One class title covers all of these positions, and they are all tested by the same examination.

B. FOUR BASIC STEPS

1) Study the announcement

How, then, can you know what subjects to study? Our best answer is: "Learn as much as possible about the class of positions for which you've applied." The exam will test the knowledge, skills and abilities needed to do the work.

Your most valuable source of information about the position you want is the official exam announcement. This announcement lists the training and experience qualifications. Check these standards and apply only if you come reasonably close to meeting them.

The brief description of the position in the examination announcement offers some clues to the subjects which will be tested. Think about the job itself. Review the duties in your mind. Can you perform them, or are there some in which you are rusty? Fill in the blank spots in your preparation.

Many jurisdictions preview the written test in the exam announcement by including a section called "Knowledge and Abilities Required," "Scope of the Examination," or some similar heading. Here you will find out specifically what fields will be tested.

2) Review your own background

Once you learn in general what the position is all about, and what you need to know to do the work, ask yourself which subjects you already know fairly well and which need improvement. You may wonder whether to concentrate on improving your strong areas or on building some background in your fields of weakness. When the announcement has specified "some knowledge" or "considerable knowledge," or has used adjectives like "beginning principles of…" or "advanced … methods," you can get a clue as to the number and difficulty of questions to be asked in any given field. More questions, and hence broader coverage, would be included for those subjects which are more important in the work. Now weigh your strengths and weaknesses against the job requirements and prepare accordingly.

3) Determine the level of the position

Another way to tell how intensively you should prepare is to understand the level of the job for which you are applying. Is it the entering level? In other words, is this the position in which beginners in a field of work are hired? Or is it an intermediate or advanced level? Sometimes this is indicated by such words as "Junior" or "Senior" in the class title. Other jurisdictions use Roman numerals to designate the level – Clerk I, Clerk II, for example. The word "Supervisor" sometimes appears in the title. If the level is not indicated by the title, check the description of duties. Will you be working under very close supervision, or will you have responsibility for independent decisions in this work?

4) Choose appropriate study materials

Now that you know the subjects to be examined and the relative amount of each subject to be covered, you can choose suitable study materials. For beginning level jobs, or even advanced ones, if you have a pronounced weakness in some aspect of your training, read a modern, standard textbook in that field. Be sure it is up to date and has general coverage. Such books are normally available at your library, and the librarian will be glad to help you locate one. For entry-level positions, questions of appropriate difficulty are chosen – neither highly advanced questions, nor those too simple. Such questions require careful thought but not advanced training.

If the position for which you are applying is technical or advanced, you will read more advanced, specialized material. If you are already familiar with the basic principles of your field, elementary textbooks would waste your time. Concentrate on advanced textbooks and technical periodicals. Think through the concepts and review difficult problems in your field.

These are all general sources. You can get more ideas on your own initiative, following these leads. For example, training manuals and publications of the government agency which employs workers in your field can be useful, particularly for technical and professional positions. A letter or visit to the government department involved may result in more specific study suggestions, and certainly will provide you with a more definite idea of the exact nature of the position you are seeking.

III. KINDS OF TESTS

Tests are used for purposes other than measuring knowledge and ability to perform specified duties. For some positions, it is equally important to test ability to make adjustments to new situations or to profit from training. In others, basic mental abilities not dependent on information are essential. Questions which test these things may not appear as pertinent to the duties of the position as those which test for knowledge and information. Yet they are often highly important parts of a fair examination. For very general questions, it is almost impossible to help you direct your study efforts. What we can do is to point out some of the more common of these general abilities needed in public service positions and describe some typical questions.

1) General information

Broad, general information has been found useful for predicting job success in some kinds of work. This is tested in a variety of ways, from vocabulary lists to questions about current events. Basic background in some field of work, such as sociology or economics, may be sampled in a group of questions. Often these are principles which have become familiar to most persons through exposure rather than through formal training. It is difficult to advise you how to study for these questions; being alert to the world around you is our best suggestion.

2) Verbal ability

An example of an ability needed in many positions is verbal or language ability. Verbal ability is, in brief, the ability to use and understand words. Vocabulary and grammar tests are typical measures of this ability. Reading comprehension or paragraph interpretation questions are common in many kinds of civil service tests. You are given a paragraph of written material and asked to find its central meaning.

3) Numerical ability

Number skills can be tested by the familiar arithmetic problem, by checking paired lists of numbers to see which are alike and which are different, or by interpreting charts and graphs. In the latter test, a graph may be printed in the test booklet which you are asked to use as the basis for answering questions.

4) Observation

A popular test for law-enforcement positions is the observation test. A picture is shown to you for several minutes, then taken away. Questions about the picture test your ability to observe both details and larger elements.

5) Following directions

In many positions in the public service, the employee must be able to carry out written instructions dependably and accurately. You may be given a chart with several columns, each column listing a variety of information. The questions require you to carry out directions involving the information given in the chart.

6) Skills and aptitudes

Performance tests effectively measure some manual skills and aptitudes. When the skill is one in which you are trained, such as typing or shorthand, you can practice. These tests are often very much like those given in business school or high school courses. For many of the other skills and aptitudes, however, no short-time preparation can be made. Skills and abilities natural to you or that you have developed throughout your lifetime are being tested.

Many of the general questions just described provide all the data needed to answer the questions and ask you to use your reasoning ability to find the answers. Your best preparation for these tests, as well as for tests of facts and ideas, is to be at your physical and mental best. You, no doubt, have your own methods of getting into an exam-taking mood and keeping "in shape." The next section lists some ideas on this subject.

IV. KINDS OF QUESTIONS

Only rarely is the "essay" question, which you answer in narrative form, used in civil service tests. Civil service tests are usually of the short-answer type. Full instructions for answering these questions will be given to you at the examination. But in case this is your first experience with short-answer questions and separate answer sheets, here is what you need to know:

1) Multiple-choice Questions

Most popular of the short-answer questions is the "multiple choice" or "best answer" question. It can be used, for example, to test for factual knowledge, ability to solve problems or judgment in meeting situations found at work.

A multiple-choice question is normally one of three types—

- It can begin with an incomplete statement followed by several possible endings. You are to find the one ending which *best* completes the statement, although some of the others may not be entirely wrong.
- It can also be a complete statement in the form of a question which is answered by choosing one of the statements listed.
- It can be in the form of a problem – again you select the best answer.

Here is an example of a multiple-choice question with a discussion which should give you some clues as to the method for choosing the right answer:

When an employee has a complaint about his assignment, the action which will *best* help him overcome his difficulty is to
A. discuss his difficulty with his coworkers
B. take the problem to the head of the organization
C. take the problem to the person who gave him the assignment
D. say nothing to anyone about his complaint

In answering this question, you should study each of the choices to find which is best. Consider choice "A" – Certainly an employee may discuss his complaint with fellow employees, but no change or improvement can result, and the complaint remains unresolved. Choice "B" is a poor choice since the head of the organization probably does not know what assignment you have been given, and taking your problem to him is known as "going over the head" of the supervisor. The supervisor, or person who made the assignment, is the person who can clarify it or correct any injustice. Choice "C" is, therefore, correct. To say nothing, as in choice "D," is unwise. Supervisors have and interest in knowing the problems employees are facing, and the employee is seeking a solution to his problem.

2) True/False Questions

The "true/false" or "right/wrong" form of question is sometimes used. Here a complete statement is given. Your job is to decide whether the statement is right or wrong.

SAMPLE: A roaming cell-phone call to a nearby city costs less than a non-roaming call to a distant city.

This statement is wrong, or false, since roaming calls are more expensive.
This is not a complete list of all possible question forms, although most of the others are variations of these common types. You will always get complete directions for

answering questions. Be sure you understand *how* to mark your answers – ask questions until you do.

V. RECORDING YOUR ANSWERS

Computer terminals are used more and more today for many different kinds of exams.

For an examination with very few applicants, you may be told to record your answers in the test booklet itself. Separate answer sheets are much more common. If this separate answer sheet is to be scored by machine – and this is often the case – it is highly important that you mark your answers correctly in order to get credit.

An electronic scoring machine is often used in civil service offices because of the speed with which papers can be scored. Machine-scored answer sheets must be marked with a pencil, which will be given to you. This pencil has a high graphite content which responds to the electronic scoring machine. As a matter of fact, stray dots may register as answers, so do not let your pencil rest on the answer sheet while you are pondering the correct answer. Also, if your pencil lead breaks or is otherwise defective, ask for another.

Since the answer sheet will be dropped in a slot in the scoring machine, be careful not to bend the corners or get the paper crumpled.

The answer sheet normally has five vertical columns of numbers, with 30 numbers to a column. These numbers correspond to the question numbers in your test booklet. After each number, going across the page are four or five pairs of dotted lines. These short dotted lines have small letters or numbers above them. The first two pairs may also have a "T" or "F" above the letters. This indicates that the first two pairs only are to be used if the questions are of the true-false type. If the questions are multiple choice, disregard the "T" and "F" and pay attention only to the small letters or numbers.

Answer your questions in the manner of the sample that follows:

> 32. The largest city in the United States is
>   A. Washington, D.C.
>   B. New York City
>   C. Chicago
>   D. Detroit
>   E. San Francisco

1) Choose the answer you think is best. (New York City is the largest, so "B" is correct.)
2) Find the row of dotted lines numbered the same as the question you are answering. (Find row number 32)
3) Find the pair of dotted lines corresponding to the answer. (Find the pair of lines under the mark "B.")
4) Make a solid black mark between the dotted lines.

VI. BEFORE THE TEST

Common sense will help you find procedures to follow to get ready for an examination. Too many of us, however, overlook these sensible measures. Indeed, nervousness and fatigue have been found to be the most serious reasons why applicants fail to do their best on civil service tests. Here is a list of reminders:

- Begin your preparation early – Don't wait until the last minute to go scurrying around for books and materials or to find out what the position is all about.
- Prepare continuously – An hour a night for a week is better than an all-night cram session. This has been definitely established. What is more, a night a week for a month will return better dividends than crowding your study into a shorter period of time.
- Locate the place of the exam – You have been sent a notice telling you when and where to report for the examination. If the location is in a different town or otherwise unfamiliar to you, it would be well to inquire the best route and learn something about the building.
- Relax the night before the test – Allow your mind to rest. Do not study at all that night. Plan some mild recreation or diversion; then go to bed early and get a good night's sleep.
- Get up early enough to make a leisurely trip to the place for the test – This way unforeseen events, traffic snarls, unfamiliar buildings, etc. will not upset you.
- Dress comfortably – A written test is not a fashion show. You will be known by number and not by name, so wear something comfortable.
- Leave excess paraphernalia at home – Shopping bags and odd bundles will get in your way. You need bring only the items mentioned in the official notice you received; usually everything you need is provided. Do not bring reference books to the exam. They will only confuse those last minutes and be taken away from you when in the test room.
- Arrive somewhat ahead of time – If because of transportation schedules you must get there very early, bring a newspaper or magazine to take your mind off yourself while waiting.
- Locate the examination room – When you have found the proper room, you will be directed to the seat or part of the room where you will sit. Sometimes you are given a sheet of instructions to read while you are waiting. Do not fill out any forms until you are told to do so; just read them and be prepared.
- Relax and prepare to listen to the instructions
- If you have any physical problem that may keep you from doing your best, be sure to tell the test administrator. If you are sick or in poor health, you really cannot do your best on the exam. You can come back and take the test some other time.

VII. AT THE TEST

The day of the test is here and you have the test booklet in your hand. The temptation to get going is very strong. Caution! There is more to success than knowing the right answers. You must know how to identify your papers and understand variations in the type of short-answer question used in this particular examination. Follow these suggestions for maximum results from your efforts:

1) Cooperate with the monitor

The test administrator has a duty to create a situation in which you can be as much at ease as possible. He will give instructions, tell you when to begin, check to see that you are marking your answer sheet correctly, and so on. He is not there to guard you, although he will see that your competitors do not take unfair advantage. He wants to help you do your best.

2) Listen to all instructions

Don't jump the gun! Wait until you understand all directions. In most civil service tests you get more time than you need to answer the questions. So don't be in a hurry. Read each word of instructions until you clearly understand the meaning. Study the examples, listen to all announcements and follow directions. Ask questions if you do not understand what to do.

3) Identify your papers

Civil service exams are usually identified by number only. You will be assigned a number; you must not put your name on your test papers. Be sure to copy your number correctly. Since more than one exam may be given, copy your exact examination title.

4) Plan your time

Unless you are told that a test is a "speed" or "rate of work" test, speed itself is usually not important. Time enough to answer all the questions will be provided, but this does not mean that you have all day. An overall time limit has been set. Divide the total time (in minutes) by the number of questions to determine the approximate time you have for each question.

5) Do not linger over difficult questions

If you come across a difficult question, mark it with a paper clip (useful to have along) and come back to it when you have been through the booklet. One caution if you do this – be sure to skip a number on your answer sheet as well. Check often to be sure that you have not lost your place and that you are marking in the row numbered the same as the question you are answering.

6) Read the questions

Be sure you know what the question asks! Many capable people are unsuccessful because they failed to *read* the questions correctly.

7) Answer all questions

Unless you have been instructed that a penalty will be deducted for incorrect answers, it is better to guess than to omit a question.

8) Speed tests

It is often better NOT to guess on speed tests. It has been found that on timed tests people are tempted to spend the last few seconds before time is called in marking answers at random – without even reading them – in the hope of picking up a few extra points. To discourage this practice, the instructions may warn you that your score will be "corrected" for guessing. That is, a penalty will be applied. The incorrect answers will be deducted from the correct ones, or some other penalty formula will be used.

9) Review your answers

If you finish before time is called, go back to the questions you guessed or omitted to give them further thought. Review other answers if you have time.

10) Return your test materials

If you are ready to leave before others have finished or time is called, take ALL your materials to the monitor and leave quietly. Never take any test material with you. The monitor can discover whose papers are not complete, and taking a test booklet may be grounds for disqualification.

VIII. EXAMINATION TECHNIQUES

1) Read the general instructions carefully. These are usually printed on the first page of the exam booklet. As a rule, these instructions refer to the timing of the examination; the fact that you should not start work until the signal and must stop work at a signal, etc. If there are any *special* instructions, such as a choice of questions to be answered, make sure that you note this instruction carefully.

2) When you are ready to start work on the examination, that is as soon as the signal has been given, read the instructions to each question booklet, underline any key words or phrases, such as *least*, *best*, *outline*, *describe* and the like. In this way you will tend to answer as requested rather than discover on reviewing your paper that you *listed without describing*, that you selected the *worst* choice rather than the *best* choice, etc.

3) If the examination is of the objective or multiple-choice type – that is, each question will also give a series of possible answers: A, B, C or D, and you are called upon to select the best answer and write the letter next to that answer on your answer paper – it is advisable to start answering each question in turn. There may be anywhere from 50 to 100 such questions in the three or four hours allotted and you can see how much time would be taken if you read through all the questions before beginning to answer any. Furthermore, if you come across a question or group of questions which you know would be difficult to answer, it would undoubtedly affect your handling of all the other questions.

4) If the examination is of the essay type and contains but a few questions, it is a moot point as to whether you should read all the questions before starting to answer any one. Of course, if you are given a choice – say five out of seven and the like – then it is essential to read all the questions so you can eliminate the two that are most difficult. If, however, you are asked to answer all the questions, there may be danger in trying to answer the easiest one first because you may find that you will spend too much time on it. The best technique is to answer the first question, then proceed to the second, etc.

5) Time your answers. Before the exam begins, write down the time it started, then add the time allowed for the examination and write down the time it must be completed, then divide the time available somewhat as follows:

- If 3-1/2 hours are allowed, that would be 210 minutes. If you have 80 objective-type questions, that would be an average of 2-1/2 minutes per question. Allow yourself no more than 2 minutes per question, or a total of 160 minutes, which will permit about 50 minutes to review.
- If for the time allotment of 210 minutes there are 7 essay questions to answer, that would average about 30 minutes a question. Give yourself only 25 minutes per question so that you have about 35 minutes to review.

6) The most important instruction is to *read each question* and make sure you know what is wanted. The second most important instruction is to *time yourself properly* so that you answer every question. The third most important instruction is to *answer every question*. Guess if you have to but include something for each question. Remember that you will receive no credit for a blank and will probably receive some credit if you write something in answer to an essay question. If you guess a letter – say "B" for a multiple-choice question – you may have guessed right. If you leave a blank as an answer to a multiple-choice question, the examiners may respect your feelings but it will not add a point to your score. Some exams may penalize you for wrong answers, so in such cases *only*, you may not want to guess unless you have some basis for your answer.

7) Suggestions
   a. Objective-type questions
      1. Examine the question booklet for proper sequence of pages and questions
      2. Read all instructions carefully
      3. Skip any question which seems too difficult; return to it after all other questions have been answered
      4. Apportion your time properly; do not spend too much time on any single question or group of questions
      5. Note and underline key words – *all, most, fewest, least, best, worst, same, opposite,* etc.
      6. Pay particular attention to negatives
      7. Note unusual option, e.g., unduly long, short, complex, different or similar in content to the body of the question
      8. Observe the use of "hedging" words – *probably, may, most likely,* etc.
      9. Make sure that your answer is put next to the same number as the question
      10. Do not second-guess unless you have good reason to believe the second answer is definitely more correct
      11. Cross out original answer if you decide another answer is more accurate; do not erase until you are ready to hand your paper in
      12. Answer all questions; guess unless instructed otherwise
      13. Leave time for review

   b. Essay questions
      1. Read each question carefully
      2. Determine exactly what is wanted. Underline key words or phrases.
      3. Decide on outline or paragraph answer

4. Include many different points and elements unless asked to develop any one or two points or elements
5. Show impartiality by giving pros and cons unless directed to select one side only
6. Make and write down any assumptions you find necessary to answer the questions
7. Watch your English, grammar, punctuation and choice of words
8. Time your answers; don't crowd material

8) Answering the essay question

Most essay questions can be answered by framing the specific response around several key words or ideas. Here are a few such key words or ideas:

M's: manpower, materials, methods, money, management
P's: purpose, program, policy, plan, procedure, practice, problems, pitfalls, personnel, public relations
    a. Six basic steps in handling problems:
        1. Preliminary plan and background development
        2. Collect information, data and facts
        3. Analyze and interpret information, data and facts
        4. Analyze and develop solutions as well as make recommendations
        5. Prepare report and sell recommendations
        6. Install recommendations and follow up effectiveness

    b. Pitfalls to avoid
        1. *Taking things for granted* – A statement of the situation does not necessarily imply that each of the elements is necessarily true; for example, a complaint may be invalid and biased so that all that can be taken for granted is that a complaint has been registered
        2. *Considering only one side of a situation* – Wherever possible, indicate several alternatives and then point out the reasons you selected the best one
        3. *Failing to indicate follow up* – Whenever your answer indicates action on your part, make certain that you will take proper follow-up action to see how successful your recommendations, procedures or actions turn out to be
        4. *Taking too long in answering any single question* – Remember to time your answers properly

IX. AFTER THE TEST

Scoring procedures differ in detail among civil service jurisdictions although the general principles are the same. Whether the papers are hand-scored or graded by machine we have described, they are nearly always graded by number. That is, the person who marks the paper knows only the number – never the name – of the applicant. Not until all the papers have been graded will they be matched with names. If other tests, such as training and experience or oral interview ratings have been given, scores will be combined. Different parts of the examination usually have different weights. For example, the written test might count 60 percent of the final grade, and a rating of training and experience 40 percent. In many jurisdictions, veterans will have a certain number of points added to their grades.

After the final grade has been determined, the names are placed in grade order and an eligible list is established. There are various methods for resolving ties between those who get the same final grade – probably the most common is to place first the name of the person whose application was received first. Job offers are made from the eligible list in the order the names appear on it. You will be notified of your grade and your rank as soon as all these computations have been made. This will be done as rapidly as possible.

People who are found to meet the requirements in the announcement are called "eligibles." Their names are put on a list of eligible candidates. An eligible's chances of getting a job depend on how high he stands on this list and how fast agencies are filling jobs from the list.

When a job is to be filled from a list of eligibles, the agency asks for the names of people on the list of eligibles for that job. When the civil service commission receives this request, it sends to the agency the names of the three people highest on this list. Or, if the job to be filled has specialized requirements, the office sends the agency the names of the top three persons who meet these requirements from the general list.

The appointing officer makes a choice from among the three people whose names were sent to him. If the selected person accepts the appointment, the names of the others are put back on the list to be considered for future openings.

That is the rule in hiring from all kinds of eligible lists, whether they are for typist, carpenter, chemist, or something else. For every vacancy, the appointing officer has his choice of any one of the top three eligibles on the list. This explains why the person whose name is on top of the list sometimes does not get an appointment when some of the persons lower on the list do. If the appointing officer chooses the second or third eligible, the No. 1 eligible does not get a job at once, but stays on the list until he is appointed or the list is terminated.

X. HOW TO PASS THE INTERVIEW TEST

The examination for which you applied requires an oral interview test. You have already taken the written test and you are now being called for the interview test – the final part of the formal examination.

You may think that it is not possible to prepare for an interview test and that there are no procedures to follow during an interview. Our purpose is to point out some things you can do in advance that will help you and some good rules to follow and pitfalls to avoid while you are being interviewed.

What is an interview supposed to test?

The written examination is designed to test the technical knowledge and competence of the candidate; the oral is designed to evaluate intangible qualities, not readily measured otherwise, and to establish a list showing the relative fitness of each candidate – as measured against his competitors – for the position sought. Scoring is not on the basis of "right" and "wrong," but on a sliding scale of values ranging from "not passable" to "outstanding." As a matter of fact, it is possible to achieve a relatively low score without a single "incorrect" answer because of evident weakness in the qualities being measured.

Occasionally, an examination may consist entirely of an oral test – either an individual or a group oral. In such cases, information is sought concerning the technical knowledges and abilities of the candidate, since there has been no written examination for this purpose. More commonly, however, an oral test is used to supplement a written examination.

Who conducts interviews?

The composition of oral boards varies among different jurisdictions. In nearly all, a representative of the personnel department serves as chairman. One of the members of the board may be a representative of the department in which the candidate would work. In some cases, "outside experts" are used, and, frequently, a businessman or some other representative of the general public is asked to serve. Labor and management or other special groups may be represented. The aim is to secure the services of experts in the appropriate field.

However the board is composed, it is a good idea (and not at all improper or unethical) to ascertain in advance of the interview who the members are and what groups they represent. When you are introduced to them, you will have some idea of their backgrounds and interests, and at least you will not stutter and stammer over their names.

What should be done before the interview?

While knowledge about the board members is useful and takes some of the surprise element out of the interview, there is other preparation which is more substantive. It *is* possible to prepare for an oral interview – in several ways:

1) Keep a copy of your application and review it carefully before the interview

This may be the only document before the oral board, and the starting point of the interview. Know what education and experience you have listed there, and the sequence and dates of all of it. Sometimes the board will ask you to review the highlights of your experience for them; you should not have to hem and haw doing it.

2) Study the class specification and the examination announcement

Usually, the oral board has one or both of these to guide them. The qualities, characteristics or knowledges required by the position sought are stated in these documents. They offer valuable clues as to the nature of the oral interview. For example, if the job involves supervisory responsibilities, the announcement will usually indicate that knowledge of modern supervisory methods and the qualifications of the candidate as a supervisor will be tested. If so, you can expect such questions, frequently in the form of a hypothetical situation which you are expected to solve. NEVER go into an oral without knowledge of the duties and responsibilities of the job you seek.

3) Think through each qualification required

Try to visualize the kind of questions you would ask if you were a board member. How well could you answer them? Try especially to appraise your own knowledge and background in each area, *measured against the job sought*, and identify any areas in which you are weak. Be critical and realistic – do not flatter yourself.

4) Do some general reading in areas in which you feel you may be weak

For example, if the job involves supervision and your past experience has NOT, some general reading in supervisory methods and practices, particularly in the field of human relations, might be useful. Do NOT study agency procedures or detailed manuals. The oral board will be testing your understanding and capacity, not your memory.

5) Get a good night's sleep and watch your general health and mental attitude

You will want a clear head at the interview. Take care of a cold or any other minor ailment, and of course, no hangovers.

What should be done on the day of the interview?

Now comes the day of the interview itself. Give yourself plenty of time to get there. Plan to arrive somewhat ahead of the scheduled time, particularly if your appointment is in the fore part of the day. If a previous candidate fails to appear, the board might be ready for you a bit early. By early afternoon an oral board is almost invariably behind schedule if there are many candidates, and you may have to wait. Take along a book or magazine to read, or your application to review, but leave any extraneous material in the waiting room when you go in for your interview. In any event, relax and compose yourself.

The matter of dress is important. The board is forming impressions about you – from your experience, your manners, your attitude, and your appearance. Give your personal appearance careful attention. Dress your best, but not your flashiest. Choose conservative, appropriate clothing, and be sure it is immaculate. This is a business interview, and your appearance should indicate that you regard it as such. Besides, being well groomed and properly dressed will help boost your confidence.

Sooner or later, someone will call your name and escort you into the interview room. *This is it.* From here on you are on your own. It is too late for any more preparation. But remember, you asked for this opportunity to prove your fitness, and you are here because your request was granted.

What happens when you go in?

The usual sequence of events will be as follows: The clerk (who is often the board stenographer) will introduce you to the chairman of the oral board, who will introduce you to the other members of the board. Acknowledge the introductions before you sit down. Do not be surprised if you find a microphone facing you or a stenotypist sitting by. Oral interviews are usually recorded in the event of an appeal or other review.

Usually the chairman of the board will open the interview by reviewing the highlights of your education and work experience from your application – primarily for the benefit of the other members of the board, as well as to get the material into the record. Do not interrupt or comment unless there is an error or significant misinterpretation; if that is the case, do not hesitate. But do not quibble about insignificant matters. Also, he will usually ask you some question about your education, experience or your present job – partly to get you to start talking and to establish the interviewing "rapport." He may start the actual questioning, or turn it over to one of the other members. Frequently, each member undertakes the questioning on a particular area, one in which he is perhaps most competent, so you can expect each member to participate in the examination. Because time is limited, you may also expect some rather abrupt switches in the direction the questioning takes, so do not be upset by it. Normally, a board member will not pursue a single line of questioning unless he discovers a particular strength or weakness.

After each member has participated, the chairman will usually ask whether any member has any further questions, then will ask you if you have anything you wish to add. Unless you are expecting this question, it may floor you. Worse, it may start you off on an extended, extemporaneous speech. The board is not usually seeking more information. The question is principally to offer you a last opportunity to present further qualifications or to indicate that you have nothing to add. So, if you feel that a significant qualification or characteristic has been overlooked, it is proper to point it out in a sentence or so. Do not compliment the board on the thoroughness of their examination – they have been sketchy, and you know it. If you wish, merely say, "No thank you, I have nothing further to add." This is a point where you can "talk yourself out" of a good impression or fail to present an important bit of information. Remember, *you close the interview yourself.*

The chairman will then say, "That is all, Mr. _____, thank you." Do not be startled; the interview is over, and quicker than you think. Thank him, gather your belongings and take your leave. Save your sigh of relief for the other side of the door.

How to put your best foot forward

Throughout this entire process, you may feel that the board individually and collectively is trying to pierce your defenses, seek out your hidden weaknesses and embarrass and confuse you. Actually, this is not true. They are obliged to make an appraisal of your qualifications for the job you are seeking, and they want to see you in your best light. Remember, they must interview all candidates and a non-cooperative candidate may become a failure in spite of their best efforts to bring out his qualifications. Here are 15 suggestions that will help you:

1) Be natural – Keep your attitude confident, not cocky

If you are not confident that you can do the job, do not expect the board to be. Do not apologize for your weaknesses, try to bring out your strong points. The board is interested in a positive, not negative, presentation. Cockiness will antagonize any board member and make him wonder if you are covering up a weakness by a false show of strength.

2) Get comfortable, but don't lounge or sprawl

Sit erectly but not stiffly. A careless posture may lead the board to conclude that you are careless in other things, or at least that you are not impressed by the importance of the occasion. Either conclusion is natural, even if incorrect. Do not fuss with your clothing, a pencil or an ashtray. Your hands may occasionally be useful to emphasize a point; do not let them become a point of distraction.

3) Do not wisecrack or make small talk

This is a serious situation, and your attitude should show that you consider it as such. Further, the time of the board is limited – they do not want to waste it, and neither should you.

4) Do not exaggerate your experience or abilities

In the first place, from information in the application or other interviews and sources, the board may know more about you than you think. Secondly, you probably will not get away with it. An experienced board is rather adept at spotting such a situation, so do not take the chance.

5) If you know a board member, do not make a point of it, yet do not hide it

Certainly you are not fooling him, and probably not the other members of the board. Do not try to take advantage of your acquaintanceship – it will probably do you little good.

6) Do not dominate the interview

Let the board do that. They will give you the clues – do not assume that you have to do all the talking. Realize that the board has a number of questions to ask you, and do not try to take up all the interview time by showing off your extensive knowledge of the answer to the first one.

7) Be attentive

You only have 20 minutes or so, and you should keep your attention at its sharpest throughout. When a member is addressing a problem or question to you, give him your undivided attention. Address your reply principally to him, but do not exclude the other board members.

8) Do not interrupt

A board member may be stating a problem for you to analyze. He will ask you a question when the time comes. Let him state the problem, and wait for the question.

9) Make sure you understand the question

Do not try to answer until you are sure what the question is. If it is not clear, restate it in your own words or ask the board member to clarify it for you. However, do not haggle about minor elements.

10) Reply promptly but not hastily

A common entry on oral board rating sheets is "candidate responded readily," or "candidate hesitated in replies." Respond as promptly and quickly as you can, but do not jump to a hasty, ill-considered answer.

11) Do not be peremptory in your answers

A brief answer is proper – but do not fire your answer back. That is a losing game from your point of view. The board member can probably ask questions much faster than you can answer them.

12) Do not try to create the answer you think the board member wants

He is interested in what kind of mind you have and how it works – not in playing games. Furthermore, he can usually spot this practice and will actually grade you down on it.

13) Do not switch sides in your reply merely to agree with a board member

Frequently, a member will take a contrary position merely to draw you out and to see if you are willing and able to defend your point of view. Do not start a debate, yet do not surrender a good position. If a position is worth taking, it is worth defending.

14) Do not be afraid to admit an error in judgment if you are shown to be wrong

The board knows that you are forced to reply without any opportunity for careful consideration. Your answer may be demonstrably wrong. If so, admit it and get on with the interview.

15) Do not dwell at length on your present job

The opening question may relate to your present assignment. Answer the question but do not go into an extended discussion. You are being examined for a *new* job, not your present one. As a matter of fact, try to phrase ALL your answers in terms of the job for which you are being examined.

Basis of Rating

Probably you will forget most of these "do's" and "don'ts" when you walk into the oral interview room. Even remembering them all will not ensure you a passing grade. Perhaps you did not have the qualifications in the first place. But remembering them will help you to put your best foot forward, without treading on the toes of the board members.

Rumor and popular opinion to the contrary notwithstanding, an oral board wants you to make the best appearance possible. They know you are under pressure – but they also want to see how you respond to it as a guide to what your reaction would be under the pressures of the job you seek. They will be influenced by the degree of poise you display, the personal traits you show and the manner in which you respond.

ABOUT THIS BOOK

This book contains tests divided into Examination Sections. Go through each test, answering every question in the margin. At the end of each test look at the answer key and check your answers. On the ones you got wrong, look at the right answer choice and learn. Do not fill in the answers first. Do not memorize the questions and answers, but understand the answer and principles involved. On your test, the questions will likely be different from the samples. Questions are changed and new ones added. If you understand these past questions you should have success with any changes that arise. Tests may consist of several types of questions. We have additional books on each subject should more study be advisable or necessary for you. Finally, the more you study, the better prepared you will be. This book is intended to be the last thing you study before you walk into the examination room. Prior study of relevant texts is also recommended. NLC publishes some of these in our Fundamental Series. Knowledge and good sense are important factors in passing your exam. Good luck also helps. So now study this Passbook, absorb the material contained within and take that knowledge into the examination. Then do your best to pass that exam.

EXAMINATION SECTION

EXAMINATION SECTION
TEST 1

DIRECTIONS: Each question or incomplete statement is followed by several suggested answers or completions. Select the one the BEST answers the question or completes the statement. *PRINT THE LETTER OF THE CORRECT ANSWER IN THE SPACE AT THE RIGHT.*

1. Which of the following events would typically cause the greatest amount of stress in a person's life?

    A. A major change in financial status
    B. Vacation
    C. Pregnancy
    D. Marital separation

1.____

2. A local shopping center has experienced a recent rash of shoplifting. Officer Jones is patrolling the mall parking lot frequently. Which situation below should Officer Jones regard as most suspicious?

    A. A man running out a store entrance with a shopping bag from the store under his arm.
    B. A car parked for a long time near the front entrance of the store.
    C. A woman loading a pile of clothes, some with plastic security tags still attached, into the trunk of her car.
    D. A young man walking around looking in through the windows of various parked cars.

2.____

3. An officer is faced with the responsibility of telling a woman her husband has been murdered. While the officers should phrase the news as gently as possible, he or she should also demonstrate empathy nonverbally. The best way to do this is to

    A. stand with the arms crossed
    B. hold the woman closely
    C. maintain eye contact
    D. tell the woman you understand her pain

3.____

4. Cognitive symptoms of anxiety include

    A. rapid heart rate
    B. feelings of fear or helplessness
    C. poor social functioning
    D. euphoria

4.____

5. Which of the following is MOST likely to help a person to improve her attitude?

    A. Avoiding people who make her feel bad about herself
    B. Learning to become more goal-oriented
    C. Learning to look more clearly at her own faults
    D. Taking charge of an unruly situation

5.____

6. A suspect has been handcuffed, but refuses to take a seat in the patrol car after several requests. The arresting officer should

6.____

A. tap the suspect behind the knees with the baton, just hard enough so that the suspect's legs will fold and he can be inserted into the car
B. tighten the handcuffs until the pain compels compliance
C. try to frighten the suspect with threats
D. inform the suspect of the consequences for resisting arrest

7. Each of the following is likely to be a cause of stress on the job, EXCEPT　　7.____

A. work overload
B. differences in organizational and personal values
C. a narrowly-defined role
D. time pressures

8. In communicating with people, especially in stressful or high-conflict situations, nonver-　　8.____
bal communication is

A. more important than the verbal message
B. less important than the verbal message
C. universal across all cultures
D. typically contradictory to the verbal message

9. Problem-oriented police work does NOT　　9.____

A. help officers get to the roots of a crime problem
B. offer a proactive model for policing
C. focus on responding to calls for service
D. have any impact on preventing or reducing crime

10. The difference between assertiveness and aggressiveness is that　　10.____

A. assertiveness is not potentially harmful to others
B. aggressiveness involves strangers
C. aggressiveness has to do with achieving goals
D. assertiveness is always negative

11. As an officer and his partner arrive to investigate a reported domestic disturbance, the　　11.____
husband and wife are still arguing. In the presence of the officers, each spouse makes a
verbal threat of physical harm against the other. In resolving this conflict, the FINAL step
that should be taken by the officers is to

A. indicate the consequences if this behavior continues
B. empathize with each of the spouses
C. present the spouses with problem-solving strategies
D. describe the behaviors that appeared to cause the disturbance

12. Elements of community policing include　　12.____
　　　I.　the police
　　　II.　the business community
　　　III.　the media
　　　IV.　religious institutions

A. I and II　　　　　　　　　　　　　　B. I, II and III
C. I and III　　　　　　　　　　　　　　D. I, II, III and IV

2

13. In a grocery store parking lot, a pair of officers arrest both the buyer and seller in an alleged drug transaction in a grocery store parking lot. After the suspects have been handcuffed and placed in a patrol car, one of the officers notices a wad of bills on the ground where the transaction took place. The officer pockets the money and decides to keep it, telling herself that the money is "dirty" and that she has more of a right to it than either of the criminal suspects. Legally, the officer has committed a crime; ethically, she has committed a(n)

    A. rationalization
    B. kickback
    C. stereotyping
    D. deviance

13.____

14. Probably the most effective way to deal with on-the-job stress is to

    A. find alternative employment
    B. take early retirement
    C. participate in a personal wellness program
    D. acquire assertiveness skills that will help confront the people responsible for the stress

14.____

Questions 15 and 16 deal with the following situation: A pharmacist has complained to the police department that several drug addicts in his neighborhood have been attempting to obtain drugs illegally, usually by passing fake prescriptions.

15. Which of the following people should arouse the most suspicion when approaching the prescription counter?

    A. A middle-aged woman who appears homeless and is poorly groomed
    B. A young African-American male in a hooded sweatshirton a hot day
    C. A man in his thirties who glances around furtively and brings a large amount of nonprescription items to the counter for purchase
    D. None of the above should be regarded as suspicious on the basis of their appearance alone

15.____

16. After refusing to fill several prescriptions, the pharmacist describes or gives each of the prescriptions to an investigating officer. Which of the following most warrants investigation?

    A. A written prescription that is covered with several coffee rings
    B. A prescription written on a Post-It note
    C. A written prescription for pain killers with a date indicating it was written more than a week ago
    D. A prescription that is phoned in by a doctor

16.____

17. An individual's personality, whether normal or deviant, will always

    A. refer to the person's deep inner self, rather than just superficial aspects
    B. involve unique characteristics that are all different from another person's
    C. be a product of social and cultural environments, with no biological foundation
    D. be organized into patterns that are observable and measurable to some degree

17.____

18. Change in a person's life that is due to personal growth is almost always

    A. negative   B. dramatic
    C. positive   D. minor

18._____

19. Residents in an urban neighborhood have complained of a recent increase in gang-related graffiti in their community. Which of the following should be regarded as most suspicious by an officer on patrol?

    A. One young man walking down the street and flashing gang signs at passing cars
    B. A pair of teenagers riding their bicycles in a tenement parking lot late at night
    C. A group of teenagers hanging out in a convenience store parking lot, leaning against a wall that is covered with graffiti.
    D. A group of teenagers hanging out in a convenience store parking lot. One of the teenagers has a spray paint can.

19._____

20. Common symptoms of stress include each of the following, EXCEPT

    A. digestive problems
    B. sluggishness
    C. sleep problems
    D. emotional instability

20._____

21. The general goal of community policing is

    A. a lower overall crime rate
    B. conviction of criminals who are caught in the community
    C. fewer violent crimes
    D. a higher quality of life in the community

21._____

22. In most settings, the simplest and most effective method of stopping sexual harassment is to

    A. threaten the person with legal or administrative consequences
    B. ignore it
    C. avoid the person as much as possible
    D. ask or tell the person to stop

22._____

23. Of the following types of crime, the one most likely to have a widespread impact on a victim's community is

    A. hate or bias crime
    B. workplace violence
    C. theft
    D. sexual assault

23._____

24. Functional roles of the police include
    I. Crime prevention
    II. Order maintenance
    III. Public service
    IV. Criminal prosecution

    A. I only   B. I and II
    C. I, II and III   D. I, II, III and IV

24._____

25. A pre-existing thought or belief that people have about members of a given group- 25.____
whether the belief is positive, negative, or neutral-is

    A. ethnocentrism
    B. a stereotype
    C. self-centeredness
    D. discrimination

KEY (CORRECT ANSWERS)

1.	D		11.	A
2.	C		12.	D
3.	C		13.	A
4.	B		14.	C
5.	B		15.	D
6.	D		16.	B
7.	C		17.	D
8.	A		18.	B
9.	C		19.	D
10.	A		20.	B

21.	D
22.	D
23.	A
24.	C
25.	B

TEST 2

DIRECTIONS: Each question or incomplete statement is followed by several suggested answers or completions. Select the one the BEST answers the question or completes the statement. *PRINT THE LETTER OF THE CORRECT ANSWER IN THE SPACE AT THE RIGHT.*

1. Role expectations for police officers generally

    A. are consistent across the country, with a strong focus on peacekeeping
    B. change from community to community, depending on the local culture
    C. direct them to be more lenient with juvenile offenders
    D. direct them to be self-reliant in both preventing and investigating crime

1._____

2. Officer Shinjo takes a complaint from a woman who says she is being stalked by a man who is a classmate in one of her night business courses. The man has sent her unwanted gifts and left numerous unanswered telephone messages, but she did not become concerned until last night, when she noticed the man following her home from class. She asks Officer Shinjo what to do about the situation. At least part of Officer Shinjo's advice to the woman should include the suggestion that she

    A. immediately apply for a restraining order
    B. create a logbook to document each of the stalking incidents in as much detail as possible
    C. answer one of the man's telephone calls and try to explain that the unwanted attention is making her uncomfortable
    D. call the man herself and threaten legal action if he doesn't stop bothering her

2._____

3. Which of the following is an element of self-direction?

    A. Knowing when to seek help from others
    B. Being able to get from one geographic location to another without a map
    C. Establishing and reaching both short- and long-term goals
    D. Adopting healthier lifestyle habits

3._____

4. Each of the following factors is typically associated with ethnicity, EXCEPT

    A. culture   B. language
    C. economic status   D. physical characteristics

4._____

5. Among the communication skills necessary for effective communication with people, the foundation upon which all others are based is considered to be

    A. confrontation   B. authoritativeness
    C. attending behavior   D. observation

5._____

6. Which of the following offers the best definition of the word "ethics?"

    A. An individual's means of obtaining what he wants from and for other people in a society
    B. Standards of conduct that express a society's concept of right and wrong
    C. A formal code of conduct that delineates a strict set of rules and a framework for punishment
    D. Morality and the consequences of behaviors

6._____

7. Which of the following is a measurement of a rate?   7.____

    A. The ratio of the number of new African American arrestees for drug-related crimes
        in the 35-49 age bracket during a specific year, compared to the number of African
        Americans in the same age group in the entire community
    B. The number of white females, aged 18-25, who are arrested each year on child
        endangerment charges
    C. The percentage change in the number of property crimes in a given year, com-
        pared to the previous year.
    D. The ratio of the number of persons currently under prosecution for violent crimes to
        the number of people, aged 14-55, in the entire community

8. In recent weeks, several patrons at a local restaurant have had their cars broken into by   8.____
    having a window smashed in, and then having valuable items taken from the car. Officer
    Jackson is patrolling restaurant parking lot. Which situation below should she regard as
    most suspicious?

    A. A young man in a hooded sweatshirt walking around the parking lot at lunchtime,
        carrying a long, heavy flashlight.
    B. A car parked so as to partially block other cars from exiting the parking lot
    C. A man's voice raised in anger coming from the parking lot
    D. Several young men leaning against the outside of the parking lot fence in the early
        evening, bouncing a basketball and apparently waiting for the arrival of another
        person.

9. Among the skills important to effective communication with people, the most complex   9.____
    and difficult to master are those that help to

    A. encourage
    B. confront
    C. influence
    D. summarize

10. The first step in dealing with an alcohol or drug addiction is to   10.____

    A. admit there is a problem
    B. talk to a counselor or close friend
    C. stop taking the drug or drinking alcohol
    D. join a support group or enter a rehabilitation center

11. Key elements of police professionalism include   11.____
        I.   an advanced education
        II. a clearly stated code of ethics
        III. accountability through peer review
        IV. demonstrated understanding of the field's core body of knowl edge

    A. I and II
    B. I, III and IV
    C. II, III and IVs
    D. I, II, III and IV

12. A factor that makes a police officer susceptible to corruption is that the officer   12.___

    A. is typically different from most members of society
    B. can be sure that if a suspect is arrested, the suspect will be prosecuted and punished
    C. is usually better off financially than most of the people she interacts with in carrying out her duties
    D. has the professional discretion not to enforce the law

13. In resolving an ethical dilemma, a police officer's FIRST step should generally be to   13.___

    A. identify the ethical issues that are in conflict
    B. identify the people and organizations likely to be affected by the decision
    C. consult with colleagues and appropriate experts
    D. examine the reasons in favor of and opposed to each possible course of action

14. During a lengthy interview with a witness, an officer decides to use "reflection of meaning" strategies in order to clarify the information he's being given. This strategy would involve each of the following, EXCEPT   14.___

    A. trying to paraphrase longer statements offered by the witness
    B. closing with a check on the witness's words, such as "So do I understand this correctly?"
    C. beginning sentences with phrases such as "You mean...." or "Sounds as if you saw...."
    D. offering an interpretation of the witness's words

15. Officer McGee is meeting with several community members to determine a course of action for reducing gang-related activities in the area. Each of the following is a guideline to be used by an officer in building a constructive relationship with community members, EXCEPT   15.___

    A. viewing community members as equals
    B. adopting a completely neutral tone of voice when speaking with people
    C. using a shared vocabulary of easily understood, nonoffensive words
    D. asking for the input of community members before making any suggestions

16. In solving a complex problem, the first step is always to   16.___

    A. develop a plan
    B. gather information
    C. define the problem
    D. envision contingencies

17. Role conflict can occur when an officer encounters two sets of expectations that are inconsistent with each other. Role strain can occur when an officer's role is limited by what he or she is authorized to do. The main difference between these two is that   17.___

    A. role conflict is relatively rare among police officers
    B. role conflict can be resolved; role strain cannot
    C. role strain creates stressful situations for officers
    D. role strain has a greater influence on the officer's exercise of discretion

18. Generally, police community relations differs from public relations, in that they   18.____

    A. consider the needs of the community first
    B. are much more successful in reducing social problems
    C. are without inherent spheres of interest
    D. encourage two-way communications

19. Factors that place a man at risk as a potential batterer include each of the following,   19.____
EXCEPT

    A. poverty
    B. drug or alcohol use
    C. 30-45 years of age
    D. witnessing spousal abuse between parents

20. The four major categories of commonly abused substances include   20.____

    A. stimulants
    B. alcohol
    C. nicotine
    D. caffeine

21. After receiving their monthly assistance payments from the local social services agency,   21.____
some members of the homeless community immediately use the money to carry out
drug transactions. In his patrol of the area around the agency, which situation below
should Officer Garcia regard as most suspicious?

    A. A group of several homeless people who meet every day in a local park, where
       they sit together for about three hours and then move on
    B. A homeless woman who walks up and down the entire length of a busy city street
       all day long, endlessly smoking cigarettes
    C. An abandoned car that sits on a privately-owned lot and is used as a sleeping
       place by several homeless people throughout the day
    D. A single man remaining in the same area for several hours at a time, during which
       many homeless people approach him and greet him with handshakes

22. The most significant factor that requires police to perform functions other than law   22.____
enforcement is

    A. greater public trust relative to other agencies or institutions
    B. a broader resource base
    C. round-the-clock availability
    D. the level of police interaction with community members

23. A "minority" group is a group that is discriminated against on the basis of   23.____

    A. physical or cultural characteristics
    B. the size of the group relative to the majority
    C. race
    D. the group's degree of conformity to the norms of the majority

24. An officer is talking with a resident of a high-crime urban neighborhood about a recent increase in drug-related activities. Because of the active police presence in the area, some residents are suspicious of the police. Each of the following nonverbal cues is a likely indicator of distrust on the part of a listener, EXCEPT

24.____

   A. holding arms crossed over one's chest
   B. steady eye contact
   C. clenched jaw
   D. shoulders angled away from speaker

25. Personality characteristics necessary for the successful performance of police duties include

25.____

   I. dependent style in problem-solving
   II. emotional expressiveness in interpersonal communication
   III. cohesiveness in group performance
   IV. emotional restraint

   A. I and III
   B. I, II and IV
   C. II, III and IV
   D. I, II, III and IV

KEY (CORRECT ANSWERS)

1.	B		11.	D
2.	B		12.	D
3.	C		13.	A
4.	C		14.	D
5.	C		15.	B
6.	B		16.	C
7.	B		17.	B
8.	A		18.	D
9.	C		19.	C
10.	A		20.	A

21.	D
22.	C
23.	A
24.	B
25.	C

EXAMINATION SECTION
TEST 1

DIRECTIONS: Each question or incomplete statement is followed by several suggested answers or completions. Select the one the BEST answers the question or completes the statement. *PRINT THE LETTER OF THE CORRECT ANSWER IN THE SPACE AT THE RIGHT.*

1. Officer Hayes has arrived at the scene of an automobile accident to find the two drivers arguing heatedly in the middle of the intersection, where their two cars remain entangled by their front bumpers. Traffic has backed up on all four sides of the intersection. As Officer Hayes approaches, the two drivers each begin to tell their side of the story at the same time. As they grow more agitated and begin to call each other names, one of the drivers threatens the other with physical harm. In this situation, Officer Hayes' first action should be to

    A. ask each driver to stand on an opposite corner of the intersection and wait for him to begin documenting the accident
    B. call a tow truck to clear the accident from the intersection
    C. arrest the driver who made the threat
    D. ask the drivers to pull their cars out of the intersection and off to the side of the road

1.____

2. Probably the most important thing a police officer can do to build and strengthen a trusting relationship with community members is to

    A. patrol the area often and conspicuously
    B. listen to them in a respectful and nonjudgemental way
    C. make sure people understand his background and qualifications
    D. establish clear, reachable goals for improving the community

2.____

3. Which of the following is NOT a factor that should influence an officer's exercise of discretion?

    A. Clear statutes and protocols
    B. Informal expectations of legislatures and the public
    C. Use of force
    D. Limited resources

3.____

4. The term for the policing style which emphasizes order maintenance is _____ style.

    A. service
    B. coercive
    C. watchman
    D. legalistic

4.____

5. Officer Torres, a community service law enforcement officer, approaches the home of recent Vietnamese immigrants to speak to several community members gathered there. He notices several pairs of shoes on the front porch. It is reasonable for Officer Torres to assume that

    A. the people in the home are superstitious
    B. the house must have some religious significance

5.____

C. if he removes his own shoes before entering, it will be perceived as a sign of respect
D. the homeowners are having their carpets cleaned

6. Ethical issues are   6._____

   A. usually a problem only in individual behaviors
   B. relevant to all aspects of police work
   C. usually referred to a board or committee for decision-making
   D. the same as legal issues

7. In using the "reflection of meaning" technique in a client interview, a social worker should   7._____
   do each of the following, EXCEPT

   A. Begin with a sentence stem such as "You mean..." or "Sounds like you believe..."
   B. Offer an interpretation of the client's words.
   C. Add paraphrasing of longer client statements.
   D. Close with a "check-out" such as, "Am I hearing you right?"

8. A police officer is speaking with a victim who is hearing-impaired. The police officer   8._____
   should try to do each of the following, EXCEPT

   A. speak slowly and clearly
   B. gradually increase the volume of his voice
   C. face the victim squarely
   D. reduce or eliminate any background or ambient noise

9. An officer is interviewing a witness who is a recent immigrant from China. In general, the   9._____
   officer should avoid

   A. verbal tracking or requests for clarification
   B. open-ended questions
   C. sustained eye contact
   D. attentive body language

10. Which of the following statements about rape is FALSE?   10._____

    A. The use of alcohol and drugs can reduce sexual inhibitions.
    B. Rape is a crime of violence.
    C. Rape is a crime that can only be committed against women.
    D. It is not a sustainable legal charge if the partner has already consented to sex in the past.

11. A person's individual code of ethics is typically determined by each of the following fac-   11._____
    tors, EXCEPT

    A. reason
    B. religion
    C. emotion
    D. law

12. Officer Long, new to the urban precinct where he is assigned patrol, has received a pair of complaints from two customers about the owner of a local convenience store, who works the cash register on most days. According to one customer, the owner became angry and ordered her out of the store after she had asked the price of a certain item. The other customer claims that on another occasion, the owner pulled a handgun from behind the counter and trained it on him as he walked slowly out of the store with his hands up. Each of the customers has lived in the neighborhood for many years and has never before seen or heard of any strange behavior on the owner's part.
In investigating these complaints, Officer Long should suspect that

12.____

    A. the owner should be considered armed and dangerous, and any entry into the store should be made with weapons drawn
    B. the cause of the problem is most likely the onset of a serious psychological disturbance
    C. the customers may have reasons to be untruthful about the convenience store owner
    D. the store owner has probably experienced a recent trauma, such as a robbery attempt or a personal loss

13. Typical signs and symptoms of stress include

13.____

    I. weakened immune system
    II. prolonged, vivid daydreams
    III. insomnia
    IV. depression

    A. I only
    B. I, III and IV
    C. III and IV
    D. I, II, III and IV

14. Other than solid, ethical police work, an officer's best defense against a lawsuit or complaint is usually

14.____

    A. detailed case records
    B. a capable advocate
    C. a vigorous counterclaim against the plaintiff
    D. the testimony of professional character witnesses

15. Assertive people

15.____

    A. avoid stating feelings, opinions, or desires
    B. appear passive, but behave aggressively
    C. state their views and needs directly
    D. appear aggressive, but behave passively

16. In the non-verbal communication process, meaning is most commonly provided by

16.____

    A. body language
    B. touch
    C. tone of voice
    D. context

17. The most obvious practical benefit that deviance has on a society is the

    A. advancement of the status quo
    B. vindication of new laws
    C. inducement to reach cultural goals
    D. promotion of social unity

    17.____

18. What is the term for policing that focuses on providing a wider and more thorough array of social services to defeat the social problems that cause crime?

    A. Reflective policing
    B. Order maintenance
    C. Social engineering
    D. Holistic policing

    18.____

19. The term "active listening" mostly refers to a person's ability to

    A. both listen and accomplish other tasks at the same time
    B. take an active role in determining which information is provided by the speaker
    C. concentrate on what is being said
    D. indicate with numerous physical cues that he/she is listening

    19.____

20. Police officers in any jurisdiction are most likely to receive calls about

    A. threats
    B. suspicious persons
    C. petty theft or property crime
    D. disturbances, such as family arguments

    20.____

21. Which of the following is NOT a physiological explanation for rape?

    A. uncontrollable sex drive
    B. lack of available partners
    C. reaction to repressed desires
    D. consequence of the natural selection process.

    21.____

22. Which of the following is an element of self-discipline?

    A. Establishing and reaching short-term goals
    B. Establishing and reaching long-term goals
    C. Taking an honest look at one's lifestyle and making conscious changes toward improvement
    D. Taking an honest look at one's personality and revealing traits, both good and bad, to others

    22.____

23. Most of the events in a person's life are the result of

    A. chance events
    B. a sense of intuition
    C. individual choices and decisions
    D. the decisions of one's parents or other authority figures

    23.____

24. Which of the following is the most effective way for a department to limit the discretion exercised by police officers?　24.____

   A. Open and flexible departmental directives
   B. Close supervision by departmental management
   C. Broadening role definitions for officers.
   D. Statutory protection from civil liability lawsuits

25. Police officers who demonstrate critical thinking skills are also more likely to demonstrate each of the following, EXCEPT　25.____

   A. the ability to empathize
   B. the tendency to criticize
   C. self-awareness
   D. reflective thinking

KEY (CORRECT ANSWERS)

1. A		11. D	
2. B		12. D	
3. A		13. B	
4. C		14. A	
5. C		15. C	
6. B		16. A	
7. B		17. D	
8. B		18. D	
9. C		19. C	
10. D		20. D	

21. C
22. C
23. C
24. B
25. B

TEST 2

DIRECTIONS: Each question or incomplete statement is followed by several suggested answers or completions. Select the one the BEST answers the question or completes the statement. *PRINT THE LETTER OF THE CORRECT ANSWER IN THE SPACE AT THE RIGHT.*

1. Officer Park responds to a domestic disturbance call to find a mother and her two young children huddled together in the living room, all of them crying. The mother explains that her husband is no longer there; he flew into a fit of rage and then stormed out to join his friends for a night of drinking. Officer Park's first action would most likely be to

    A. determine the location of the husband
    B. contact the appropriate social services agency, to arrange a consultation
    C. try to calm the family down and ask the mother to explain what happened
    D. refer the mother to a local battered-spouse shelter

1.____

2. Most commonly, the reason for crimes involving stranger violence is

    A. anger
    B. retaliation
    C. hate
    D. robbery

2.____

3. For a police officer, "burst stress" is most likely to be caused by

    A. a shootout
    B. financial troubles
    C. departmental politics
    D. substance abuse

3.____

4. The most significant factor in whether a person achieves success in his/her personal life, school, and career is

    A. intelligence
    B. a positive attitude
    C. existing financial resources
    D. innate ability

4.____

5. Typically, a professional code of ethics

    A. embodies a broad picture of expected moral conduct.
    B. is voluntary
    C. provides specific guidance for performance in situations
    D. are decided by objective ethicists outside of the profession

5.____

6. Components recognized by contemporary society as elements of sexual harassment include
    I. abuse of power
    II. immature behavior
    III. sexual desire
    IV. hormonal imbalance

6.____

A. I only
B. I and III
C. II and III
D. I, II, III and IV

7. The phrase "substance abuse" is typically defined as   7.____

    A. an addiction to an illegal substance
    B. the continued use of a psychoactive substance even after it creates problems in a person's life
    C. the overuse of an illegal substance
    D. a situation in which a person craves a drug and organizes his or her life around obtaining it

8. The humanist perspective of behavior holds that people who commit crimes or otherwise act badly are   8.____

    A. willfully disregarding societal norms
    B. reacting to the deprivation of basic needs
    C. suffering from a psychological illness
    D. experiencing a moral lapse

9. Which of the following is NOT involved in the process of empathic listening?   9.____

    A. actually hearing exactly what the other person is saying
    B. searching for the "hidden meanings" behind statements
    C. listening without judgement
    D. communicating that you're hearing what the other person is saying, both verbally and nonverbally

10. Which of the following is NOT a component in developing a stress-resistant lifestyle?   10.____

    A. Finding leisure time
    B. Eating nutritious foods
    C. Getting enough sleep
    D. Seeking financial independence

11. Which of the following was NOT a factor that led to the expansion of a community policing model?   11.____

    A. Information obtained at a crime scene during a preliminary investigation was the most important factor determining the probability of an arrest.
    B. Police response times typically had little to do with the probability of making an arrest.
    C. Traditional "preventive patrols" generally failed to reduce crime.
    D. People who knew police officers personally often tried to take advantage of them.

12. Most of the correspondence in a pyramid scheme that has defrauded several elderly victims has been traced to a post office box in a rural area. Probably the simplest and most efficient way of arresting the suspect(s) in this case would be to   12.____

A. use an elderly man as a "victim" to lure the suspects into an attempt to defraud him
B. address a letter to the post office box asking the user to come in for questioning
C. check Postal Service records to see who is leasing the post office box
D. physically observe the post office box for a while, to see who is using it

13. The process of hiring a police officer typically involves each of the following, EXCEPT   13.____

    A. technical preparation
    B. medical examination
    C. background checks
    D. physical ability test

14. The most common form of rape is _____ rape.   14.____

    A. stranger
    B. acquaintance
    C. sadistic rape
    D. spousal rape

15. Officer Stevens and his partner respond to a domestic disturbance call involving a father   15.____
and his teenage daughter. As the officers arrive at their home, the two are still arguing
heatedly, but when the officers enter, the daughter retreats to the kitchen, where she continues crying. The father explains that his wife, the daughter's mother, died last year, and
the daughter's behavior and school performance have suffered as a result. The father is
afraid that the daughter is falling in with the wrong crowd, and may be getting involved
with drugs. He is afraid for her and doesn't know what to do.
Within the scope of his police role, the most appropriate action for Officer Stevens to
take in this case would be to

    A. warn both the father and the daughter of the potential consequences of conviction
on a charge of disturbing the peace
    B. refer the father and the daughter to a social services or counseling agency
    C. inform the daughter of the drug statutes that may apply in her case as a way to
influence her choices
    D. question the daughter about her feelings surrounding the death of her mother

16. During an interview, a suspect confesses to the rape of a co-worker that occurred in the   16.____
office after the rest of the employees had left for the day. The suspect says he was tor-
mented by the seductive behavior of the co-worker until he could no longer stand it. He
was himself a victim, he says. In this case, the suspect is making use of the psychological defense mechanism known as

    A. projection
    B. regression
    C. denial
    D. sublimation

17. Which of the following is NOT a good stress-reduction strategy?   17.____

    A. Spend some time each day doing absolutely nothing
    B. Become more assertive
    C. Develop a hobby
    D. Have a sense of humor

18. The term for the policing style which emphasizes problem-solving is _____ style.   18.____

    A. watchman
    B. order maintenance
    C. service
    D. legalistic

19. According to current rules and statutes, any employer   19.____

    A. may inquire as to a job applicant's age or date of birth
    B. may keep on file information regarding an employee's race, color, religion, sex, or national origin.
    C. may refuse employment to someone without a car
    D. must give a woman who has taken time off for maternity leave her same job and salary when she is ready to return to work

20. During a conversation with the mother of a teenage boy who has been arrested twice for shoplifting, an officer attempts to be an active listener as the mother explains why she thinks the boy is having so much trouble. Being an active listener includes each of the following strategies, EXCEPT   20.____

    A. putting the speaker at ease
    B. interrupting with questions to clarify meaning
    C. summarizing the speaker's major ideas and feelings
    D. withholding criticism

21. Which of the following is NOT a characteristic of the typical poverty-class family?   21.____

    A. Female-headed, single-parent families
    B. Unwed parents
    C. Isolated from neighbors and relatives
    D. High divorce rates

22. When speaking with community members about improving the quality of life in the neighborhood, an officer should look for signs of social desirability bias among the people with whom he's talking. Social desirability bias often causes people to   22.____

    A. judge other people based on their social role rather than inner character
    B. attribute their successes to skill, while blaming external factors for failures
    C. modify their interactions or behaviors based on what they think is acceptable to others
    D. contend for leadership positions

23. For a number of reasons, Officer Stone thinks a fellow officer might have a drinking problem, and decides to talk to her about it. The officer says she doesn't have a drinking problem; she doesn't even take a drink until after it gets dark. Her answer indicates that she   23.____

    A. doesn't have a drinking problem
    B. is probably a social drinker
    C. drinks more during the winter months
    D. is in denial

19

24. Factors which shape the police role include each of the following, EXCEPT 24.____

    A. individual goals
    B. role expectations
    C. role acquisition
    D. multiple-role phenomenon

25. "Deviance" is a social term denoting 25.____

    A. any violation of norms
    B. any serious violation of norms
    C. a type of nonconforming behavior recognizable in all cultures
    D. a specific set of crime statistics

KEY (CORRECT ANSWERS)

1. C			11. D
2. D			12. D
3. A			13. A
4. B			14. B
5. A			15. B
6. A			16. A
7. B			17. A
8. B			18. C
9. B			19. B
10. D			20. B

21. C
22. C
23. D
24. A
25. A

POLICE SCIENCE

EXAMINATION SECTION
TEST 1

DIRECTIONS: Each question or incomplete statement is followed by several suggested answers or completions. Select the one that *BEST* answers the question or completes the statement. *PRINT THE LETTER OF THE CORRECT ANSWER IN THE SPACE AT THE RIGHT.*

1. The police department is charged with the preservation of the public peace, the preven-   1._____
    tion of crime and so on. In order to carry out these duties the police commissioner is
    given many powers.
    The *one* of the following which is *NOT* a power or duty of the commissioner is to

    A.   issue, revoke and suspend licenses for taxi drivers
    B.   generally supervise and inspect the activities of pawnbrokers
    C.   erect and operate a telegraph system for police work
    D.   have charge of all institutions of the city for the care and custody of criminals
    E.   guard the public health.

2. The police department works in cooperation with the health and sanitation departments.   2._____
    Members of the department, therefore, give to officials of these two departments all
    proper assistance in carrying out their duties.
    A function which is *LEAST* representative of those performed by *either* of these
    departments is to

    A.   keep a record of births and deaths in the city
    B.   maintain and operate city-owned hospitals
    C.   move and dispose of refuse
    D.   adopt rules specifying the kind of ashes and garbage the city will collect
    E.   alter, amend or repeal any part of the sanitary code.

3. The police commissioner, upon the requisition of the department of health, details suit-   3._____
    able officers and men to the service of such department of health for the purpose of
    enforcement of the provisions of the sanitary code. Of the following activities, the *one*
    which is *LEAST* affected by the provisions of the sanitary code is the

    A.   sale of drugs   B.   sale of food and drink
    C.   board and care of children
    D.   placing of wall paper on the walls of tenement houses
    E.   renting of buildings as dwelling places

4. A thief committed a felony by stealing a sum of money. Of the following, the fact which   4._____
    would determine for the *most* part whether the maximum offense he could be charged
    with is grand or petit larceny is:

    A.   The age of the thief
    B.   Whether he intended to commit a serious crime
    C.   The county in which the crime was committed
    D.   Whether it was a first or second offense
    E.   The amount of money

5. You are getting the description of a lost diamond bracelet. Of the following, the MOST important piece of information, in addition to knowing that the missing item is a diamond bracelet, is:

    A. Value - $10,000
    B. Material - platinum
    C. Diamonds - many small and several large diamonds
    D. Owner - Mrs. H. Jones
    E. Design - Two intertwining snakes

5._____

6. You are watching a great number of people leave a ball game. Of the persons who are described below, the one whom it would be EASIEST to spot would be:

    A. Female; age 15; height 5'6"; weight 130 lbs; long straight black hair
    B. Male; age 20; height 5'8"; weight 150 lbs.; missing toe on right foot
    C. Male; age 60; height 5'7"; weight 170 lbs.; all false teeth
    D. Male; age 25; height 6'3"; weight 220 lbs.; pockmarked
    E. Female; age 35; height 5'4"; weight 150 lbs.; wears glasses

6._____

7. You are preparing a description of a woman to be broadcast .
Of the following characteristics, the one which would be of MOST value to a man driving a squad car is:

    A. Wanted for murder   B. Age 45 years
    C. Height 6'1"   D. Smokes very heavily
    E. Frequents moving picture theaters

7._____

8. Stationed at your post, you are given the description of a vehicle which has been stolen. Of the following characteristics, the one which will permit you to eliminate MOST EAS-ILY a large number of vehicles is:

    A. No spare tire Make
    B. Buick, two-door coupe, 2002
    C. Motor number - 16x432
    D. Tires 750x16, white-walled
    E. Color - black

8._____

9. A man is making a great deal of undue noise in the street. Of the following, the MOST valid reason for not giving him a summons is that

    A. there is obviously no intention to annoy anyone
    B. the man is selling newspapers
    C. it is a first offense
    D. the noise is caused by a defective exhaust pipe
    E. the man is repairing his automobile

9._____

10. A famous detective said that he always assumes every case of death to be a case of suicide and then looks for clues to prove his case.
The BEST evaluation of this procedure is that it is

    A. desirable, as it gives a definite starting point
    B. undesirable, as it sets up a formal procedure
    C. undesirable, as it precludes the use of a formal procedure
    D. undesirable, as it might tend to blind the investigation to clues which do not fit his assumption

10._____

    E.   *desirable,* as it permits the investigator to proceed on a case without too much thinking

11.   Where a satisfactory adjustment can be made without arresting the delinquent minor, it is done. Court action is only taken where it seems best for the minor or the community.
Of the following, the *BEST* justification for this procedure is that

    A.   court cases are costly to the community
    B.   rehabilitation of the delinquent minor is of primary importance
    C.   arresting minors may become a source of inconvenience if not discouraged
    D.   juvenile delinquency can increase if juvenile delinquents are not arrested
    E.   punishment is only a means to an end and ,in consequence, should be used with care

11._____

12.   During your tour of duty, you find an obviously insane person.
For you to take him to the station house, which is four short blocks away, at once would be

    A.   *desirable,* as the man may not know where he is
    B.   *undesirable,* it would take you away from your rounds
    C.   *undesirable,* it would be better to call the station house
    D.   *undesirable,* it would be more expeditious to call a hospital
    E.   *desirable,* as it would settle the matter with a minimum of time taken from your rounds

12._____

13.   If possible, the principal witnesses, especially the most trustworthy ones, should be heard *before* the suspect is interrogated.
The *MOST* valid reason for this procedure is that

    A.   the investigator will tend to be more adequately informed when he questions the suspect
    B.   waiting to be questioned increases the pressure on the suspect
    C.   the suspect has to wait at any rate
    D.   all witnesses should be heard before the suspect
    E.   trustworthy witnesses tend to become untrustworthy if kept waiting

13._____

14.   It is important that the policeman or detective establish the fact that the crime reported is *bona fide.*
This procedure may be *BEST* evaluated as

    A.   *necessary,* as many crimes are reported which have not taken place
    B.   *unnecessary,* as in only few cases are crimes simulated
    C.   *unnecessary,* as general investigation will show the nature of the crime without any emphasis on validity
    D.   *unnecessary,* as it may take considerable time better spent in apprehending the criminal
    E.   *necessary,* as it gives the investigator a starting point

14._____

15.   The four witnesses to the bank robbery, including the bank president and the cashier, were left together for one hour in the president's office at the bank before they were questioned.
This type of procedure is

15._____

A. *desirable and considerate,* as there is no point in treating respectable citizens as criminals
B. *unwise,* as it permits undue pressure to be brought upon some of the witnesses
C. *unwise,* as it permits an exchange of actual and imagined details which may result in invalid testimony
D. *unwise,* as the president may not want the others in his office
E. *wise,* as it keeps the witnesses all in one place

16. You are on your way to report for an assignment when you see two men fighting on the street.   16.____
For you to attempt to stop the fight would be

A. *unjustified;* it is none of your business
B. *justified; a* fight between individuals may turn into a riot
C. *unjustified;* you may get hurt with the result that you will not be able to report for duty
D. *justified;* as a policeman it is your duty to see that the public peace is kept
E. *unjustified;* the men do not want anyone to intrude

17. Patrolling your post, you notice a crap game in progress. The three men involved have   17.____
been previously warned.
The *BEST* action to take would be to

A. call for additional police help
B. ignore the situation
C. break up the game and take the dice
D. inform the group that you want the game to stop
E. arrest the group

18. While patrolling your post, you notice several people in two groups enter an old aban-   18.____
doned house by means of the rear entrance.
The *BEST* action to take would be to

A. call headquarters notifying your superior of the occurrence
B. ignore the situation
C. enter the house, gun drawn
D. arrest all the people
E. note the occurrence by an entry in your memorandum book

19. On a dark background,bloodstains are often difficult to recognize. When searching for   19.____
bloodstains in such cases, one should use a flashlight, even in the daytime.
Of the following, the *BEST* reason for this procedure is that

A. it is important to get as much light as possible
B. the contrast around the edges of the light is great
C. artificial light may make differentiation between the blood and the background pos-sible
D. the light will cause the dark background to seem lighter
E. the movement of the flashlight will cause a moving reflection

20. When a defendant claims that the presence of blood sprinkles on his clothing is due to the fact that he has touched such clothing with bloody hands, one can immediately conclude that he is lying.
The fact upon which this conclusion is based is *most nearly* that

    A. nothing absorbs blood
    B. blood does not sprinkle
    C. fingerprints would have been left by the defendant if he had touched the clothing
    D. bloody hands will not leave the described mark
    E. the defendant's hands were bloody

20.____

21. With respect to traffic regulations, the law provides that, when it is deemed necessary, a police officer is authorized to give orders and instructions contrary to any provision of these laws and regulations for the purpose of expeditiously moving traffic.
Of the following, the *MOST* direct justification for this provision is that

    A. expeditious moving of traffic usually requires changing regulations
    B. fixed traffic laws and regulations cannot cover all possible events
    C. police officers must have authorization to perform their duties
    D. police officers must be able to give instructions contrary to law
    E. moving traffic requires changing regulations

21.____

22. With respect to minor traffic violations, the police officer should be guided *FOREMOST* by the consideration that

    A. violations must be punished
    B. most violations are deliberate
    C. the aim is to discourage violations
    D. some violations are unintentional
    E. violators are, in effect, criminals

22.____

23. In taking a statement from a defendant which may be presented in court, it is *MOST* desirable that the answers to the first questions asked should indicate

    A. how the person is involved in the case
    B. that no threats or promises have been used
    C. the reasons for the statement
    D. in a concise manner the scope of the statements
    E. any peculiar circumstances surrounding the case

23.____

24. One of the first steps a member of the emergency squad will take upon finding a package suspected to contain a time-bomb is to immerse it in lubricating oil.
Of the following, the *BEST* reason for this action is that the lubricating oil

    A. has a cooling effect and, therefore, will prevent an explosion
    B. will prevent any sudden shock from being transmitted to the bomb
    C. is a non-conductor of electricity
    D. has a low specific gravity which will tend to keep the bomb immersed
    E. will tend to stop the works of a clock with the oil

24.____

25. An officer using hand signals is directing traffic at a congested intersection. It is *LEAST* important that the   25.____

    A. officer be visible
    B. officer be accessible
    C. officer be distinguishable
    D. signs used by the officer be simple
    E. signs used by the officer be uniform

_____

KEY (CORRECT ANSWERS)

1.	D		11.	B
2.	B		12.	E
3.	D		13.	A
4.	E		14.	A
5.	E		15.	C
6.	D		16.	D
7.	C		17.	E
8.	B		18.	A
9.	C		19.	C
10.	D		20.	D

21.	B
22.	C
23.	B
24.	E
25.	B

_____

TEST 2

DIRECTIONS: Each question or incomplete statement is followed by several suggested answers or completions. Select the one that *BEST* answers the question or completes the statement. *PRINT THE LETTER OF THE CORRECT ANSWER IN THE SPACE AT THE RIGHT.*

1. A writ which directs a detaining agent to produce a prisoner at a designated place and time, together with the day and cause of his detention, is *MOST* correctly called a writ of   1.____

    A. mandamus   B. execution   C. habeas corpus
    D. surety   E. extradition

2. The purpose and effect of the section are to abolish the distinction which, heretofore, existed in cases of felony between a *principal,* and an *accessory* before the fact. The word "accessory," as used in this sentence, means, most nearly,   2.____

    A. appendage   B. assistant   C. complement
    D. situation existing   E. additional

3. The word "principal," as used in the sentence in question 2, means, most nearly,   3.____

    A. prime mover   B. probity   C. motive
    D. maximum   E. tenet

4. Arraignment is, most nearly: 4.____

    A. The statement of pleading on the part of the people of the state regarding an offense in question.
    B. Directing the arrest of an offender against whom an indictment has been found.
    C. Preparation of a prisoner to appear before a court for sentence.
    D. The assembling of all the charges and evidence supporting the charges.
    E. The reading under the jurisdiction of a court of an indictment or information to a defendant and delivering a copy to him.

5. The bullet to be examined is at first inspected for *adhering* particles. The word "adhering" means, most nearly,   5.____

    A. small   B. deforming   C. detaching
    D. clinging   E. loose

6. To constitute an attempt to commit a crime, an *overt* act, beyond mere preparation, in furtherance of that design, must be done. The word "overt," as used in this sentence, means, most nearly,   6.____

    A. important   B. open   C. planned
    D. serious   E. criminal

7. Any person who by *duress* interferes with the free exercise of the elective *franchise* by any voter is guilty of a misdemeanor. The word "duress," as used in this sentence, means, most nearly,   7.____

    A. any illegal means   B. any fraudulent device
    C. abduction   D. misdirection
    E. compulsion

8. The word "franchise," as used in the sentence in question 7, means, most nearly,   8.____

    A. indulgence   B. prerogative
    C. charter (as for public utility)
    D. permission   E. obligation

9. *Corroboration* of the criminal's identity should be obtained, if possible, from persons   9.____
other than the victim. The word "corroboration," as used in this sentence, means, most
nearly,

    A. authentication   B. vindication   C. description
    D. deduction   E. apprehension

10. "Venue" means, most nearly,   10.____

    A. a list of persons summoned for jury service
    B. intense malice caused by an unbalanced mind
    C. the place within which a jury must be gathered and the case tried
    D. material witnesses for the defense
    E. an illegal sale

11. Where the language of an *instrument* has a settled legal meaning, its construction is not   11.____
open to evidence.
The word "instrument," as used in this sentence, means, most nearly,

    A. the formal expression of a legal agreement
    B. a court decision   C. any legal act
    D. any means of accomplishment   E. an implement

12. "Zoning laws" relate, most nearly, to   12.____

    A. city boundaries   B. police jurisdiction
    C. legal ownership of property
    D. regulation of traffic
    E. regulation of use and construction of buildings

13. A "plaintiff" means, most nearly, a person   13.____

    A. who has been confined in a prison
    B. who sues another person
    C. who is suspected of committing a crime
    D. against whom a charge of breaking a law has been made
    E. who requires the services of an attorney

14. The accomplishment of theft or larceny from the person or immediate presence of   14.____
another in possession thereof by force or intimidation is

    A. swindle   B. peculation   C. robbery
    D. burglary   E. pilfering

15. The procedure for the surrender of an alleged criminal by one state to another having   15.____
jurisdiction to try the charge is called

    A. extradition   B. indictment   C. rendition
    D. sedition   E. legal pursuit

16. Contradictory testimony from witnesses claiming to have seen the same event is not
infrequent. Every day in our courts of law men swear in good faith to having seen things
which on cross-examination, they admit they were not in a position to observe clearly.
This paragraph asserts, most nearly, that eye-witnesses of good faith should be
expected

    A. sometimes to be upset emotionally by hostile cross-examination
    B. never to give contradictory testimony
    C. sometimes to observe inaccurately
    D. to contradict themselves
    E. sometimes to swear to testimony which they know in advance to be false

16._____

17. A "crime" is an act committed or omitted in violation of a public law either forbidding or
commanding it.
This statement implies, most nearly, that

    A. crimes can be omitted
    B. a forbidding act if omitted is a crime
    C. an act of omission may be criminal
    D. to commit an act not commanded is criminal
    E. some acts are acts of commission

17._____

18. He who by command, counsellor assistance procures another to commit a crime is, in
morals and in law, as culpable as the visible actor himself, for the reason that the criminal
act, whichever it may be, is imputable to the person who conceived it and set the forces
in motion for its actual accomplishment.
Of the following, the MOST accurate inference from the above sentence is that

    A. a criminal act does not have to be committed for a crime to be committed
    B. acting as counselor for a criminal is a crime
    C. the mere counseling of a criminal act can never be a crime if no criminal act is committed
    D. only the visible actor himself can be criminal
    E. a person acting only as an adviser may be guilty of committing a criminal act

18._____

19. The large number of fatal motor-vehicle accidents renders necessary the organization of
special units in the police department to cope with the technical problems encountered in
such investigations.
The generalization which can be inferred MOST DIRECTLY from this statement is that

    A. large problems require specialists
    B. technical problems require specialists
    C. many police problems require special handling
    D. many policemen are specialists
    E. the number of motor-vehicle accidents which are fatal is large

19._____

20. An explanation is relevant to a problem if it expresses connections between a set of facts
and the fact being investigated; it is irrelevant otherwise.
According to this statement, an explanation is not relevant to a problem if it

    A. expresses a connection between the fact being investigated and a set of facts
    B. denies the existence of any positive connection between a set of facts and the fact being investigated

20._____

C. expresses a false connection between a set of facts and the fact being investigated
D. expresses no connection between a set of facts and the fact being investigated
E. expresses only a few of the connections between a set of facts and the fact being investigated

21. In examining the scene of a homicide one should not only look for the usual, standard traces - fingerprints, footprints, etc. - but should also have eyes open for details which at first glance may not seem to have any connection with the crime.
The *MOST* logical inference to be drawn from this statement is that

A. in general, standard traces are not important
B. sometimes one should not look for footprints
C. usually only the usual, standard traces are important
D. one cannot tell in advance what will be important
E. details which have no connection with the crime may be important

21._____

22. Pistols with the same number of barrel grooves may be differentiated by the direction of the twist of the rifling, which may be either to the left or to the right. Of the following statements, the *one* which can *MOST* accurately be inferred from the statement is that

A. most pistols have the same number of grooves
B. some pistols have rifling twisted both left and right
C. the direction of the twist in any pistol can be either left or right
D. pistols with different numbers of grooves are rifled differently
E. all pistols have grooves

22._____

23. Normally, traces of arsenic are found in the nails, skin, hair, etc. This fact must be considered when examining a dead body if poisoning is suspected. Quantities of arsenic less than 0.1 milligram ; may be regarded as originating from the body itself.
The inference which can *MOST* logically be made from this statement is that

A. the presence of arsenic in the body indicates poisoning
B. arsenic is normally contained in the body and only a dose as large as .1 gram is lethal
C. traces of arsenic must be considered when examining a dead body
D. the presence of arsenic in a body does not prove poisoning
E. when examining a dead body, arsenic poisoning should be considered

23._____

24. While the safe burglar can ply his trade the year round, the loft man is more seasonal in his activities, since only at certain periods of the year is a substantial amount of valuable merchandise stored in lofts.
The generalization which this statement *BEST* illustrates is that

A. nothing is ever completely safe from a thief
B. there are safe burglars and loft burglars
C. some types of burglary are seasonal
D. the safe burglar considers "safecracking" a trade
E. there are different kinds of thieves

24._____

25. The successful prosecution of an incendiary depends upon a close collaboration
between the prosecutor and the investigator.
The *MOST* accurate inference that can be drawn from this statement is that

    A. collaboration between prosecutor and investigator is always necessary
    B. in most cases of incendiaries, successful prosecution is difficult without collaboration between the prosecutor and the investigator
    C. successful prosecution of other types of crime generally requires collaboration
    D. prosecutors must have the essential attributes of an investigator in order to prosecute an incendiary successfully
    E. a successful incendiary depends upon a close collaboration between the prosecutor and the investigator

25.____

KEY (CORRECT ANSWERS)

1. C		11. A	
2. A		12. E	
3. B		13. B	
4. E		14. C	
5. D		15. A	
6. B		16. C	
7. E		17. C	
8. B		18. E	
9. A		19. B	
10. C		20. D	

21. D
22. C
23. D
24. C
25. B

TEST 3

Each question or incomplete statement is followed by several suggested answers or completions. Select the one that *BEST* answers the question or completes the statement. *PRINT THE LETTER OF THE CORRECT ANSWER IN THE SPACE AT THE RIGHT.*

1. A disquieting proportion of those committing crimes against property are young persons who do not rob and steal for a steady income but for the opportunity which such crimes provide to indulge in conspicuous spending.
A statement which, most nearly, sums up the thought of this statement is that

    A. young persons usually rob and steal for pleasure
    B. conspicuous spending frequently leads to robbery
    C. people who indulge in conspicuous spending are young thieves
    D. some young people perform criminal acts in order to get spending money
    E. older thieves use robbery as a means for a steady income

1.____

2. No matter how efficient a police force may be, and no matter how careful to observe civil liberties of long standing, it will always have to fight its way against an undercurrent of opposition and criticism from some of the very elements which it is paid to serve and pro-tect; and to which it is, in the last analysis, responsible. This is the enduring problem of a police force in a democracy.
Of the following statements, the *one* which substantially restates a thought made in this statement is that

    A. police forces must expect some opposition from honest, upright citizens
    B. some police forces are not democratic
    C. police forces must expect opposition from criminal elements of the population
    D. police forces in a democracy are efficient
    E. the police force is responsible for fighting an undercurrent of opposition

2.____

3. The *specific* problem raised by the statement in question 2 is that it is difficult to

    A. observe civil liberties of long standing
    B. serve and protect elements of the population
    C. deal with an inherent opposition to police forces
    D. analyze critically police functions
    E. treat specific problems of a police

3.____

4. The tendency for an increase in crime during the winter is most pronounced in the case of robbery, which shows a 50 percent fluctuation from minimum to maximum levels. The variation in the lengths of days and nights with the changing seasons has a direct influ-ence here, since the winter months provide more hours of darkness during which rob-beries, burglaries and larcenies may be committed. Of the following, the *CHIEF* implication of the above statement is that

    A. crime is prevalent during the winter months
    B. the influence of the seasons on crime varies from year to year
    C. the number of robberies probably also varies from day to day
    D. robbery is a common crime
    E. most robberies are committed during darkness

4.____

5. A "felony" is a crime punishable by death or imprisonment in a state prison, and any other crime is a misdemeanor. According to this statement, the *decisive* distinction between "felony" and "misdemeanor" is the

    A. degree of criminality   B. type of crime
    C. place of incarceration   D. length of imprisonment
    E. judicial jurisdiction

5.____

Questions 6-9.

DIRECTIONS: Answer Questions 6 to 9 on the basis of the following statement:

Disorderly conduct, in the abstract, does not constitute any crime known to law; it is only when it "tends to a breach of the peace" under the circumstances detailed in section 1458 of the Consolidation Act that it constitutes a minor offense cognizable by the police magistrate of the city, and when it in fact threatens to disturb the peace it is a misdemeanor as well under section 675 of the penal code as at common law, and not within the jurisdiction of the police magistrate, but of the court of special sessions.

6. Of the following, the *MOST* accurate statement on the basis of the above paragraph is that

6.____

    A. an act which merely threatens to disturb the peace is not a crime
    B. disorderly conduct, by itself, is not a crime
    C. some types of disorderly conduct are indictable
    D. a minor offense may or may not be cognizable by the police
    E. some facts threaten to disturb the peace

7. Of the following, the *LEAST* accurate statement on the basis of the above paragraph is that

7.____

    A. disorderly conduct which threatens to disturb the peace is within the jurisdiction of a police magistrate
    B. disorderly conduct which "tends to a breach of the peace" may constitute a minor offense
    C. section 1458 of the Consolidation Act discusses a "breach of the peace"
    D. disorderly conduct which "tends to a breach of the peace" is not the same as that which threatens to disturb the peace
    E. the court of special sessions considers some cases resulting from disorderly conduct

8. The above paragraph distinguishes *LEAST* sharply between

8.____

    A. jurisdiction of a police magistrate and jurisdiction of the court of special sessions
    B. disorderly conduct as a crime and disorderly conduct as no crime
    C. what "tends to a breach of the peace" and what threatens to disturb the peace
    D. a minor offense and a misdemeanor
    E. the penal code and the common law

9. Of the following generalizations, the *one* which is *BEST* illustrated by the above paragraph is that

9.____

A. acts which in themselves are not criminal may become criminal as a result of their effect
B. abstract conduct may, in and of itself, be criminal
C. criminal acts are determined by results rather than by intent
D. an act which is criminal to begin with may not be criminal if it fails to have the desired effect
E. all law consists of a detailing of circumstances under which a crime is committed

10. While the number of arrests of persons under 16 years of age for murder or manslaughter was the same this year as last year, the percentage of arrests made in this age group decreased in comparison with all arrests for murder or manslaughter.
The *one* of the following conclusions which is *MOST* accurate on the basis of this statement, is that the

    10._____

A. total number of arrests in the under-16-year age group increased
B. total number of murder or manslaughter arrests increased
C. total number of arrests in the 16-year-or-over age group for murder or man-salughter decreased
D. percentage of arrests in the 16-year-or-over age group for murder or manslaughter decreased
E. number of arrests for manslaughter or murder for the under-16-year age group decreased

11. An automobile rapidly gets out of control, mounts a sidewalk and hits a woman. The woman is injured.
In all cases, you *should*

    11._____

A. apply an antiseptic to her wounds
B. treat her for shock
C. carry her to the nearest doctor
D. make a splint for any broken members
E. wash any open wounds with clean water

12. Upon entering an apartment, you find that a man attempted to commit suicide by turning on the gas jets.
Of the following, the *FIRST* action you should take is to

    12._____

A. begin artificial respiration
B. remove the patient from the room
C. call for help
D. keep the neighbors out of the room
E. continue artificial respiration until natural breathing is restored

13. As the child was discovered to be suffering from multiple abrasions, the older man washed the wounds with cold water. This action was

    13._____

A. *desirable;* it was important to wash wounds
B. *undesirable;* it might have introduced a cause of infection
C. *desirable;* cold water kills bacteria, the cause of infection
D. *undesirable;* cold water does *not* kill bacteria, the cause of infection
E. *desirable;* it permitted the extent of the wounds to be determined

14. A knowledge of "pressure points" would be *MOST* useful in giving first aid in case of 14.____

    A. shock   B. a burn   C. drowning
    D. electrocution   E. bleeding

15. In cases of first-degree burns, any good burn ointment, vaseline or bicarbonate of soda 15.____
may be used.
Of the following, the *MAIN* reason for applying any of these is that

    A. they prevent infection
    B. they prevent the bandage from sticking to the wound
    C. they prevent the burn from penetrating deeper
    D. first-degree burns are not serious and special medication is unnecessary
    E. they exclude air from the burned parts

Questions 16-25.

DIRECTIONS: Questions 16 to 25 relate to the report of an accident. Under "A" you are given
the regulations governing filling out the report form.
Under "B" you are given the completed report upon the basis of which you are to answer the
questions.
    "A" - 1. A report form will be filled out for each person injured.
2. Be brief, but do not omit any information which can help the Department reduce number of
accidents. If it is necessary, use more than one card. 3. Under "Details" enter all important facts
not reported elsewhere on the card which may be pertinent to the completeness of the report
as: the specific traffic violation, if any; whether the injured person was crossing not at crossing;
crossing against lights; the direction the vehicle was proceeding and if making right or left turn;
attending surgeon, etc. If the officer is an eyewitness, he should be able to determine the cause.
    "B" - Report:
INJURED PERSON: Julius Morgan; SEX, Male; AGE: 52.
ADDRESS: 2110 Fairwell Rd.
PLACE OF OCCURRENCE: 72nd St. and Broadway; DATE: 3.12.07
ACCIDENT: Yes; NO. OF PERSONS INVOLVED: 12; TIME, 10 a.m.
NATURE OF INJURY: Right forearm, fractured.
STRUCK BY: Auto No. 3
DRIVER INVOLVED: Auto 1, Harry Baldwin, 11 Far St. - Lic. 2831 owner; Auto 2, Roger Lin-
coln, 106 Near Ave. - Lic. 1072 owner; Auto 3, Albert Pierson, 32 Open Rd. - Lic. 566 owner.
DETAILS: (1) Vehicle 1 came out of 72nd St. just as the lights along 72nd St. were changing to
green going west. (2) Vehicle 2 proceding north along Broadway continued across the intersection as the lights in his direction turned red. (3) Vehicle 1 colliding with Vehicle 2 turning
said vehicle over and throwing it into the path of Vehicle 3 going east along 72nd St. (4) This
had manifold results: other vehicles were struck; a hydrant was obliterated; several pedestrians were injured; there was considerible property damage; and three riders in the cars
involved were killed. (5) This was a very tragic accident.

16. In the report, the *one* of the following words which was *misspelled* is: 16.____

    A. fractured   B. owner   C. vehicle
    D. proceding   E. none of the foregoing

17. In the report, the *one* of the following words which was *misspelled* is :　　　17.____

    A. continuied   B. across   C. intersection
    D. colliding   E. none of the foregoing

18. In the report, the *one* of the following words which was *misspelled* is:　　　18.____

    A. manifold   B. obliterated   C. pedestrians
    D. considerible   E. none of the foregoing

19. In the report, the one of the following words which was *used incorrectly* is:　　　19.____

    A. manifold   B. obliterated   C. intersection
    D. fractured   E. colliding

20. In the report, under "Details," there are several errors in grammar.　　　20.____
Of the changes listed below, a change which will *CORRECT* an existing error in *grammar* is:

    A. Change sentence (1) to, "Vehicle 1, going west, came out of 72nd St. just as the lights along 72nd St. were changing to green."
    B. Change sentence (2) to, "Vehicle 2 proceded north along Broadway continuied across the intersection as the lights in his direction turned red."
    C. Change sentence (3) to, "Vehicle 1 colliding with vehicle 2 turns said vehicle over and throwing it into the path of vehicle 3 going east along 72nd St."
    D. Change sentence (4) to, "This has had manifold results: there was considerible property damage; a hydrant was obliterated; and several pedestrians were injured."
    E. None of the foregoing changes

21. A change which will *CORRECT* an existing error in *grammar* is :　　　21.____

    A. Change sentence (1) to, "Vehicle 1 came out of 72nd St. just as the lights along 72nd St. changed to green going west."
    B. Change sentence (2) to, "Vehicle 2 proceding north along Broadway continuied across the intersection when the light in his direction turned red."
    C. Change sentence (3) to, "Vehicle 1 collided with vehicle 2 ,turning said vehicle over and throwing it into the path of vehicle 3 going east along 72nd St."
    D. Change all semicolons in sentence (4) to commas.
    E. None of the foregoing changes

22. Of the following critical evaluations of the report, the *MOST CORRECT* is that it is a　　　22.____

    A. *good* report; it gives a graphic description of the accident
    B. *bad* report; the damage to the cars is not given in detail
    C. *bad* report; there is no indication of what happened to the 11 persons other than Morgan who were involved
    D. *good* report; it is summary and conclusive
    E. *good* report; it is very brief

23. Of the following, the report indicates *most clearly*　　　23.____

    A. the driver at fault
    B. that Morgan was a pedestrian
    C. that the reporting officer was an eyewitness

D. the names of all the drivers involved
E. that some city property was damaged

24. Of the following, the report indicates *LEAST* clearly

    24.____

    A. the time of the accident
    B. the direction in which Baldwin was driving
    C. how the accident might have been avoided
    D. the number of persons involved
    E. the injury to Morgan

25. From the report, as submitted, it is *most reasonable* to infer that

    25.____

    A. Baldwin was at fault
    B. the information is too hazy to determine the guilty person
    C. Lincoln was at fault
    D. something was wrong with the light system
    E. the accident was the fault of no one person

26. Authorities state that all officers should check their weapons when responding to the scene of a crime.
The *one* of the following which indicates the BEST time *and* manner for them to check their weapons for this purpose, would be while the vehicle is

    26.____

    A. *en route* to the scene, with the weapons pointed toward the floor of the vehicle
    B. *en route* to the scene, with the weapons pointed toward the roof of the vehicle
    C. *standing,* with the weapons pointed toward the floor of the vehicle
    D. *standing,* with the weapons pointed toward the roof of the vehicle.
    E. right before an arrest

27. According to various authorities, it would be MOST correct to state, with respect to youthful shoplifters, that they, *generally,*

    27.____

    A. shoplift because a deep inner tension or compulsion induces an irresistible desire to steal
    B. do not try to sell for profit the shoplifted articles
    C. shoplift for merchandise with high resale value
    D. take things which they need greatly when committing their act of shoplifting
    E. get a "high" from stealing

28. The basic fact which has made fingerprinting the *principal* and *most absolutely* certain method of criminal identification is that

    28.____

    A. even the vaguest of fingerprint impressions left at the scene of a crime invariably leads the police to a positive identification of the perpetrator being sought
    B. no two persons possess fingerprints which fall into the same general patterns
    C. each person has a set of uniquely distinctive and never-changing fingerprints
    D. every fingertip makes a print that can fit into only one out of only four general patterns
    E. fingerprints are the easiest methods of identification

29. Police officers are advised to hold their initial interview with juvenile suspects as soon as possible after the arrest or detention.
This precaution is of value CHIEFLY in order to

    A. evaluate anti-social attitudes in the suspects and encourage them to adopt a more adult outlook

    B. inform the suspects of the officers' constructive aims and eliminate their fear of impending punishment

    C. counteract the harmful parental or other adult influences underlying the suspects' criminal behavior

    D. demonstrate the officers' interest in the suspects and help prevent their building up an alibi

    E. get a confession before it's too late

29.____

30. Of the following, the efficiency of an interrogator is measured BEST by his ability to bring the subject to the point where the subject

    A. chooses to be of assistance

    B. identifies himself, although subconsciously, with police goals

    C. appreciates the inherent difficulty of the police investigative task

    D. realizes the futility of non-cooperation

    E. becomes afraid not to cooperate

30.____

KEY (CORRECT ANSWERS)

1.	D	11.	B	21.	C
2.	A	12.	B	22.	C
3.	C	13.	D	23.	E
4.	E	14.	E	24.	C
5.	C	15.	E	25.	B
6.	B	16.	D	26.	C
7.	A	17.	A	27.	B
8.	E	18.	D	28.	C
9.	A	19.	B	29.	D
10.	B	20.	A	30.	A

EXAMINATION SECTION
TEST 1

DIRECTIONS: Each question or incomplete statement is followed by several suggested answers or completions. Select the one that BEST answers the question or completes the statement. *PRINT THE LETTER OF THE CORRECT ANSWER IN THE SPACE AT THE RIGHT.*

1. A sergeant tells a patrolman to perform a certain duty.   1.____
   If the patrolman does not completely understand the order, he should

   A. carry out the order to the best of his ability and then request further information if necessary
   B. carry out the order to the best of his ability so that he does not give the appearance of being unable to follow orders
   C. inform the sergeant that he does not understand the order
   D. request clarification from a more experienced patrolman

2. While on patrol, you are informed by the manager of a supermarket that an object which   2.____ appears to be a homemade bomb has been discovered in his market.
   Your FIRST action should be to

   A. go to the market and make sure that everyone leaves it immediately
   B. go to the market, examine the bomb, and then decide what action is to be taken
   C. question the manager in detail in an effort to determine whether this is really a bomb
   D. telephone the Bomb Squad for instructions as to how the bomb should be rendered harmless

3. A patrolman on post would be MOST likely to make a regular hourly signal-box call to his   3.____ precinct, rather than an immediate call, when he

   A. discovers a traffic signal light which is not functioning properly
   B. discovers what appears to be an abandoned car on his post
   C. notices a street name sign which has been damaged
   D. overhears a conversation relating to a possible disturbance between two groups of teenagers

4. A patrolman is on post, and a citizen sees him *ringing in* on a street police call box to the   4.____ station house. The citizen asks him what the purpose of the box is.
   Of the following, the BEST course of action for the officer to follow in this situation is to

   A. speak to the desk officer over the call box phone and get his permission to answer the question
   B. suggest that he write to the Community Relations Office of the Police Department for complete information
   C. tactfully suggest to the man it is a police matter and hence confidential
   D. tell the man what the call box is and what it is used for

5. The MOST reasonable advice that a patrolman can give to a merchant who asks what he   5.____ should do if he receives a telephone call from a person he doesn't recognize regarding an alleged emergency at his store after ordinary business hours is that the merchant should go to the store and, if police officers are not at the scene, he should

A. continue past the store and call the police for assistance
B. continue past the store, and return and enter it if there doesn't appear to be an emergency
C. enter the store and ascertain whether the alleged emergency exists
D. enter the store only if there is no one apparently loitering in the vicinity

6. A patrolman is asked by a citizen the location of a candy store which the patrolman knows is under observation for suspected bookmaking activity.
In such a situation, the patrolman should

6.____

A. give the proper directions to the citizen
B. give the proper directions to the citizen, but tell him the store is under observation
C. state that he does not know the location of the store
D. tell the citizen that he may be arrested if the store is raided

7. *Whenever a crime has been committed, the criminal, has disturbed the surroundings in one way or another by his presence.*
The LEAST valid deduction for the police to make from this statement is that

7.____

A. clues are thus present at all crime scenes
B. even the slightest search at crime scenes will turn up conclusive evidence
C. the greater the number of criminals involved in a crime, the greater the number of clues likely to be available
D. the completely clueless crime is rarely encountered in police work

8. It is suggested that a suspect should not be permitted to walk in or about the scene of a crime where fingerprints may be present until a thorough search has been made for such evidence.
This suggested procedure is

8.____

A. *good;* the suspect would, if permitted to walk about the scene, smear all fingerprints that might be found by police investigators
B. *bad;* the return of a suspect to the scene of a crime provides an opportunity to obtain additional fingerprints from the suspect
C. *good;* if the suspect handled any objects at the scene, the value of any original fingerprints, as evidence, might be seriously impaired
D. *bad;* the return of a suspect to the scene of a crime provides an opportunity to identify objects that had been handled during the commission of the crime

9. Of the following, the one which is the purpose of the police fingerprinting procedure is the

9.____

A. identification of deceased persons
B. identification of the guilty
C. protection of the innocent
D. recognition of first offenders

10. A patrolman is the first one to arrive at the scene of a murder. A suspect offers to make a statement to him concerning the crime. The patrolman refuses to accept the statement.
The patrolman's action was

10.____

A. *good;* interrogation of suspects should be performed by experienced detectives
B. *poor;* the suspect may later change his mind and refuse to make any statement

C. *good;* the patrolman will be too busy maintaining order at the scene to be able to accept the statement

D. *poor;* a statement made by the suspect would quickly solve the crime

11. The scene of a crime is the area within the immediate vicinity of the specific location of the crime in which evidence might be found. This definition serves as an acceptable working guide for the discovery of evidence by the police because 11.____

    A. evidence found outside the crime scene can be just as valuable as evidence found nearby

    B. it assigns the finding of evidence to those responsible for its discovery

    C. it is likely that the most important evidence will be found within the area of the crime scene

    D. evidence found within the area of the crime scene is more readily accepted

12. It is important that the police give proper attention to the investigation of apparently minor, as well as major, complaints made by citizens.
Of the following, the one which is the MOST valid reason for doing so is that 12.____

    A. minor complaints are frequently of great importance to the complainant

    B. minor complaints are more readily disposed of

    C. minor complaints may be an indication of a serious police problem

    D. police efficiency is determined by their attitude towards citizen complaints

13. Hearsay evidence may be defined as testimony by one person that another person told him about a criminal act which that other person had witnessed.
Hearsay evidence is usually NOT admissible in a criminal trial MAINLY because 13.____

    A. hearsay evidence is consistently biased and deliberately distorted

    B. hearsay evidence is usually not relevant to the issues of the case

    C. such evidence is usually distorted by both the original witness and the person to whom he stated his observations

    D. the witness to the criminal act is not being cross-examined under oath

14. Arrests should not be given too much weight in the appraisal of a policeman's perfor- mance since a large number of arrests does not necessarily indicate that a man is doing a good police job.
This statement is 14.____

    A. *true;* factors other than the total of arrests must also be considered in judging police effectiveness

    B. *false;* the basic job of the police is to suppress crime and the surest measure of this is the number of arrests made

    C. *true;* arrest figures are not indicative in any way of a patrolman's efficiency

    D. *false;* although some policemen are in a better position to make arrests than oth- ers, the law of averages should operate to even this out

15. Arson is a particularly troublesome crime for the police. Of the following statements, the one which is the MOST important reason why this is so is that 15.____

    A. arsonists usually seek the protection of darkness for their crimes

    B. arsons occur so infrequently that the police lack a definite approach

C. important evidence is frequently destroyed by the fire itself
D. witnesses find it difficult to distinguish arsonists from other criminals

16. Undoubtedly, the police have an important contribution to make to the welfare of youth. Of the following, the PRINCIPAL reason for this is that   16._____

   A. effectiveness is a result of experience and the police have had the longest experience in youth work
   B. no other agency can make use of the criminal aspects of the law as effectively as the police
   C. the police are in a strategic position to observe children actually or potentially delinquent and the conditions contributing thereto
   D. welfare agencies lack an understanding of the problems of youth

17. Adolescents, whether delinquent or not, are especially sensitive to the attitudes of their own small group and are more responsive to the judgments of their companions than to those of their own family.
According to this statement, it would be MOST accurate to conclude that   17._____

   A. adolescents are concerned more with their gang's opinion of them than with their own families' reaction to their behavior
   B. adolescents are more personally sensitive to criticism of their conduct than adults
   C. adolescent misbehavior can best be approached through the family
   D. adolescent misbehavior is often caused by the lack of parental interest

18. It is safe to say that the significant patterns of behavior conveyed by movies, press, or radio must reach individuals whose behavior resistance is low, in order to be influential. It follows from the above statement that it would be MOST desirable to   18._____

   A. consider the public press a negative factor in the developmental pattern of individuals
   B. encourage youth to imitate significant patterns of behavior which they observe
   C. exclude all children from attending movies which portray patterns of behavior of an anti-social nature
   D. prevent exposure of potentially delinquent children to unfavorable influences

19. The suggestion has been made that the Police Department issue identification cards to be used by juveniles over 21 who wish to drink alcoholic beverages in bars.
The one of the following which is NOT a valid criticism of this proposal is that it might   19._____

   A. appear to bestow positive social approval on the consumption of alcoholic beverages by youths
   B. induce more youngsters to congregate in bars
   C. lead to a *black market* in counterfeit identification cards
   D. shield youths from exposure to unwholesome situations

20. An apparently senile man informs a patrolman that he is returning from a visit to his daughter and that he is unable to find his way back home because he has forgotten his address.
Of the following courses of action, the FIRST one that should be taken by the patrolman is to   20._____

A. question the man in an effort to establish his identity
B. request the police missing persons section to describe to you any person recently reported as missing
C. suggest that the man return to his daughter for travel directions to his home
D. telephone a description of the man to the precinct station house

21. Of the following facts about a criminal, the one which would be of MOST value in apprehending and identifying the criminal would be that he

    A. drives a black Cadillac 1988 sedan with chrome license plate holders
    B. invariably uses a .38 caliber Colt blue-steel revolver with walnut stock and regulation front sight
    C. talks with a French accent and frequently stutters
    D. usually wears 3-button single-breasted *Ivy League* suits and white oxford cloth button-down-collar shirts

21.____

22. A pawnshop dealer has submitted to the police an accurate and complete description of a wristwatch which he recently purchased from a customer.
    The one of the following factors that would be MOST important in determining whether this wristwatch was stolen is the

    A. degree of investigative perseverance demonstrated by the police
    B. exactness of police records describing stolen property
    C. honesty and neighborhood reputation of the pawnbroker
    D. time interval between the purchase of the wristwatch by the pawnbroker and his report to the police

22.____

23. · A patrolman noticed a man fumbling at the controls of an automobile, starting with a lurch, grinding the gears, and then driving on the wrong side of the street. The patrolman signaled the car to stop, warned the driver about his driving, and permitted him to depart. This procedure was

    A. *right;* it is good public relations for the police to caution rather than punish inadvertent violations
    B. of law
    C. *wrong;* the patrolman should have arrested the driver for driving while in an intoxicated condition
    D. *right;* the bad driving probably was due to nervousness caused by the presence of the patrolman
    E. *wrong;* the patrolman should have investigated the possibility that this was a stolen car

23.____

24. A patrolman at the scene of a serious vehicular accident requests two witnesses to the accident not to speak to each other until he has received from each of them a statement concerning the accident.
    The MOST likely reason for this request by the patrolman is that if the witnesses were allowed to speak to each other at this time, they might

    A. become involved in a violent quarrel over what actually occurred
    B. change their opinion so that identical statements to the police would result

24.____

C. discuss the possibility of a bribe offer to either of them by one of the operators involved in the accident
D. have their original views of the accident somewhat altered by hearing each other's view of the accident

25. Patrolman Z is directing traffic when he observes a car approaching him which appears to meet the description of a car stolen several days previously. Patrolman Z signals the driver of this car to stop. The car does not stop or slacken its speed and proceeds past Patrolman Z. In an effort to stop the car, Patrolman Z fires several shots at the car. The action of Patrolman Z was

    25.____

A. *improper;* Patrolman Z should know that pistol marksmanship is not always accurate, even at relatively close ranges
B. *proper;* it is legally justifiable to fire at an escaping felon
C. *improper;* it is possible that the driver misunderstood the patrolman's signal to stop
D. *proper;* Patrolman Z was on foot duty and there was no other immediately available means of halting the car

26. Assume that a recent study showed a 2% increase in highway fatalities in the first six months of 2007 over the last six months of 2006.
Of the following factors, generally the LEAST important one to include in a report evaluating this study is the

    26.____

A. age and sex distribution of drivers
B. total number of automobiles in use
C. total number of miles automobiles were driven
D. total population

27. Tests have shown that sound waves set up by a siren have a greater intensity ahead than at either side or at the rear of a police car.
On the basis of this statement, it would be MOST reasonable for the operator of a police car, when responding to the scene of an emergency and using the siren, to expect that a motorist approaching an intersection from

    27.____

A. a side street may not stop his vehicle as soon as a more distant motorist directly ahead of the police car
B. directly ahead may not stop his vehicle as soon as a more distant motorist approaching from the rear of the police car
C. directly ahead may not stop his vehicle as soon as a more distant motorist approaching from the side of the police car
D. the rear of the police car may stop his vehicle before the less distant motorist approaching from the street

28. An alarm broadcast for criminals escaping by car directs policemen to observe occupants of all cars, even occupants in cars not meeting the description of the fleeing car. The MOST likely reason for this is that

    28.____

A. cars of the same make are not distinctive enough to be of any recognition value
B. the car's appearance may have been greatly altered after the crime was committed
C. the criminals may have disguised themselves after the commission of the crime
D. the escaping criminals may change to a different car after leaving the scene

29. Five minutes after receiving an alarm for a blue 1980 Buick four-door sedan which had been used as a get-away car by bank robbers, a radio patrol team spots and stops a car which seems to fit the description.
The one of the following which is MOST likely to indicate the need for further careful investigation is that the
29.____

    A. car has a cracked rear side window
    B. driver does not have a registration certificate for this car
    C. rear license plate is rusted
    D. occupants of the car consist of three poorly dressed men

30. A foot patrolman who is several blocks away observes a woman being dragged into a car, which drives off very rapidly.
Of the following, his FIRST action should be to
30.____

    A. call headquarters from the nearest call box or public telephone
    B. commandeer a bus and pursue the other car
    C. shoot in the direction of the scene as a warning
    D. step into a hallway and await the approach of the car

31. A citizen requests police assistance in locating his adult son who has not been home for a period of twenty-four hours. Questioning of the citizen reveals no reason for the son's absence.
The MOST appropriate of the following actions that the police should take is to
31.____

    A. advise the citizen to contact all nearby hospitals and then contact the police again if this is not successful
    B. conduct a thorough investigation in an attempt to locate the missing son
    C. politely inform the citizen that no police action will be taken since the son is an adult
    D. suggest that the citizen wait several days; and if his son has not then returned home, they will accept the complaint

32. A patrolman is guarding the entrance of an apartment in which a homicide occurred. While awaiting the arrival of the detectives assigned to the case, he is approached by a newspaper reporter who asks to be admitted. The patrolman refuses to admit him.
The patrolman's action was
32.____

    A. *wrong;* the police should cooperate with the press
    B. *right;* the reporter might unintentionally destroy evidence if admitted
    C. *wrong;* experienced police reporters can be trusted to act intelligently in this situation
    D. *right;* this reporter should not be given an advantage over other newspaper men

33. A radio patrolman investigating a reported store hold-up, which occurred shortly before his arrival, enters the store. The salesclerk who witnessed the hold-up starts telling the patrolman, in a confused and excited manner, what had happened.
The BEST course for the patrolman to follow initially is to
33.____

    A. ask the clerk to write out an account of what had happened
    B. let the clerk tell her story without interruption
    C. try to confine the clerk to answering relevant questions
    D. wait until the clerk calms down before taking her statement

34. A phone call is received at police headquarters indicating that a burglary is now taking place in a large loft building. Several radio motor patrol teams are dispatched to the scene.
    In order to prevent the escape of the burglars, the two patrolmen arriving first at the building, knowing that there is at least one entrance on each of the four sides of the building, should FIRST

    A. station themselves at diagonally opposite corners, outside of the building
    B. enter the building and proceed to search for the criminals
    C. station themselves at the most likely exit from the building
    D. enter the building and remain on the ground floor, attempting to keep all stairways under observation

34.____

Questions 35-56.

DIRECTIONS: In each of Questions 35 through 56, select the lettered word which means MOST NEARLY the same as the capitalized word. Place the letter which corresponds to your choice in the space at the right.

35. AVARICE   35.____

    A. flight   B. greed   C. pride   D. thrift

36. PREDATORY   36.____

    A. offensive   B. plundering
    C. previous   D. timeless

37. VINDICATE   37.____

    A. clear   B. conquer   C. correct   D. illustrate

38. INVETERATE   38.____

    A. backward   B. erect   C. habitual   D. lucky

39. DISCERN   39.____

    A. describe   B. fabricate   C. recognize   D. seek

40. COMPLACENT   40.____

    A. indulgent   B. listless
    C. overjoyed   D. satisfied

41. ILLICIT   41.____

    A. insecure   B. unclear   C. unlawful   D. unlimited

42. PROCRASTINATE   42.____

    A. declare   B. multiply   C. postpone   D. steal

43. IMPASSIVE   43.____

    A. calm   B. frustrated
    C. thoughtful   D. unhappy

44. AMICABLE

   A. cheerful   B. flexible   C. friendly   D. poised

45. FEASIBLE

   A. breakable   B. easy
   C. likeable   D. practicable

KEY (CORRECT ANSWERS)

1. C	11. C	21. C	31. B	41. C
2. A	12. C	22. B	32. B	42. C
3. C	13. D	23. D	33. C	43. A
4. D	14. A	24. D	34. A	44. C
5. A	15. C	25. C	35. B	45. D
6. A	16. C	26. D	36. B	
7. B	17. A	27. A	37. A	
8. C	18. D	28. B	38. C	
9. B	19. D	29. B	39. C	
10. B	20. A	30. A	40. D	

TEST 2

DIRECTIONS: Each question or incomplete statement is followed by several suggested answers or completions. Select the one that BEST answers the question or completes the statement. *PRINT THE LETTER OF THE CORRECT ANSWER IN THE SPACE AT THE RIGHT.*

1. INNOCUOUS   1.____
   - A. harmless
   - C. insincere
   - B. insecure
   - D. unfavorable

2. OSTENSIBLE   2.____
   - A. apparent
   - B. hesitant
   - C. reluctant
   - D. showy

3. INDOMITABLE   3.____
   - A. excessive
   - C. unreasonable
   - B. unconquerable
   - D. unthinkable

4. CRAVEN   4.____
   - A. cowardly
   - B. hidden
   - C. miserly
   - D. needed

5. ALLAY   5.____
   - A. discuss
   - B. quiet
   - C. refine
   - D. remove

6. ALLUDE   6.____
   - A. denounce
   - B. refer
   - C. state
   - D. support

7. NEGLIGENCE   7.____
   - A. carelessness
   - C. objection
   - B. denial
   - D. refusal

8. AMEND   8.____
   - A. correct
   - B. destroy
   - C. end
   - D. list

9. RELEVANT   9.____
   - A. conclusive
   - C. obvious
   - B. careful
   - D. related

10. VERIFY   10.____
   - A. challenge
   - B. change
   - C. confirm
   - D. reveal

11. INSIGNIFICANT   11.____
   - A. incorrect
   - C. unimportant
   - B. limited
   - D. undesirable

Questions 12-16.

DIRECTIONS: Questions 12 through 16 are to be answered on the basis of the graphs shown below.

CLEARANCE RATES FOR CRIMES AGAINST THE PERSON

2004

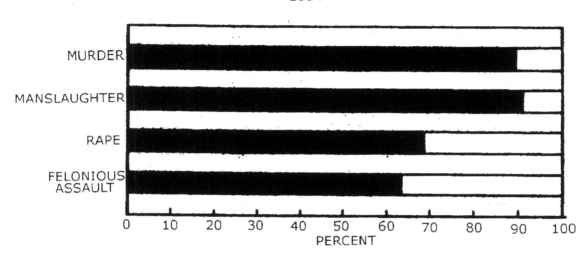

2005

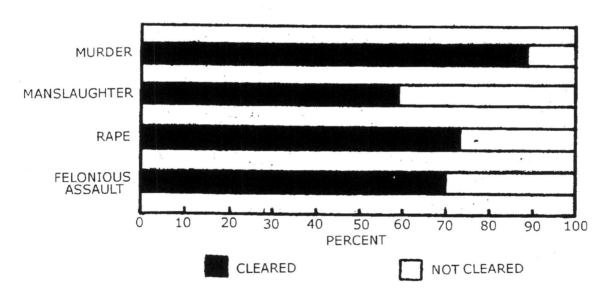

NOTE: The clearance rate is defined as the percentage of reported cases which were closed
by the police through arrests or other means.

12.   According to the above graphs, the AVERAGE clearance rate for all four crimes for 2005   12._____

    A.   was greater than in 2004
    B.   was less than in 2004
    C.   was the same as in 2004
    D.   cannot properly be compared to the 2004 figures

13. According to the above graphs, the crimes which did NOT show an increasing clearance rate from 2004 to 2005 were

    A. manslaughter and murder
    B. rape and felonious assault
    C. manslaughter and felonious assault
    D. rape and murder

13.____

14. According to the above graphs, the average clearance rate for the two year period 2004-2005 was SMALLEST for the crime of

    A. murder   B. manslaughter
    C. rape   D. felonious assault

14.____

15. If, in 2005, 63 cases of reported felonious assault remained *not cleared,* then the total number of felonious assault cases reported that year was MOST NEARLY

    A. 90   B. 150   C. 210   D. 900

15.____

16. In comparing the graphs for 2004 and 2005, it would be MOST accurate to state that

    A. it is not possible to compare the total number of crimes cleared in 2004 with the total number cleared in 2005
    B. the total number of crimes reported in 2004 is greater than the number in 2005
    C. there were fewer manslaughter cases cleared during 2004 than in 2005
    D. there were more rape cases cleared during 2005 than manslaughter cases cleared in the same year

16.____

17. A radio motor patrol car finds it necessary to travel at 90 miles per hour for a period of 1 minute and 40 seconds. The number of miles which the car travels during this period is

    A. 1 5/6   B. 2   C. 2 1/2   D. 3 3/4

17.____

18. A radio motor patrol car has to travel a distance of 15 miles in an emergency. If it does the first two-thirds of the distance at 40 m.p.h. and the last third at 60 m.p.h., the total number of minutes required for the entire run is MOST NEARLY

    A. 15   B. 20   C. 22 1/2   D. 25

18.____

19. A patrol car had 11 1/2 gallons of gasoline at the beginning of a trip of 196 miles and 5 1/2 gallons at the end of the trip. During the trip, gasoline was bought for $10.85 at a cost of $1.55 per gallon.
The average number of miles driven per gallon of gasoline is MOST NEARLY

    A. 14   B. 14.5   C. 15   D. 15.5

19.____

20. There are 15 patrolmen assigned to a certain operation. One-third earn $42,000 per year, three earn $44,100 per year, one earns $49,350 per year, and the rest earn $55,810 per year.
The average annual salary of these patrolmen is MOST NEARLY

    A. $47,500   B. $48,000   C. $48,500   D. $49,000

20.____

21. In 2006, the cost of patrol car maintenance and repair was $2,500 more than in 2005, representing an increase of 10%.
The cost of patrol car maintenance and repair in 2006 was MOST NEARLY

    A. $2,750   B. $22,500   C. $25,000   D. $27,500

21.____

22. A police precinct has an assigned strength of 180 men. Of this number, 25% are not available for duty due to illness, vacations, and other reasons. Of those who are available for duty, 1/3 are assigned outside of the precinct for special emergency duty.
The ACTUAL available strength of the precinct, in terms of men immediately available for precinct duty, is

    A. 45   B. 60   C. 90   D. 135

22.____

23. Five police officers are taking target practice.
The number of rounds fired by each and the percentage of perfect shots is as follows:

Officer	Rounds Fired	Perfect Shots
R	80	30%
S	70	40%
T	75	60%
U	92	25%
V	96	66 2/3%

The average number of perfect shots fired by them is MOST NEARLY

    A. 30   B. 36   C. 42   D. 80

23.____

24. A dozen 5-gallon cans of paint weigh 494 pounds. Each can, when empty, weighs 3 pounds.
The weight of one gallon of paint is MOST NEARLY _____ lbs.

    A. 5   B. 6 1/2   C. 7 1/2   D. 8

24.____

Questions 25-26.

DIRECTIONS: Questions 25 and 26 are to be answered SOLELY on the basis of the following paragraph.

The medical examiner may contribute valuable data to the investigator of fires which cause fatalities. By careful examination of the bodies of any victims, he not only establishes cause of death, but may also furnish, in many instances, answers to questions relating to the identity of the victim and the source and origin of the fire. The medical examiner is of greatest value to law enforcement agencies because he is able to determine the exact cause of death through an examination of tissue of apparent arson victims. Thorough study of a burned body or even of parts of a burned body will frequently yield information which illuminates the problems confronting the arson investigator and the police.

25. According to the above paragraph, the MOST important task of the medical examiner in the investigation of arson is to obtain information concerning the

    A. identity of arsonists   B. cause of death
    C. identity of victims   D. source and origin of fires

25.____

26. The CENTRAL thought of the above paragraph is that the medical examiner aids in the solution of crimes of arson when   26.____

    A. a person is burnt to death
    B. identity of the arsonist is unknown
    C. the cause of the fire is known
    D. trained investigators are not available

Questions 27-30.

DIRECTIONS: Questions 27 through 30 are to be answered SOLELY on the basis of the following paragraph.

    A foundling is an abandoned child whose identity is unknown. Desk officers shall direct the delivery, by a policewoman if available, of foundlings actually or apparently under two years of age to the American Foundling Hospital, or if actually or apparently two years of age or over, to the Children's Center. In all other cases of dependent or neglected children, other than foundlings, requiring shelter, desk officers shall provide for obtaining such shelter as follows: between 9 A.M. and 5 P.M., Monday through Friday, by telephone direct to the Bureau of Child Welfare, in order to ascertain the shelter to which the child shall be sent; at all other times, direct the delivery of a child actually or apparently under two years of age to the American Foundling Hospital, or if the child is actually or apparently two years of age or over to the Children's Center.

27. According to the above paragraph, it would be MOST correct to state that   27.____

    A. a foundling as well as a neglected child may be delivered to the American Foundling Hospital
    B. a foundling but not a neglected child may be delivered to the Children's Center
    C. a neglected child requiring shelter, regardless of age, may be delivered to the Bureau of Child Welfare
    D. the Bureau of Child Welfare may determine the shelter to which a foundling may be delivered

28. According to the above paragraph, the desk officer shall provide for obtaining shelter for a neglected child, apparently under two years of age, by   28.____

    A. directing its delivery to Children's Center if occurrence is on a Monday between 9 A.M. and 5 P.M.
    B. telephoning the Bureau of Child Welfare if occurrence is on a Sunday
    C. directing its delivery to the American Foundling Hospital if occurrence is on a Wednesday at 4 P.M.
    D. telephoning the Bureau of Child Welfare if occurrence is at 10 A.M. on a Friday

29. According to the above paragraph, the desk officer should direct delivery to the American Foundling Hospital of any child who is   29.____

    A. actually under 2 years of age and requires shelter
    B. apparently under two years of age and is neglected or dependent
    C. actually 2 years of age and is a foundling
    D. apparently under 2 years of age and has been abandoned

30. A 12-year-old neglected child requiring shelter is brought to a police station on Thursday   30._____
    at 2 P.M.
    Such a child should be sent to

    A. a shelter selected by the Bureau of Child Welfare
    B. a shelter selected by the desk officer
    C. the Children's Center
    D. the American Foundling Hospital when a brother or sister, under 2 years of age,
        also requires shelter

Questions 31-33.

DIRECTIONS: Questions 31 through 33 are to be answered SOLELY on the basis of the fol-
               lowing paragraph.

In addition to making the preliminary investigation of crimes, patrolmen should serve as eyes,
ears, and legs for the detective division. The patrol division may be used for surveillance, to
serve warrants and bring in suspects and witnesses, and to perform a number of routine tasks
for the detectives which will increase the time available for tasks that require their special skills
and facilities. It is to the advantage of individual detectives, as well as of the detective division,
to have patrolmen working in this manner; more cases are cleared by arrest and a greater proportion of stolen property is recovered when, in addition to the detective regularly assigned, a
number of patrolmen also work on the case. Detectives may stimulate the interest and participation of patrolmen by keeping them currently informed of the presence, identity, or description,
hangouts, associates, vehicles and method of operation of each criminal known to be in the
community.

31. According to the above paragraph, a patrolman should   31._____

    A. assist the detective in certain of his routine functions
    B. be considered for assignment as a detective on the basis of his patrol performance
    C. leave the scene once a detective arrives
    D. perform as much of the detective's duties as time permits

32. According to the above paragraph, patrolmen should aid detectives by   32._____

    A. accepting assignments from detectives which give promise of recovering stolen
        property
    B. making arrests of witnesses for the detective's interrogation
    C. performing all special investigative work for detectives
    D. producing for questioning individuals who may aid the detective in his investigation

33. According to the above paragraph, detectives can keep patrolmen interested by   33._____

    A. ascertaining that patrolmen are doing investigative work properly
    B. having patrolmen directly under his supervision during an investigation
    C. informing patrolmen of the value of their efforts in crime prevention
    D. supplying the patrolmen with information regarding known criminals in the commu-
        nity

Questions 34-35.

DIRECTIONS: Questions 34 and 35 are to be answered SOLELY on the basis of the following paragraph.

State motor vehicle registration departments should and do play a vital role in the prevention and detection of automobile thefts. The combatting of theft is, in fact, one of the primary purposes of the registration of motor vehicles. In 2003, there were approximately 61,309,000 motor vehicles registered in the United States. That same year, some 200,000 of them were stolen. All but 6 percent have been or will be recovered. This is a very high recovery ratio compared to the percentage of recovery of other stolen personal property. The reason for this is that automobiles are carefully identified by the manufacturers and carefully registered by many of the states.

34. The CENTRAL thought of the above paragraph is that there is a close relationship between the

    A. number of automobiles registered in the United States and the number stolen
    B. prevention of automobile thefts and the effectiveness of police departments in the United States
    C. recovery of stolen automobiles and automobile registration
    D. recovery of stolen automobiles and of other stolen property

34.____

35. According to the above paragraph, the high recovery ratio for stolen automobiles is due to

    A. state registration and manufacturer identification of motor vehicles
    B. successful prevention of automobile thefts by state motor vehicle departments
    C. the fact that only 6% of stolen vehicles are not properly registered
    D. the high number of motor vehicles registered in the United States

35.____

Questions 36-39.

DIRECTIONS: Questions 36 through 39 are to be answered SOLELY on the basis of the following paragraph.

It is not always understood that the term *physical evidence* embraces any and all objects, living or inanimate. A knife, gun, signature, or burglar tool is immediately recognized as physical evidence. Less often is it considered that dust, microscopic fragments of all types, even an odor, may equally be physical evidence and often the most important of all. It is well established that the most useful types of physical evidence are generally microscopic in dimensions, that is, not noticeable by the eye and, therefore, most likely to be overlooked by the criminal and by the investigator. For this reason, microscopic evidence persists for months or years after all other evidence has been removed and found inconclusive. Naturally, there are limitations to the time of collecting microscopic evidence as it may be lost or decayed. The exercise of judgment as to the possibility or profit of delayed action in collecting the evidence is a field in which the expert investigator should judge.

36. The one of the following which the above paragraph does NOT consider to be physical evidence is a

    A. criminal thought
    C. raw onion smell
    B. minute speck of dust
    D. typewritten note

36.____

37. According to the above paragraph, the rechecking of the scene of a crime   37.____

    A. is useless when performed years after the occurrence of the crime
    B. is advisable chiefly in crimes involving physical violence
    C. may turn up microscopic evidence of value
    D. should be delayed if the microscopic evidence is not subject to decay or loss

38. According to the above paragraph, the criminal investigator should   38.____

    A. give most of his attention to weapons used in the commission of the crime
    B. ignore microscopic evidence until a request is received from the laboratory
    C. immediately search for microscopic evidence and ignore the more visible objects
    D. realize that microscopic evidence can be easily overlooked

39. According to the above paragraph,   39.____

    A. a delay in collecting evidence must definitely diminish its value to the investigator
    B. microscopic evidence exists for longer periods of time than other physical evidence
    C. microscopic evidence is generally the most useful type of physical evidence
    D. physical evidence is likely to be overlooked by the criminal and by the investigator

Questions 40-42.

DIRECTIONS: Questions 40 through 42 are to be answered SOLELY on the basis of the following paragraph.

    Sometimes, but not always, firing a gun leaves a residue of nitrate particles on the hands. This fact is utilized in the paraffin test which consists of applying melted paraffin and gauze to the fingers, hands, and wrists of a suspect until a cast of approximately 1/8 of an inch is built up. The heat of the paraffin causes the pores of the skin to open and release any particles embedded in them. The paraffin cast is then removed and tested chemically for nitrate particles. In addition to gunpowder, fertilizers, tobacco ashes, matches, and soot are also common sources of nitrates on the hands.

40. Assume that the paraffin test has been given to a person suspected of firing a gun and   40.____
that nitrate particles have been found.
It would be CORRECT to conclude that the suspect

    A. is guilty
    B. is innocent
    C. may be guilty or innocent
    D. is probably guilty

41. In testing for the presence of gunpowder particles on human hands, the characteristic of   41.____
paraffin which makes it MOST serviceable is that it

    A. causes the nitrate residue left by a fired gun to adhere to the gauze
    B. is waterproof
    C. melts at a high temperature
    D. helps to distinguish between gunpowder nitrates and other types

42. According to the above paragraph, in the paraffin test, the nitrate particles are removed   42._____
from the pores because the paraffin

    A. enlarges the pores
    B. contracts the pores
    C. reacts chemically with nitrates
    D. dissolves the particles

Questions 43-45.

DIRECTIONS: Questions 43 through 45 are to be answered SOLELY on the basis of the following paragraph.

Pickpockets operate most effectively when there are prospective victims in either heavily congested areas or in lonely places. In heavily populated areas, the large number of people about them covers the activities of these thieves. In lonely spots, they have the advantage of working unobserved. The main factor in the pickpocket's success is the selection of the *right* victim. A pickpocket's victim must, at the time of the crime, be inattentive, distracted, or unconscious. If any of these conditions exist, and if the pickpocket is skilled in his operations, the stage is set for a successful larceny. With the coming of winter, the crowds move southward and so do most of the pickpockets. However, some pickpockets will remain in certain areas all year around. They will concentrate on theater districts, bus and railroad terminals, hotels, or large shopping centers. A complete knowledge of the methods of this type of criminal and the ability to recognize them come only from long years of experience in performing patient surveillance and trailing of them. This knowledge is essential for the effective control and apprehension of this type of thief.

43. According to this paragraph, the pickpocket is LEAST likely to operate in a   43._____

    A. baseball park with a full capacity attendance
    B. subway station in an outlying area late at night
    C. moderately crowded dance hall
    D. over-crowded department store

44. According to the above paragraph, the one of the following factors which is NOT neces-   44._____
sary for the successful operation of the pickpocket is that

    A. he be proficient in the operations required to pickpockets
    B. the *right* potential victims be those who have been the subject of such a theft previously
    C. his operations be hidden from the view of others
    D. the potential victim be unaware of the actions of the pickpocket

45. According to the above paragraph, it would be MOST correct to conclude that police   45._____
officers who are successful in apprehending pickpockets

    A. are generally those who have had lengthy experience in recognizing all types of criminals
    B. must, by intuition, be able to recognize potential *right* victims
    C. must follow the pickpockets in their southward movement
    D. must have acquired specific knowledge and skills in this field

KEY (CORRECT ANSWERS)

1. A	11. C	21. D	31. A	41. A
2. A	12. B	22. C	32. D	42. A
3. B	13. A	23. B	33. D	43. C
4. A	14. D	24. C	34. C	44. B
5. B	15. C	25. B	35. A	45. D
6. B	16. A	26. A	36. A	
7. A	17. C	27. A	37. C	
8. A	18. B	28. D	38. D	
9. D	19. C	29. D	39. C	
10. C	20. C	30. A	40. C	

EXAMINATION SECTION
TEST 1

DIRECTIONS: Each question or incomplete statement is followed by several suggested answers or completions. Select the one that BEST answers the question or completes the statement. *PRINT THE LETTER OF THE CORRECT ANSWER IN THE SPACE AT THE RIGHT.*

1. The basic purpose of patrol is to create a public impression of police presence every-where so that potential offenders will think there is no opportunity for successful miscon-duct.
   In the assignment of police personnel, the type of police activity that MOST NEARLY realizes this purpose is

   A. traffic summons duty
   B. traffic duty
   C. patrol of all licensed premises
   D. patrol by the detective force
   E. radio motor patrol

   1.____

2. A patrolman, who is asked by a civilian about a legal matter, directs him to the appropri-ate court.
   Of the following information given by the patrolman, the item which is LEAST likely to be useful to the civilian is

   A. hours during which the court is in session
   B. location of the court
   C. name of the Magistrate sitting in this court
   D. location of the complaint clerk within the court building
   E. transportation directions necessary to get to the court

   2.____

3. An officer discovers two teenaged gangs, numbering about 50 boys, engaged in a free-for-all fight.
   The BEST immediate course for the officer to adopt is to

   A. call the station house for reinforcements
   B. fire over the heads of the boys and order them to disperse
   C. arrest the ringleaders
   D. call upon adult bystanders to assist him in restoring order
   E. attempt to stop the fight by using his club

   3.____

4. A radio motor patrol team arrives on the scene a few minutes after a pedestrian has been killed on a busy street by a hit-and-run driver.
   After obtaining a description of the car, the FIRST action the officer should take is to

   A. radio a description of the fleeing car to precinct headquarters
   B. try to overtake the fleeing car
   C. obtain complete statements from everyone at the scene
   D. call for an ambulance
   E. inspect the site of the accident for clues

   4.____

5. A police officer is approached by an obviously upset woman who reports that her husband is missing.
The FIRST thing the officer should do is to

    A. check with the hospitals and the police station
    B. tell the woman to wait a few hours and call the police station if her husband has not returned by then
    C. obtain a description of the missing man so that an alarm can be broadcast
    D. ask the woman why she thinks her husband is missing
    E. make certain that the woman lives in his precinct

5.____

6. A violin is reported as missing from the home of Mrs. Brown.
It would be LEAST important to the police, before making a routine check of pawnshops, to know that this violin

    A. is of a certain unusual shade of red
    B. has dimensions which are different from those of most violins
    C. has a well-known manufacturer's label stamped inside the violin
    D. has a hidden number given to the police by the owner
    E. has one tuning key with a chip mark on it in the shape of a triangle

6.____

7. In making his rounds, an officer should follow the same route and schedule each time.
The suggested procedure is

    A. *good;* a fixed routine enables the officer to proceed methodically and systematically
    B. *poor;* criminals can avoid observation by studying the officer's routine
    C. *good;* without a fixed routine, an officer may overlook some of his many duties
    D. *poor;* a fixed routine reduces an officer's alertness and initiative
    E. *good;* residents in the area covered will have more confidence in police efficiency

7.____

8. Police officers should call for ambulances to transport injured people to the hospital rather than use patrol cars for this purpose.
Of the following, the MOST valid reason for this policy is that

    A. there is less danger of aggravating injuries
    B. patrol cars cannot be spared from police duty
    C. patrol cars are usually not equipped for giving emergency first aid
    D. medical assistance reaches the injured person sooner
    E. responsibility for treating injured people lies with the Department of Hospitals

8.____

9. A businessman requests advice concerning good practice in the use of a safe in his business office. The one of the following points which should be stressed MOST in the use of safes is that

    A. a safe should not be placed where it can be seen from the street
    B. the combination should be written down and carefully hidden in the office
    C. a safe located in a dark place is more tempting to a burglar than one which is located in a well-lighted place
    D. factors of size and weight alone determine the protection offered by a safe
    E. the names of the manufacturer and the owner should be painted on the front of the safe

9.____

10. During a quarrel on a crowded city street, one man stabs another and flees. An officer   10._____
arriving at the scene a short time later finds the victim unconscious, calls for an ambulance, and orders the crowd to leave.
His action was

   A. *bad;* there may have been witnesses to the assault among the crowd
   B. *good;* it is proper first aid procedure to give an injured person room and air
   C. *bad;* the assailant is probably among the crowd
   D. *good;* a crowd may destroy needed evidence
   E. *bad;* it is poor public relations for the police to order people about needlessly

11. An officer walking his post at 3 A.M. notices heavy smoke coming out of a top floor win-   11._____
dow of a large apartment house.
Of the following, the action he should take FIRST is to

   A. make certain that there really is a fire
   B. enter the building and warn all the occupants of the apartment house
   C. attempt to extinguish the fire before it gets out of control
   D. call the Fire Department
   E. call precinct headquarters for Fire Department help

12. Two rival youth gangs have been involved in several minor clashes. The youth officer   12._____
working in their area believes that a serious clash will occur if steps are not taken to prevent it.
Of the following, the LEAST desirable action for the officer to take in his effort to head
off trouble is to

   A. arrest the leaders of both groups as a warning
   B. warn the parents of the dangerous situation
   C. obtain the cooperation of religious and civic leaders in the community
   D. alert all social agencies working in that neighborhood
   E. report the situation to his superior

13. Police officers are instructed to pay particular attention to anyone apparently making   13._____
repairs on an auto parked on a street.
The MOST important reason for this rule is that

   A. the auto may be parked illegally
   B. the person making the repairs may be obstructing traffic
   C. working on autos is prohibited on certain streets
   D. many people injure themselves while working on autos
   E. the person making the repairs may be stealing the auto

14. After making an arrest of a criminal, the officer is LEAST likely to request some kind of   14._____
transportation if the

   A. prisoner is apparently a violent mental patient
   B. distance to be traveled is considerable
   C. prisoner is injured
   D. prisoner is in an alcoholic stupor
   E. prisoner talks of escaping

15. The Police Department, in an effort to prevent losses due to worthless checks, suggests   15.____
to merchants that they place near the cash register a card stating that the merchant
reserves the right to require positive identification and fingerprints from all persons who
cash checks.
This procedure is

    A. *poor;* the merchant's regular customers may be offended by compulsory finger-
        printing
    B. *poor;* the taking of fingerprints would not deter the professional criminal
    C. *good;* the police criminal files may be enlarged by the addition of all fingerprints
        taken
    D. *poor;* this system could not work unless the fingerprinting was made mandatory
    E. *good;* the card might serve to discourage persons from attempting to cash worth-
        less checks

16. A factory manager asks an officer to escort his payroll clerk to and from the local bank   16.____
when payroll money is withdrawn. The officer knows that it is against departmental policy
to provide payroll escort service.
The officer should

    A. refuse and explain why he cannot do what is requested
    B. refer the manager to his precinct commander
    C. tell the manager that police officers have more important tasks
    D. advise the manager that he will provide this service if other duties do not interfere
    E. suggest that paychecks be issued to employees

17. A motorist who has been stopped by a motorcycle police officer for speeding acts rudely.   17.____
He hints about his personal connections with high officials in the city government and
demands the officer's name and shield number.
The officer should

    A. arrest the motorist for threatening an officer in the performance of his duty
    B. give his name and shield number without comment
    C. ignore the question since his name and shield number will be on the summons he
        is about to issue
    D. give his name and shield number but add to the charges against the motorist
    E. ask the motorist why he wants the information and give it only if the answer is sat-
        isfactory

18. Tire skidmarks provide valuable information to policemen investigating automobile acci-   18.____
dents.
The MOST important information obtained from this source is the

    A. condition of the road at the time of the accident
    B. effectiveness of the automobile's brakes
    C. condition of the tires
    D. point at which the driver first saw the danger
    E. speed of the automobile at the time of the accident

19. An officer observes several youths in the act of looting a peanut-vending machine. The   19.____
youths flee in several directions as he approaches, ignoring his order to halt. The officer
then shoots at them, and they halt and are captured.
The officer's action was

A. *right;* it was the most effective way of capturing the criminals
B. *wrong;* extreme measures should not be taken in apprehending petty offenders
C. *right;* provided that there was no danger of shooting innocent bystanders
D. *wrong;* this is usually ineffective when more than one offender is involved
E. *right;* it is particularly important to teach juvenile delinquents respect for the law

20. Before permitting automobiles involved in an accident to depart, an officer should take certain measures.
Of the following, it is LEAST important that the officer make certain that

    20._____

A. both drivers are properly licensed
B. the automobiles are in safe operating condition
C. the drivers have exchanged names and license numbers
D. the drivers are physically fit to drive
E. he obtains the names and addresses of drivers and witnesses

21. A detective, following a tip that a notorious bank robber is to meet a woman in a certain restaurant, is seated in a booth from which he can observe people entering and leaving. While waiting, he notices a flashily dressed woman get up from a table and slip by the cashier without paying her check. The detective ignored the incident and continued watching for the wanted man.
This course of action was

    21._____

A. *correct;* the woman probably forgot to pay her bill
B. *incorrect;* he should have arrested the woman since *a bird in the hand is worth two in the bush*
C. *correct;* it is not the duty of the police department to protect businessmen from loss due to their own negligence
D. *incorrect;* he should have followed the woman since she may lead to the bank robber
E. *correct;* the detective should not risk losing the bank robber by checking on this incident

22. All officers are required to maintain a record of their daily police activity in a memorandum book.
The LEAST likely reason for this requirement is to

    22._____

A. make it unnecessary for the officer to remember police incidents
B. give supervisors information concerning the officer's daily work
C. serve as a possible basis to refute unjustified complaints against the officer
D. make a record of information that may have a bearing on a court action
E. record any action which may later require an explanation

23. Police officers have a duty to take into custody any person who is actually or apparently mentally ill. Of the following cases, the one LEAST likely to fall under this provision of the law is the

    23._____

A. quarrelsome person who makes unjustifiable accusations
B. elderly man who appears confused and unable to dress or feed himself
C. young man who sits on the sidewalk curb staring into space and, when questioned, gives meaningless answers
D. man who shouts obscenities at strangers in the streets
E. woman who accuses waiters of attempting to poison her

24. An officer should not take notes while first questioning a suspect.   24.____
     Of the following, the MOST important reason for this procedure is that

     A. information obtained at this time will probably not be truthful
     B. unessential facts can be eliminated if statements are written later
     C. the physical reactions of the suspect during interrogation can be better observed
     D. the exact wording is of no importance
     E. the statement will be better organized if written later

25. An officer should know the occupations and habits of the people on his beat. In heavily   25.____
     populated districts, however, it is too much to ask that the officer know all the people on
     his beat.
     If this statement is correct, the one of the following which would be the MOST practical
     course for an officer to follow is to

     A. concentrate on becoming acquainted with the oldest residents of the beat
     B. limit his attention to people who work as well as live in the district
     C. limit his attention to people with criminal records
     D. concentrate on becoming acquainted with key people such as janitors, bartenders,
         and local merchants
     E. concentrate on becoming acquainted with the newest residents of the beat

26. An officer off-duty but in uniform recognizes a stolen car parked outside of a tavern. He   26.____
     notices that the radiator of the car is warm, indicating recent use.
     Of the following, the MOST practical course for the officer to follow is to

     A. enter the tavern and ask aloud for the driver of the car
     B. stand in a nearby doorway and watch the car
     C. search for the officer on the beat and report the facts to him
     D. telephone the station house as soon as he arrives home
     E. enter the tavern and privately ask the bartender if he knows who owns the car

27. When a person is arrested, he is always asked whether he uses narcotics, regardless of   27.____
     the charge against him.
     Of the following, the MOST important reason for asking this question is that

     A. drug addicts can be induced to confess by withholding narcotics from them
     B. the theft of narcotics is becoming a serious police problem
     C. criminals are usually drug addicts
     D. many drug addicts commit crimes in order to obtain money for the purchase of nar-
         cotics
     E. it may be possible to convict the suspect of violation of the narcotics law

28. Of the following types of crimes, increased police vigilance would probably be LEAST   28.____
     successful in preventing

     A. murder   B. burglary
     C. prostitution   D. automobile thefts
     E. robbery

29. The Police Department has been hiring civilian women to direct traffic at school cross- 29.____
ings.
The MOST important reason for this policy is

    A. to stimulate civic interest in police problems
    B. to dramatize the traffic safety problem
    C. that women are more careful of the safety of children
    D. that young school children have more confidence in women who are mothers of
        their playmates
    E. to free policemen for regular patrol duty

30. Of the following, the fact that makes it MOST difficult to identify stolen cars is that 30.____

    A. thieves frequently damage stolen cars
    B. many cars are similar in appearance
    C. thieves frequently disguise stolen cars
    D. owners frequently don't report stolen cars which are covered by insurance
    E. owners frequently delay reporting the theft

31. When testifying in a criminal case, it is MOST important that a policeman endeavor to 31.____

    A. avoid technical terms which may be unfamiliar to the jury
    B. lean over backwards in order to be fair to the defendant
    C. assist the prosecutor even if some exaggeration is necessary
    D. avoid contradicting other prosecution witnesses
    E. confine his answers to the questions asked

32. When investigating a burglary, a policeman should obtain as complete descriptions as 32.____
possible of articles of value which were stolen, but should list, without describing, stolen
articles which are relatively valueless.
This suggested procedure is

    A. *poor;* what is valueless to one person may be of great value to another
    B. *good;* it enables the police to concentrate on recovering the most valuable articles
    C. *poor;* articles of little value frequently provide the only evidence connecting the
        suspect to the crime
    D. *good;* the listing of the inexpensive items is probably incomplete
    E. *poor;* the police should make the same effort to recover all stolen property, regard-
        less of value

33. At 10 A.M. on a regular school day, an officer notices a boy about 11 years old wandering 33.____
in the street. When asked the reason he is not in school, he replies that he attends
school in the neighborhood, but that he felt sick that morning. The officer then took the
boy to the principal of the school.
This method of handling the situation was

    A. *bad;* the officer should have obtained verification of the boy's illness
    B. *good;* the school authorities are best equipped to deal with the problem
    C. *bad;* the officer should have obtained the boy's name and address and reported
        the incident to the attendance officer
    D. *good;* seeing the truant boy escorted by an officer will deter other children from tru-
        ancy
    E. *bad;* the principal of a school should not be saddled with a truancy problem

34. During an investigation of a robbery, an officer caught one of the witnesses contradicting   34.____
himself on one point. Upon questioning, the witness readily admitted the contradiction.
The officer should conclude that

    A. the witness was truthful but emotionally disturbed by the experience
    B. all of the statements of the witness should be disregarded as untrustworthy
    C. the statements of the witness should be investigated carefully
    D. the witness was trying to protect the guilty person
    E. contradictions of this sort are inevitable

35. A woman was found dead by her estranged husband in the kitchen of a ground floor   35.____
apartment. The husband stated that, although the apartment was full of gas and tightly
closed, all the burners of the kitchen range were shut. The husband had gone to the
apartment to get some clothes. When an officer arrived, the apartment was still heavy
with gas fumes.
Of the following, the MOST likely explanation for these circumstances is that

    A. gas seeped into the apartment under the door from a defective gas furnace in the
basement
    B. the husband has given false information to mislead the police
    C. the woman changed her mind about committing suicide and shut off the jets just
before she collapsed
    D. a leak in the kitchen range had developed
    E. the woman had died from some other cause than asphyxiation

36. An officer on post hears a cry for help from a woman in a car with two men. He   36.____
approaches the car and is told by the woman that the men are kidnapping her. The men
claim to be the woman's husband and doctor and state that they are taking her to a private mental hospital.
Of the following, the BEST course for the officer is to

    A. take all of them to the station house for further questioning
    B. permit the woman to depart and arrest the men
    C. call for an ambulance to take the woman to the nearest city mental hospital
    D. accompany the car to the private mental hospital
    E. permit the car to depart on the basis of the explanation

37. Social security cards are not acceptable proof of identification for police purposes.   37.____
Of the following, the MOST important reason for this rule is that the social security card

    A. is easily obtained
    B. states on its face *for social security purposes - not for identification*
    C. is frequently lost
    D. does not contain the address of the person
    E. does not contain a photograph, description, or fingerprints of the person

38. Many well-meaning people have proposed that officers in uniform not be permitted to   38.____
arrest juveniles.
This proposal is

    A. *good;* the police are not equipped to handle juvenile offenders
    B. *bad;* juvenile offenders would lose respect for all law enforcement agencies
    C. *good;* offending juveniles should be segregated from hardened criminals
    D. *bad;* frequently it is the uniformed officer who first comes upon the youthful
offender
    E. *good;* contact with the police would prevent any rehabilitative measures from being
taken

39. An off-duty policeman was seated in a restaurant when two men entered, drew guns, and robbed the cashier. The policeman made no effort to prevent the robbery or apprehend the criminals. Later, he justified his conduct by stating that a policeman when off-duty is a private citizen with the same duties and rights of all private citizens.
The policeman's conduct was

    A. *wrong;* a policeman must act to prevent crimes and apprehend criminals at all times
    B. *right;* he was out of uniform at the time of the robbery
    C. *wrong;* he had his gun with him at the time of the robbery
    D. *right;* it would have been foolhardy for him to intervene when outnumbered by armed robbers
    E. *wrong;* he should have obtained the necessary information and descriptions after the robbers left

39._____

40. Drivers with many convictions for traffic law violations sometimes try to conceal this record by cutting off the lower part of the operator's license and attaching to it a clean section from a blank application form.
An officer who stops a driver and notices that his operator's license is torn and held together by transparent tape should FIRST

    A. verify the driver's explanation of the torn license
    B. examine both parts of the license to see if they match
    C. request additional proof of identity
    D. take the motorist to the station house for further questioning
    E. check the records of the Bureau of Motor Vehicles for unanswered summonses

40._____

Questions 41-60.

DIRECTIONS: In answering Questions 41 through 60, select the lettered word or phrase which means MOST NEARLY the same as the word in capitals.

41. IMPLY

    A. agree to   B. hint at   C. laugh at
    D. mimic   E. reduce

41._____

42. APPRAISAL

    A. allowance   B. composition   C. prohibition
    D. quantity   E. valuation

42._____

43. DISBURSE

    A. approve   B. expend   C. prevent
    D. relay   E. restrict

43._____

44. POSTERITY

    A. back payment   B. current procedure   C. final effort
    D. future generations   E. rare specimen

44._____

45. PUNCTUAL

    A. clear   B. honest   C. polite
    D. prompt   E. prudent

45._____

46. PRECARIOUS

    A. abundant   B. alarmed   C. cautious
    D. insecure   E. placid

46.____

47. FOSTER

    A. delegate   B. demote   C. encourage
    D. plead   E. surround

47.____

48. PINNACLE

    A. center   B. crisis   C. outcome
    D. peak   E. personification

48.____

49. COMPONENT

    A. flattery   B. opposite   C. part
    D. revision   E. trend

49.____

50. SOLICIT

    A. ask   B. prohibit   C. promise
    D. revoke   E. surprise

50.____

51. LIAISON

    A. asset   B. coordination   C. difference
    D. policy   E. procedure

51.____

52. ALLEGE

    A. assert   B. break   C. irritate
    D. reduce   E. wait

52.____

53. INFILTRATION

    A. consumption   B. disposal   C. enforcement
    D. penetration   E. seizure

53.____

54. SALVAGE

    A. announce   B. combine   C. prolong
    D. save   E. try

54.____

55. MOTIVE

    A. attack   B. favor   C. incentive
    D. patience   E. tribute

55.____

56. PROVOKE

    A. adjust   B. incite   C. leave
    D. obtain   E. practice

56.____

57. SURGE

    A. branch   B. contract   C. revenge
    D. rush   E. want

57.____

58. MAGNIFY

    A. attract   B. demand   C. generate
    D. increase   E. puzzle

59. PREPONDERANCE

    A. decision   B. judgment   C. outweighing
    D. submission   E. warning

60. ABATE

    A. assist   B. coerce   C. diminish
    D. indulge   E. trade

Questions 61-65

DIRECTIONS: Questions 61 through 65 are to be answered on the basis of the table which appears on the following page.

VALUE OF PROPERTY STOLEN - 2002 AND 2003

LARCENY

Category	2002		2003	
	Number of Offenses	Value of Stolen Property	Number of Offenses	Value of Stolen Property
Pocket-picking	20	$ 1,950	10	$ 950
Purse- snatching	175	5,750	20	12,500
Shoplifting	155	7,950	225	17,350
Automobile thefts	1040	127,050	860	108,000
Thefts of auto accessories	1135	34,950	970	24,400
Bicycle thefts	355	8,250	240	6,350
All other thefts	1375	187,150	1300	153,150

61. Of the total number of larcenies reported for 2002, automobile thefts accounted for MOST NEARLY

    A. 5%   B. 15%   C. 25%
    D. 50%   E. 75%

62. The LARGEST percentage decrease in the value of the stolen property from 2002 to 2003 was in the category of

    A. pocket-picking   B. automobile thefts
    C. thefts of automobile accessories   D. bicycle thefts
    E. all other thefts

63. In 2003, the average amount of each theft was LOWEST for the category of

    A. pocket-picking
    B. purse-snatching
    C. shoplifting
    D. thefts of auto accessories
    E. bicycle thefts

64. The category which had the LARGEST numerical reduction in the number of offenses from 2002 to 2003 was

    A. pocket-picking
    B. automobile thefts
    C. thefts of auto accessories
    D. bicycle thefts
    E. all other thefts

65. When the categories are ranked for each year, according to the number of offenses committed in each category (largest number to rank first), the number of categories which will have the same rank in 2002 as in 2003 is

    A. 3   B. 4   C. 5
    D. 6   E. 7

66. A parade is marching up an avenue for 60 city blocks.
A sample count of the number of people watching the parade on one side of the street in the block is taken, first, in a block near the end of the parade, and then in a block at the middle; the former count is 4000 and the latter is 6000.
If the average for the entire parade is assumed to be the average of the two samples, then the estimated number of persons watching the entire parade is MOST NEARLY

    A. 240,000   B. 300,000   C. 480,000
    D. 600,000   E. 720,000

67. Suppose that the revenue from parking meters in a city was 5% greater in 2002 than in 2001, and 2% less in 2003 than in 2002.
If the revenue in 2001 was $1,500,000, then the revenue in 2003 was

    A. $1,541,500   B. $1,542,000   C. $1,542,500
    D. $1,543,000   E. $1,543,500

68. A radio motor patrol car completes a ten mile trip in twenty minutes.
If it does one-half the distance at a speed of twenty miles an hour, its speed, in miles per hour, for the remainder of the distance must be

    A. 30   B. 40   C. 50
    D. 60   E. 70

69. A public beach has two parking areas. Their capacities are in the ratio of two to one and, on a certain day, are filled to 60% and 40% of capacity, respectively.
The entire parking facilities of the beach on that day are MOST NEARLY _____ filled.

    A. 38%   B. 43%   C. 48%
    D. 53%   E. 58%

70. While on foot patrol, an officer walks north for eleven blocks, turns around and walks south for six blocks, turns around and walks north for two blocks, then makes a right turn and walks one block.
In relation to his starting point, he is now _____ blocks away and facing _____.

    A. twenty; east   B. eight; east   C. seven; west
    D. nine; north   E. seven; north

70.____

Questions 71-73.

DIRECTIONS: Questions 71 through 73 are to be answered on the basis of the following paragraph.

When police officers search for a stolen car, they first check for the color of the car, then for make, model, year, body damage, and finally license number. The first five can be detected from almost any angle, while the recognition of the license number is often not immediately apparent. The serial number and motor number, though less likely to be changed than the easily substituted license number, cannot be observed in initial detection of the stolen car.

71. According to the above paragraph, the one of the following features which is LEAST readily observed in checking for a stolen car in moving traffic is

    A. license number   B. serial number   C. model
    D. make   E. color

71.____

72. The feature of a car that cannot be determined from most angles of observation is the

    A. make   B. model   C. year
    D. license number   E. color

72.____

73. Of the following, the feature of a stolen car that is MOST likely to be altered by a car thief shortly after the car is stolen is the

    A. license number   B. motor number
    C. color   D. model
    E. minor body damage

73.____

Questions 74-75.

DIRECTIONS: Questions 74 and 75 are to be answered on the basis of the following paragraph.

The racketeer is primarily concerned with business affairs, legitimate or otherwise, and preferably those which are close to the margin of legitimacy. He gets his best opportunities from business organizations which meet the need of large sections of the public for goods or services which are defined as illegitimate by the same public, such as prostitution, gambling, illicit drugs or liquor. In contrast to the thief, the racketeer and the establishments he controls deliver goods and services for money received.

74. From the above paragraph, it can be deduced that suppression of racketeers is difficult 74.____
because

    A. victims of racketeers are not guilty of violating the law
    B. racketeers are generally engaged in fully legitimate enterprises
    C. many people want services which are not obtainable through legitimate sources
    D. the racketeers are well organized
    E. laws prohibiting gambling and prostitution are unenforceable

75. According to the above paragraph, racketeering, unlike theft, involves 75.____

    A. objects of value
    B. payment for goods received
    C. organized gangs
    D. public approval
    E. unlawful activities

Questions 76-78.

DIRECTIONS: Questions 76 through 78 are to be answered on the basis of the following paragraph.

A number of crimes, such as robbery, assault, rape, certain forms of theft and burglary, are high visibility crimes in that it is apparent to all concerned that they are criminal acts prior to or at the time they are committed. In contrast to these, check forgeries, especially those committed by first offenders, have low visibility. There is little in the criminal act or in the interaction between the check passer and the person cashing the check to identify it as a crime. Closely related to this special quality of the forgery crime is the fact that, while it is formally defined and treated as a felonious or infamous crime, it is informally held by the legally untrained public to be a relatively harmless form of crime.

76. According to the above paragraph, crimes of *high visibility* 76.____

    A. are immediately recognized as crimes by the victims
    B. take place in public view
    C. always involve violence or the threat of violence
    D. usually are committed after dark
    E. can be observed from a distance

77. According to the above paragraph, 77.____

    A. the public regards check forgery as a minor crime
    B. the law regards check forgery as a minor crime
    C. the law distinguishes between check forgery and other forgery
    D. it is easier to spot inexperienced check forgers than other criminals
    E. it is more difficult to identify check forgers than other criminals

78. As used in the above paragraph, an *infamous* crime is   78.____

    A. a crime attracting great attention from the public
    B. more serious than a felony
    C. less serious than a felony
    D. more or less serious than a felony, depending upon the surrounding circumstances
    E. the same as a felony

Questions 79-81.

DIRECTIONS: Questions 79 through 81 are to be answered on the basis of the following
                      paragraph.

    *Criminal science is largely the science of identification. Progress in this field has been
marked and sometimes very spectacular because new techniques, instruments, and facts
flow continuousiy from the scientists. But the crime laboratories are undermanned, trade
secrets still prevail, and inaccurate conclusions are often the result. However, modern gadgets cannot substitute for the skilled intelligent investigator; he must be their master.*

79. According to the above paragraph, criminal science   79.____

    A. excludes the field of investigation
    B. is primarily interested in establishing identity
    C. is based on the equipment used in crime laboratories
    D. uses techniques different from those used in other sciences
    E. is essentially secret in nature

80. Advances in criminal science have been, according to the above paragraph,   80.____

    A. extremely limited   B. slow but steady
    C. unusually reliable   D. outstanding
    E. infrequently worthwhile

81. A problem that has not been overcome completely in crime work is, according to the   81.____
    above paragraph,

    A. unskilled investigators
    B. the expense of new equipment and techniques
    C. an insufficient number of personnel in crime laboratories
    D. inaccurate equipment used in laboratories
    E. conclusions of the public about the value of this field

Questions 82-84.

DIRECTIONS: Questions 82 through 84 are to be answered on the basis of the following
                      paragraph.

    *The New York City Police Department will accept for investigation no report of a person
missing from his residence if such residence is located outside of New York City. The person
reporting same will be advised to report such fact to the police department of the locality
where the missing person lives, which will, if necessary, communicate officially with the New
York City Police Department. However, a report will be accepted of a person who is missing
from a temporary residence in New York City, but the person making the report will be
instructed to make a report also to the police department of the locality where the missing
person lives.*

82. According to the above paragraph, a report to the New York City Police Department of a missing person whose permanent residence is outside of New York City will

    A. always be investigated provided that a report is also made to his local police authorities
    B. never be investigated unless requested officially by his local police authorities
    C. be investigated in cases of temporary New York City residence, but a report should always be made to his local police authorities
    D. be investigated if the person making the report is a New York City resident
    E. always be investigated and a report will be made to the local police authorities by the New York City Police Department

82._____

83. Of the following, the MOST likely reason for the procedure described in the above paragraph is that

    A. non-residents are not entitled to free police service from New York City
    B. local police authorities would resent interference in their jurisdiction
    C. local police authorities sometimes try to unload their problems on the New York City Police
    D. local police authorities may be better able to conduct an investigation
    E. few persons are erroneously reported as missing

83._____

84. Mr. Smith, who lives in Jersey City, and Mr. Jones, who lives in Newark, arrange to meet in New York City, but Mr. Jones does not keep the appointment. Mr. Smith telephones Mr. Jones several times the next day and gets no answer. Mr. Smith believes that something has happened to Mr. Jones.
According to the above paragraph, Mr. Smith should apply to the police authorities of

    A. Jersey City
    B. Newark
    C. Newark and New York City
    D. Jersey City and New York City
    E. Newark, Jersey City, and New York City

84._____

Questions 85-87.

DIRECTIONS: Questions 85 through 87 are to be answered on the basis of the following paragraph.

Some early psychologists believed that the basic characteristic of the criminal type was inferiority of intelligence, if not outright feeble-mindedness. They were misled by the fact that they had measurements for all kinds of criminals but, until World War I gave them a draft army sample, they had no information on a comparable group of non-criminal adults. As soon as acceptable measurements could be taken of criminals and a comparable group of non-criminals, concern with feeblemindedness or with low intelligence as a type took on less and less significance in research in criminology.

85. According to the above paragraph, some early psychologists were in error because they did not 85._____

   A. distinguish among the various types of criminals
   B. devise a suitable method of measuring intelligence
   C. measure the intelligence of non-criminals as a basis for comparison
   D. distinguish between feeblemindedness and inferiority of intelligence
   E. clearly define the term *intelligence*

86. The above paragraph implies that studies of the intelligence of criminals and non-crimi-nals 86._____

   A. are useless because it is impossible to obtain comparable groups
   B. are not meaningful because only the less intelligent criminals are detected
   C. indicate that criminals are more intelligent than non-criminals
   D. indicate that criminals are less intelligent than non-criminals
   E. do not indicate that there are any differences between the two groups

87. According to the above paragraph, studies of the World War I draft gave psychologists vital information concerning 87._____

   A. adaptability to army life of criminals and non-criminals
   B. criminal tendencies among draftees
   C. the intelligence scores of large numbers of men
   D. differences between intelligence scores of draftees and volunteers
   E. the behavior of men under abnormal conditions

Questions 88-90.

DIRECTIONS: Questions 88 through 90 are to be answered on the basis of the following paragraph.

The use of a roadblock is simply an adaptation to police practices of the military concept of encirclement. Successful operation of a roadblock plan depends almost entirely on the amount of advance study and planning given to such operations. A thorough and detailed examination of the roads and terrain under the jurisdiction of a given police agency should be made with the locations of the roadblocks pinpointed in advance. The first principle to be borne in mind in the location of each roadblock is the time element. Its location must be at a point beyond which the fugitive could not have possibly traveled in the time elapsed from the commission of the crime to the arrival of the officers at the roadblock.

88. According to the above paragraph, 88._____

   A. military operations have made extensive use of roadblocks
   B. the military concept of encirclement is an adaptation of police use of roadblocks
   C. the technique of encirclement has been widely used by military forces
   D. a roadblock is generally more effective than encirclement
   E. police use of roadblocks is based on the idea of military encirclement

89. According to the above paragraph, 89._____

   A. the factor of time is the sole consideration in the location of a roadblock
   B. the maximum speed possible in the method of escape is of major importance in roadblock location

C. the time of arrival of officers at the site of a proposed roadblock is of little importance

D. if the method of escape is not known, it should be assumed that the escape is by automobile

E. a roadblock should be sited as close to the scene of the crime as the terrain will permit

90. According to the above paragraph,   90.____

   A. advance study and planning are of minor importance in the success of roadblock operations

   B. a thorough and detailed examination of all roads within a radius of fifty miles should precede the determination of a roadblock location

   C. consideration of terrain features is important in planning the location of roadblocks

   D. the pinpointing of roadblocks should be performed before any advance study is made

   E. a roadblock operation can seldom be successfully undertaken by a single police agency

---

KEY (CORRECT ANSWERS)

1. E	21. E	41. B	61. C	81. C
2. C	22. A	42. E	62. A	82. C
3. A	23. A	43. B	63. D	83. D
4. A	24. C	44. D	64. B	84. B
5. D	25. D	45. D	65. C	85. C
6. C	26. B	46. D	66. D	86. E
7. B	27. D	47. C	67. E	87. C
8. A	28. A	48. D	68. D	88. E
9. C	29. E	49. C	69. D	89. B
10. A	30. C	50. A	70. B	90. C
11. D	31. E	51. B	71. B	
12. A	32. C	52. A	72. D	
13. E	33. B	53. D	73. A	
14. E	34. C	54. D	74. C	
15. E	35. B	55. C	75. B	
16. A	36. A	56. B	76. A	
17. B	37. E	57. D	77. A	
18. E	38. D	58. D	78. E	
19. B	39. A	59. C	79. B	
20. C	40. B	60. C	80. D	

POLICE SCIENCE

EXAMINATION SECTION
TEST 1

DIRECTIONS: Each question or incomplete statement is followed by several suggested answers or completions. Select the one that BEST answers the question or completes the statement. *PRINT THE LETTER OF THE CORRECT ANSWER IN THE SPACE AT THE RIGHT.*

1. As you are patrolling your post, you observe two men running toward a parked automobile in which a driver is seated. You question the three men and you note the license number. You *should*   1.____

    A. let them go if you see nothing suspicious
    B. warn them not to be caught loitering again
    C. arrest them because they have probably committed a crime
    D. take them back with you to the place from which the two men came

2. While you are patrolling your post, you find a flashlight and a screwdriver lying near a closed bar and grill. You notice further some jimmy marks on the door.
You *should*   2.____

    A. continue patrolling your post after noting in your memorandum book what you have seen
    B. arrest any persons standing in the vicinity
    C. try to enter the bar and grill to investigate whether it has been robbed
    D. telephone the owner of the bar and grill and inform him of what you have seen outside the door

3. While you are patrolling your post, you notice that a peddler is vending merchandise. As you approach, he gathers up his wares and begins to run.
You *should*   3.____

    A. shoot at him as he is a violator of the law
    B. blow your whistle to summon other patrolmen in order to apprehend him
    C. remain for some time at this place so as to be certain that he does not return
    D. pursue him and continue patrolling your post

4. You have been assigned to a patrol post in a park during the winter months. You hear the cries of a boy who has fallen through the ice.
The FIRST thing you should do is to   4.____

    A. rush to the nearest call telephone and summon the Emergency Squad
    B. call upon passersby to summon additional patrolmen
    C. rush to the spot from which the cries came and try to save the boy
    D. rush to the spot from which the cries came and question the boy concerning his identity so that you can summon his parents

5. You have been summoned about a robbery in a station. Three men are grappling with each other. Two of the men are plainclothesmen, but their identity is not known to you. The FIRST thing you should do is to

    A. advance with your nightstick and be ready to use it as soon as you know which one is the thief

    B. use karate to stop the fighting

    C. ask any bystanders to identify the thief before you use your gun

    D. shoot the one who is most likely to be the thief, letting yourself be guided by your own experience as to the thief's identity

5.____

6. Upon arriving at the scene of an accident in which a pedestrian was struck and killed by an automobile, a police officer's first action was to clear the scene of spectators. Of the following, the PRINCIPAL reason for this action is that

    A. important evidence may be inadvertently destroyed by the crowd

    B. this is a fundamental procedure in first aid work

    C. the operator of the vehicle may escape in the crowd

    D. witnesses will speak more freely if other persons are not present

6.____

7. In questioning witnesses a police officer is instructed to avoid leading questions or questions that will suggest the answer.
Accordingly, when questioning a witness about the appearance of a suspect, it would be BEST for him to ask:

    A. What kind of hat did he wear?

    B. Did he wear a felt hat?

    C. What did he wear?

    D. Didn't he wear a hat?

7.____

8. The only personal description the police have of a particular criminal was made several years ago.
Of the following, the item in the description that will be MOST useful in identifying him at the present time is the

    A. color of his eyes   B. color of his hair

    C. number of teeth   D. weight

8.____

9. Crime statistics indicate that property crimes such as larceny, burglary and robbery, are more numerous during winter months than in summer.
The one of the following explanations that MOST adequately accounts for this situation is that

    A. human needs, such as clothing, food, heat and shelter, are greater in summer

    B. criminal tendencies are aggravated by climatic changes generally

    C. there are more hours of darkness in winter and such crimes are usually committed under cover of darkness

    D. urban areas are more densely populated during winter months, affording greater opportunity for such crimes

9.____

10. When automobile tire tracks are to be used as evidence, a plaster cast is made of them. Before the cast is made, however, a photograph of the tracks is taken. Of the following, the MOST probable reason for taking a photograph is that   10._____

    A. photographs can be duplicated more easily than castings
    B. less skill is required for photographing than casting
    C. the tracks may be damaged in the casting process
    D. photographs are more easily transported than castings

11. It is generally recommended that a patrolman, in lifting a revolver that is to be sent to the Police Laboratory for ballistics tests and fingerprint examination, do so by inserting a pencil through the trigger guard rather than into the barrel of the weapon. The reason for PREFERRING this procedure is that   11._____

    A. every precaution must be taken not to obliterate fingerprints on the weapon
    B. there is a danger of accidentally discharging the weapon by placing the pencil in the barrel
    C. the pencil may make scratches inside the barrel that will interfere with the ballistics tests
    D. a weapon can more easily be lifted by the trigger guard

12. In addressing a class of recruits, a police captain remarked: "Carelessness and failure are twins."
The one of the following that *most nearly* expresses his meaning is: 12._____

    A. Negligence seldom accompanies success
    B. Incomplete work is careless work
    C. Conscientious work is never attended by failure
    D. A conscientious person never makes mistakes

13. In taking a statement from a person who has been shot by an assailant and is not expected to live, police are instructed to ask the person: "Do you believe you are about to die?"
Of the following, the MOST probable reason for this question is   13._____

    A. the theory that a person about to die and meet his Maker will tell the truth
    B. to determine if the victim is conscious and capable of making a statement
    C. to put the victim mentally at ease and more willing to talk
    D. that the statement could not be used in court if his mind was distraught by the fear of impending death

14. If, while you are on traffic duty at a busy intersection, a pedestrian asks you for directions to a particular place, the BEST course of conduct is to   14._____

    A. ignore the question and continue directing traffic
    B. tell the pedestrian to ask a patrolman on foot patrol
    C. answer the question in a brief, courteous manner
    D. leave your traffic post only long enough to give clear and adequate directions

15. In lecturing on the law of arrest, an instructor remarked: "To go beyond is as bad as to fall short."
The one of the following which MOST nearly expresses his meaning is:

    A. Never undertake the impossible
    B. Extremes are not desirable
    C. Look before you leap
    D. Too much success is dangerous

15.____

16. Suppose you are a police officer assigned to a patrol precinct. While you are patrolling your post in the vicinity of a school, your attention is called to a man who is selling small packages to school children. You are told that this man distributes similar packages to these same children daily and that he is suspected of dealing in narcotics. Of the following, the BEST action for you to take is to

    A. pretend to be an addict and attempt to purchase narcotics from him
    B. observe the man's action yourself for several days in order to obtain grounds for arrest
    C. stop and question one or more of the children after they have transacted business with the man
    D. stop and question the man as he leaves the children

16.____

17. In the event of a poison gas attack, civil defense authorities advise civilians to

    A. open doors and windows and go to upper floors
    B. close doors and windows and go to upper floors
    C. open doors and windows and go to the basement
    D. close doors and windows and go to the basement

17.____

18. As an intelligent police officer, you should know that, of the following, the one which is LEAST likely to be followed by an increase in crime is

    A. war   B. depression
    C. poor housing   D. prosperity

18.____

19. As a police officer interested in the promotion of traffic safety, you should know that, according to recent statistics, the one group which has the *highest* number of deaths as a result of being struck in traffic is

    A. adults over 55 years of age
    B. adults between 36 and 55 years of age
    C. adults between 22 and 35 years old
    D. children up to 4 years old

19.____

20. As an intelligent police officer having a knowledge of the various types of crimes, you should know that, in recent years, the age group 16 through 25 showed the *greatest* number of arrests for

    A. grand larceny from highways and vehicles
    B. burglary
    C. rape
    D. homicide

20.____

21. As a well-informed police officer, you should know that the *greatest* number of arrests made and summonses served in recent years was for   21.____

    A. offenses against property rights
    B. general criminality
    C. bestial criminality
    D. offenses against public health, safety and policy

22. As a police officer interested in the reduction of unnecessary traffic accidents, you should know that two of the *chief* sources of such accidents to pedestrians in recent years were crossing a street   22.____

    A. against the light, and crossing past a parked car
    B. at a point other than the crossing, and crossing against the light
    C. at a point other than the crossing, and running off the sidewalk
    D. against the light, and failing to observe whether cars were making right or left turns

23. A "modus operandi" file will be MOST valuable to a new patrolman as a means of showing the   23.____

    A. methods used by criminals
    B. various bureaus and divisions of the Police Department
    C. number and nature of vehicular accidents
    D. forms used by the Police Department

24. A police officer is frequently advised to lie down before returning fire, if a person is shooting at him. This is PRIMARILY because   24.____

    A. a smaller target will thus be presented to the assailant
    B. he can return fire more quickly while in the prone position
    C. the assailant will think he has struck the police officer and cease firing
    D. it will indicate that the police officer is not the aggressor

25. In making arrests during a large riot, it is the practice of the police to take the ringleaders into custody as soon as possible. This is PRIMARILY because   25.____

    A. the police can obtain valuable information from them
    B. they deserve punishment more than the other rioters
    C. rioters need leadership and, without it, will disperse more quickly
    D. arrests of wrongdoers should always be in order of their importance

KEY (CORRECT ANSWERS)

1.	A		11.	C
2.	C		12.	A
3.	C		13.	A
4.	C		14.	C
5.	A		15.	B
6.	A		16.	C
7.	C		17.	B
8.	A		18.	D
9.	C		19.	A
10.	C		20.	B

21.	D
22.	B
23.	A
24.	A
25.	C

TEST 2

DIRECTIONS: Each question or incomplete statement is followed by several suggested answers or completions. Select the one that BEST answers the question or completes the statement. *PRINT THE LETTER OF THE CORRECT ANSWER IN THE SPACE AT THE RIGHT.*

1. Assume that you are a police officer. A woman has complained to you about a man's indecent exposure in front of a house. As you approach the house, the man begins to run. You *should*   1.____

   A. shoot to kill as the man may be a dangerous maniac
   B. fire a warning shot to try to halt the man
   C. summon other patrolmen in order to apprehend him
   D. question the woman regarding the man's identity

2. You are patrolling a parkway in a radio car with another police officer. A maroon car coming from the opposite direction signals you to stop and the driver informs you that he was robbed by three men speeding ahead of him in a black sedan. Your radio car cannot cross the center abutment.   2.____
   You *should*

   A. request the driver to make a report to the nearest precinct as your car cannot cross over to the other side
   B. make a U turn in your radio car and give chase on the wrong side of the parkway
   C. fire warning shots in the air to summon other patrolmen
   D. flash police headquarters over your radio system

3. You are on patrol duty in a crowded part of the city. You hear the traffic patrolman fire four shots in the air and cry, "Get out of his way. He's got a gun." You see a man tearing along the street dodging traffic.   3.____
   You *should*

   A. fire several shots in the air to alert other police officers
   B. give chase to the man and shoot, as it is possible that one of your shots may hit him
   C. wait for an opening in the crowds and then shoot at the man from one knee
   D. wade through the crowds and then shout at the man to stop

4. Assume that you have been assigned to a traffic post at a busy intersection. A car bearing out-of-town license plates is about to turn into a one-way street going in the opposite direction. You blow your whistle and stop the car.   4.____
   You *should then*

   A. hand out a summons to the driver in order to make an example of him, since out-of-town drivers notoriously disregard our traffic regulations
   B. pay no attention to him and let him continue in the proper direction
   C. ask him to pull over to the curb and advise him to drive to the nearest precinct to get a copy of the latest city traffic regulations
   D. call his attention to the fact that he was violating a traffic regulation and permit him to continue in the proper direction

5. A storekeeper has complained to you that every day at noon several peddlers congre-   5.____
gate outside his store in order to sell their merchandise. You *should*

    A. inform him that such complaints must be made directly to the Police Commissioner
    B. inform him that peddlers have a right to earn their living, too
    C. make it your business to patrol that part of your post around noon
    D. pay no attention to him as this storekeeper is probably a crank inasmuch as
       nobody else has complained

6. You notice that a man is limping hurriedly, leaving a trail of blood behind him. You ques-   6.____
tion him, and his explanation is that he was hurt accidentally while he was watching a
man clean a gun.
You *should*

    A. let him go as you have no proof that his story is not true
    B. have him sent to the nearest city hospital under police escort so that he may be
       questioned again after treatment
    C. ask him whether the man had a license for his gun
    D. ask him to lead you to the man who cleaned his gun so that you may question him
       further about the accident

7. There have been a series of burglaries in a certain residential area consisting of one-   7.____
family houses. You have been assigned to select a house in this area in which detectives
can wait secretly for the attempt to burglarize that house so that the burglars can be
apprehended in the act.
Which of the following would be the *BEST* house to select for this purpose? The house

    A. that was recently burglarized and from which several thousand dollars worth of
       clothing and personal property were taken
    B. whose owner reports that several times the telephone has rung but the person
       making the call hung up as soon as the telephone was answered
    C. that is smaller and looks much less pretentious than other houses in the same area
    D. that is occupied by a widower who works long hours but who lives with an invalid
       mother requiring constant nursing service

8. The two detectives noticed the man climb a ladder to the roof of a loft building. The   8.____
detectives followed the same route. They saw him break a skylight and lower himself into
the building. Through the broken skylight, one of the detectives covered the man with his
gun and told him to throw up his hands.
The action of the detectives in this situation was *faulty CHIEFLY* because

    A. one of the detectives should have remained on the ladder
    B. criminals should be caught red-handed
    C. the detectives should have made sure of the identity of the man before following
       him
    D. the possibility of another means of escape from the building should have been
       foreseen

9. Suppose that, while you are patrolling your post, a middle-aged woman informs you that three men are holding up a nearby express office. You rush immediately to the scene of the holdup. While you are still about 75 feet away, you see the three men, revolvers in their hands, emerge from the office and make for what is apparently their getaway car, which is pointed in the opposite direction. Of the following, your *FIRST* consideration in this situation should be to

   A. enter the express office in order to find out what the men have taken
   B. maneuver quickly so as to get the getaway car between you and the express office
   C. make a mental note of the descriptions of the escaping men for immediate alarm
   D. attempt to overtake the car in which the holdup men seek to escape.

9.____

10. Which of the following situations, if observed by you while on patrol, should you consider *MOST* suspicious and deserving of further investigation?

   A. A shabbily dressed youth is driving a new Cadillac
   B. An old Plymouth has been parked without lights outside an apartment house for several hours
   C. A light is on in the rear of a one-family, luxurious residence
   D. Two well-dressed men are standing at a bus stop at 2 A.M. and arguing heatedly

10.____

11. Suppose that, while on patrol late at night, you find a woman lying in the street, apparently the victim of a hit-and-run driver. She seems to be injured seriously but you wish to ask her one or two questions in order to help apprehend the hit-and-run car.
Of the following, the *BEST* question to ask is:

   A. In what direction did the car go?
   B. What time did it happen?
   C. What kind of car was it?
   D. How many persons were in the car?

11.____

12. Assume that you are driving a police car, equipped with two-way radio, along an isolated section of a parkway at 3 A.M. You note that the headlights of a car are blinking rapidly. When you stop to investigate, the driver of the car informs you that he was just forced to the side of the road by two men in a green convertible, who robbed him of a large amount of cash and jewelry at the point of a gun and then sped away. Your *FIRST* consideration in this situation should be to

   A. drive rapidly along the parkway in the direction taken by the criminals in an effort to apprehend them before they escape
   B. question the driver carefully, looking for inconsistencies indicating that he made up the whole story
   C. obtain a complete listing and identification of all materials lost
   D. notify your superior to have the parkway exits watched for a car answering the description of the getaway car

12.____

13. Suppose that you have been assigned to check the story of a witness in a holdup case. The witness states that, while sitting at her window, she observed the suspect loitering outside a cigar store. As she watched, the suspect entered a nearby liquor store. He remained there only a minute or two. Then she saw him walk out rapidly, hurry to the corner and hail a cab. Assume that Figure 1 is a scale drawing of the scene. All four corners of the intersection are occupied by tall buildings. W indicates the window at which the witness sat, C indicates the cigar store and L indicates the liquor store. On the basis of this sketch, the *BEST* reason for doubting the truthfulness of the witness is that

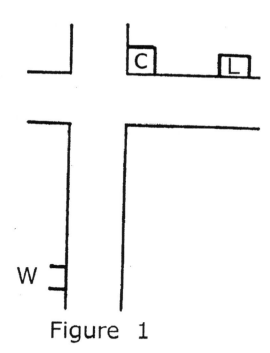

Figure 1

13.____

   A. the window is far removed from the cigar store
   B. the cigar store and the window are not on the same street
   C. distances may be distorted by a high angle of observation
   D. the liquor store cannot be seen from the window

14. Assume that you are investigating a case of reported suicide. You find the deceased sitting in a chair, sprawled over his desk, a revolver still clutched in his right hand. In your examination of the room, you find that the window is partly open. Only one bullet has been fired from the revolver. That bullet is lodged in the wall. Assume that Figure 2 is a scale drawing of the scene. D indicates the desk, C indicates the chair, W indicates the window and B indicates the bullet. The one of the following features which indicates *MOST* strongly that the deceased did *not* commit suicide is the

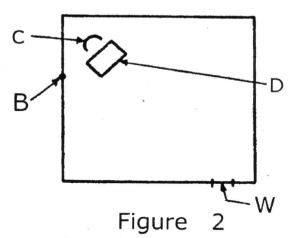

Figure 2

14.____

   A. distance between the desk and the bullet hole
   B. relative position of the bullet hole and the chair
   C. fact that the window was partly open
   D. relative position of the desk and the window

15. Driver 1 claimed that the collision occurred because, as he approached the intersection, Driver 2 started to make a left turn suddenly and at high speed, even though the light had been red against him for 15 or 20 seconds.

Suppose that you have been assigned to make a report on this accident. The position of the vehicles after the accident is indicated in Figure 3, the point in each case indicating the front of the vehicle. On the basis of this sketch, the *BEST* reason for concluding that Driver 1's statement is *false* is that Driver

A. 2's car is beyond the center of the intersection
B. 2's car is making the turn on the proper side of the road
C. 1's car is beyond the sidewalk line
D. 1's car is on the right hand side of the road

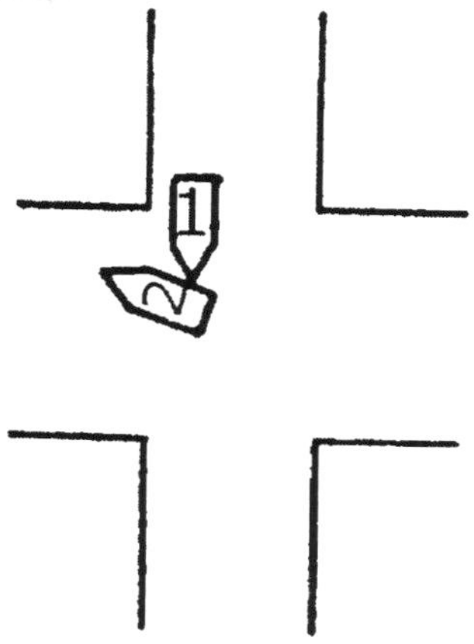

15.____

Figure 3

16. Suppose that you are a police officer investigating a complaint that a gunman is brandishing an automatic revolver in the back room of a bar and grill. Of the following, the *BEST* reason for you to exercise caution as you enter the back room is that

A. there may be a second means of exit from the room
B. the complaint may have been exaggerated
C. an automatic revolver may easily become jammed
D. the complaint mentioned only one gunman
E. the gunman may open fire without warning

16.____

17. Suppose that you have arrested a man for attempting to break into a fur shop and that you are about to escort him to a nearby precinct station.

Of the following, the *FIRST important* precaution for you to take is to make certain that

A. the man is carrying proper identification
B. no furs are missing
C. the man has a criminal record
D. the man is unarmed
E. the man's fingerprints have been carefully checked

17.____

18. While you are patrolling your post in a busy midtown area, you notice the gasoline tank of a bus burst into flame. The passengers see the fire and begin to leave the bus at once. The street is crowded with pedestrians.

Of the following, the *BEST* reason for you to clear the area of pedestrians immediately is to

A. avoid panic among the bus passengers
B. reduce the possibility of injuries due to an explosion
C. prevent the fire from spreading
D. leave room for the bus driver to maneuver the bus
E. avoid possible fatalities due to carbon monoxide fumes

18.____

19. Detectives had been following the two men for some time. At 8:10 P.M., Sunday, the sus-   19.____
pects entered a four-story apartment house. They went to the roof of the building, walked
across to an adjoining warehouse, and went down the fire escape to the second floor,
where they forced a warehouse window. Meanwhile, although the temperature was
below freezing, other detectives waited in the street below. Under the circumstances
described above, for several detectives to wait in the street was *wise CHIEFLY* because
it was

    A. possible that the suspects lived in the apartment building
    B. unlikely that the suspects would again venture out into the street
    C. desirable to block all possible avenues of escape by the suspects
    D. obvious that the warehouse windows were unlocked
    E. necessary to know the exact location of the suspects every minute of the time

20. Jones was found lying in the kitchen of his bungalow, two feet from the window. A bullet   20.____
had passed through hsi heart and was found lodged in the wall. Death must have been
instantaneous. There was a bullet hole in the lower part of the glass of the kitchen window. All doors and windows were closed and locked from within. No weapon was found
in the bungalow.
Of the following, the *MOST* valid conclusion on the basis of the above facts is that

    A. Jones was killed by a friend who escaped through the window
    B. the murderer must have had an accomplice
    C. the window was closed and locked after the murder had been committed
    D. Jones probably committed suicide
    E. Jones was shot by a person standing outside the kitchen window

21. Looking through the window of a jewelry store, a police officer sees a man take a watch   21.____
from the counter and drop it into his pocket while the jeweler is busy talking to someone
else. The man looks around the store and then walks out.
The officer should

    A. *follow* the man to see what he does with the watch as thieves of this type usually
        work in pairs
    B. *ignore* the incident; if the man were performing an illegal act,the jeweler would
        have called for help
    C. *arrest* the man, take him to the station house,and then return to obtain the jeweler's
        statement
    D. *ignore* the incident; if the man were a thief,the jeweler would not have left the
        watches unattended
    E. *stop* the man and bring him back into the shop so that both he and the jeweler can
        be questioned

22. It is quite possible to set up a general procedure which will result in the rehabilitation of   22.____
all juvenile delinquents .
This statment is, *in general,*

    A. *correct;* the major causes of all juvenile delinquency are improper home life and a
        general lack of morals; cure these and there will be no problem of juvenile delin-
        quency
    B. *not correct;* juvenile delinquency results from the generally lower moral climate;
        therefore, rehabilitation is not possible until the world climate changes

    C. *correct;* if juvenile delinquents are severely punished, rehabilitation will follow

    D. *not correct;* each case of juvenile delinquency is different and, for most effective treatment, must be handled on an individual basis

    E. *correct;* if the proper general procedure is set up, it always can be applied

23. A police officer observes a young man, who is obviously very excited, walking unusually fast and repeatedly halting to look behind him. Upon stopping the young man, the police officer finds that he is carrying a gun and has just held up a liquor store a few blocks away.
This incident illustrates that   23.____

    A. circumstances that are not suspicious in themselves frequently provide clues for the solution of crimes

    B. an experienced police officer can pick the criminal type out of a crowd by alert observation

    C. action is always to be preferred to thought

    D. a police officer should investigate suspicious circumstances

    E. a police officer who stops to think may sometimes fail to get his man

24. When making arrests, the police officer should treat all suspects in the same manner.
This suggested rule is   24.____

    A. *undesirable;* the specific problems presented should govern the police officer's actions

    B. *desirable;* this is the only democratic solution to the problem

    C. *undesirable;* police officers should not be expected to abide by rules as criminals do not

    D. *desirable;* only by setting up fixed and rigid rules can police officers know what is expected of them

    E. *undesirable;* persons who are only suspected are not criminals and should not be treated as such

25. One of the most difficult questions in a crime prevention program is to decide how many men are needed to police a particular area. There have been a number of attempts to invent a simple formula, but none has so far been successful.
Of the following reasons for this, the *MOST* probable is that   25.____

    A. men, not formulas, patrol beats

    B. many factors are involved whose relative importance has not been determined

    C. there is no information on which to base such a formula

    D. such a formula even if it were accurate would be of little use as it would be too theoretical

    E. police problems in no two areas in the city are alike in any way

---

KEY (CORRECT ANSWERS)

1.	C		11.	C
2.	D		12.	D
3.	D		13.	D
4.	D		14.	B
5.	C		15.	C
6.	B		16.	E
7.	B		17.	D
8.	D		18.	B
9.	C		19.	C
10.	D		20.	E

21.	E
22.	D
23.	D
24.	A
25.	B

———

TEST 3

DIRECTIONS: Each question or incomplete statement is followed by several suggested answers or completions. Select the one that BEST answers the question or completes the statement. *PRINT THE LETTER OF THE CORRECT ANSWER IN THE SPACE AT THE RIGHT.*

1. A police officer is testifying at the jury trial of a suspect he arrested.
   Which one of the following actions, taken by the officer while on the witness stand, is *most likely* to FAVORABLY affect the acceptance of his testimony? The officer

   A. refers to his memo book before he answers each question
   B. directs his testimony to the jury, not to the judge or counsel
   C. responds to obviously silly questions with equally silly answers
   D. carefully presents both the facts asked for and also the conclusions he is able to draw from them
   E. adds explanations and support to his answers, rather than merely replying to a question with a direct answer

   1.____

2. A police officer is interviewing the person who called the police to the scene of a crime.
   The officer wants to know whether the witness, when he entered the room to call the police, saw someone who might be the person who committed the crime.
   Which one of the following is the BEST way for the officer to phrase his question to the witness?

   A. "What did you observe when you entered the room?"
   B. "Didn't you see anyone when you entered the room?"
   C. "Was the person who committed the crime still in the room when you entered?"
   D. "Was someone who could have committed the crime in the room when you entered?"
   E. "Didn't you see someone who could have committed the crime when you entered the room?"

   2.____

3. Because of the effect that certain physical conditions have on human perception, testimony of well-intentioned witnesses is sometimes unreliable.
   Which one of the following claims by a witness (all of which are affected by physical conditions), is *most likely* to be reliable? A witness

   A. claims that a taxicab, parked at night under a sodium vapor street lamp, was yellow and not white
   B. who is farsighted, claims that he saw clearly a robbery suspect, 25 feet away, even though he was not wearing glasses at the time
   C. who had just entered a dark house from a brightly lighted street, claims that he can identify the prowler he saw escaping through the window of the house at that moment
   D. who was in a very dimly lighted area, claims to have seen a certain man wearing blue pants and a jacket of a color he could not identify
   E. who had been sitting in a movie theatre for about an hour, claims that he did not see a blue flashing light, but did see a red "exit" light; the lights were later found to be of equal brightness

   3.____

4. Two patrol officers responding to a "dispute" call find the complainant is a woman who says her neighbor is beating his child. They knock on his door and interview the man. He is drunk and alone with his 7-year-old son. The boy is badly beaten and the father is still in a rage and yells at the officers to get out.
Which one of the following, if any, *MOST* accurately states the person or agency that is both in the best position to promptly remove the child against the father's will in this situation and that also has the authority to do so?

    A. A patrol supervisor
    B. The patrol officers on the scene
    C. A youth aid division officer
    D. The family court, through issuance of a warrant authorizing the police to remove the child
    E. None of the above has authority to remove the child against the father's will.

4.____

5. A police officer has responded to a gas station robbery and is interviewing the victim. Among other things, he asks whether the victim can remember the exact words of the suspect and his manner of speech.
Which one of the following *BEST* states *both* whether or not this is an important area of investigation and also the best reason therefor?

    A. It *is not* important, because it could not be admissible as evidence in court
    B. It *is* important, because it is necessary to prove the element of intent in robbery
    C. It *is not* important, because most robbers don't say enough to determine any identifying characteristic
    D. It *is not* important, because a robbery victim will be too upset to be very accurate on this matter
    E. It *is* important, because the robber's choice of phrases is often highly characteristic and, therefore, helpful in identification

5.____

6. If the primary purpose of traffic law enforcement is the prevention of accidents, then which one of the following is the *MOST* appropriate attitude for the police to have regarding enforcing traffic laws?

    A. Police officers should attempt to issue as many citations as time permits
    B. Police officers should avoid using warnings because warnings have very little prevention value
    C. Motorists should be encouraged to comply voluntarily with traffic laws and educated regarding such laws, whenever possible
    D. To the extent possible, all traffic laws should be enforced equally, without regard to time, place, or type of violation
    E. Enforcement of traffic laws should be the sole responsibility of specialists who devote full time to accident prevention

6.____

7. A foot-patrol officer in a business district observes a man walking in front of him whom he recognizes as a wanted felon. They are at an intersection crowded with people. The suspect is not aware of the patrol officer's presence and continues across the intersection.
Which one of the following is the *BEST* place at which to make the arrest?

    A. In a restaurant or store if the suspect should enter
    B. Immediately at the intersection where he has observed the suspect
    C. At the first intersection which has little or no pedestrian movement

7.____

D. In the middle of the first block which has little or no pedestrian traffic
E. In the middle of the next block, but only if this block is still congested with pedestrians

8. **Which one** of the following cars is most *likely* to appear to a witness to be traveling *FASTER* than its *true* speed? A   8.____

A. large car   B. noisy car
C. quiet car   D. car painted a solid color
E. car painted two or more colors

9. A certain police officer was patrolling a playground area where adolescent gangs had   9.____
been causing trouble and holding drinking parties. He approached a teenage boy who
was alone and drinking from a large paper cup. He asked the boy what he was drinking
and the boy replied "Coke." The officer asked the boy for the cup and the boy refused to
give it to him. The officer then explained that he wanted to check the contents, and the
boy still refused to give it to him. The officer then demanded the cup and the boy reluc-
tantly gave it to him. The officer smelled the contents of the cup and determined that it
was, in fact, Coke. He then told the boy to move along, and emptied the Coke on the
ground.
Which one of the following is the *MOST* serious error, if any, made by the officer in
handling this situation?

A. The officer should not have made any effort to determine what was in the cup
B. The officer should not have explained to the boy why he wanted to have the cup
C. The officer should have returned the Coke to the boy and allowed the boy to stay
where he was
D. The officer should have first placed the boy under arrest before taking the cup from
him
E. None of the above since the officer made no error in handling the situation

10. A police officer assigned to some clerical duties accidentally destroys an important docu-   10.____
ment which was to be presented in court as evidence in a few days.
The *BEST* action for him to take *FIRST* in this situation is to

A. suggest that the case be postponed until more evidence can be obtained
B. immediately contact the person from whom the document was obtained and
request another copy of it
C. say nothing at this time, but admit the destruction of the document when asked for
it by his superior
D. notify his superior of the destruction of the document

11. Assume that you are a probationary police officer newly assigned to perform a certain   11.____
duty. Your superior has given you specific orders concerning a job to be done. An older
and more experienced officer who has no authority over you criticizes what you are doing
and gives you orders to do things his way.
The *BEST* action for you to take is to

A. ask your superior to direct the older patrolman to cease criticizing and giving
orders
B. continue working in accordance with the orders given you by your superior

C. stop doing the job until you have asked your superior about the situation
D. seek the advice of other experienced officers and, if they agree, follow the orders of the older officer

12. Authorities believe that delinquent behavior of children tends strongly to develop into criminal adult behavior.
The *CHIEF* significance of this statement to a police officer is that he should 12.____

   A. pay particular attention to the children of known criminals
   B. arrest all children committing delinquent acts
   C. try to correct early evidences of bad behavior
   D. administer a reasonable degree of physical punishment to the children committing such delinquent acts and warn them of immediate arrest the next time they engage in such activities

13. Of the following, the *CHIEF* reason for requiring the registration of certain firearms is that 13.____

   A. it will reduce law enforcement problems created by home-made guns
   B. uncontrolled availability of guns tends to increase law enforcement problems
   C. most criminals will not use a registered gun in committing a crime
   D. unregistered guns are often found at the scene of a crime

14. In most states no crime can occur unless there is a written law forbidding the act, and, even though an act may not be exactly in harmony with public policy, such act is not a crime unless it is expressly forbidden by legislative enactment.
According to the above statement, 14.____

   A. all acts not in harmony with public policy should be expressly forbidden by law
   B. a crime is committed only with reference to a particular law
   C. nothing contrary to public policy can be done without legislative authority
   D. legislative enactments frequently forbid actions which are exactly in harmony with public policy

15. When starting to unload a revolver, it is safest for the police officer to have the muzzle pointing 15.____

   A. upward   B. downward   C. to the left   D. to the right

16. When approaching a suspect to make an arrest, it is *LEAST* important for the police officer to guard against the possibility that the suspect may 16.____

   A. be diseased   B. have a gun
   C. use physical force   D. run away

17. The printed departmental rules may *logically* be expected to include instructions on 17.____

   A. which posts are the most dangerous
   B. where to purchase uniforms and equipment cheaply
   C. how many days a week overtime work will be required
   D. what information must be included in an accident report

18. It is well known that some people refrain from breaking the law only because they fear   18._____
subsequent punishment. This statement is *LEAST* likely to apply to the person who

    A. waits to light his cigarette after he reaches the street instead of lighting it in the station

    B. stops his car at a red light where there is a traffic officer

    C. returns the excess change he has received from a bus operator

    D. finds a brief case full of 20-dollar bills and turns it over to the police

---

KEY (CORRECT ANSWERS)

1.	B		11.	B
2.	A		12.	C
3.	B		13.	B
4.	A		14.	B
5.	E		15.	B
6.	C		16.	A
7.	D		17.	D
8.	D		18.	C
9.	C			
10.	D			

EXAMINATION SECTION
TEST 1

DIRECTIONS: Each question or incomplete statement is followed by several suggested answers or completions. Select the one that BEST answers the question or completes the statement. *PRINT THE LETTER OF THE CORRECT ANSWER IN THE SPACE AT THE RIGHT.*

1. Many officers working in the field of juvenile delinquency accept youth gangs as a natural development in community life.
   If this assumption is correct, the one of the following which would be the MOST practical course of action with respect to youth gangs is to

   A. utilize the activity of the gang, diverting it from the criminal to the constructive
   B. change the structure of community life so that gangs will no longer be a natural development
   C. ignore youth gangs and concentrate on youthful offenders
   D. encourage younger members of gangs to break away from the gang leaders
   E. set up an interesting lecture and demonstration course pointing out the evils of gang warfare

1.____

2. An officer who is called to the scene of an automobile accident questions two witnesses concerning the accident. The officer knows that the two witnesses are outstanding and upright members of the community. The two witnesses give contradictory testimony.
   He should conclude that the MOST likely reason for the contradiction is that

   A. honest, upright people do not always make the best witnesses
   B. at least one of the witnesses has been upset by the questioning
   C. people do not always observe accurately
   D. at least one of the witnesses is lying
   E. contradictions in cases of this sort are inevitable

2.____

3. An officer, making his rounds, notices that one storekeeper has not cleared the snow from the sidewalk in front of his store. After reminding the storekeeper that he is breaking the law if the sidewalk is not cleared, the officer also points out that a dangerous situation may arise if ice forms.
   This method of handling the situation by the officer is USUALLY

   A. *bad;* the storekeeper broke the law and should be punished
   B. *good;* the storekeeper will clear the sidewalk and no one will be hurt
   C. *bad;* the patrolman should have forced the storekeeper to clear the sidewalk of snow immediately
   D. *good;* threatening severe punishment is the most desirable method to achieve compliance with the law
   E. *bad;* the patrolman should not have mentioned the law but asked the storekeeper to clear the walk as a personal favor to him

3.____

4. About 9:00 P.M., an officer observes two men loitering near a neighborhood movie theatre. He has not seen either of these two men in the neighborhood before. The agent for the theatre generally deposits the night receipts in the local bank's night deposit vault between 9:00 P.M. and 9:15 P.M.
Of the following, the MOST appropriate action for the officer to take is to

    A. approach the two men and tell them that no loitering is allowed near the theatre
    B. demand that they tell him their place of residence and the reason for their presence near the theatre
    C. pay no further attention since they are obviously waiting for some friend or relative who is in the theatre
    D. enter the theatre by the side entrance and warn the manager to be prepared for a possible attempt at robbery
    E. station himself so that he can observe their further actions until the theatre's money has been deposited

4.____

5. An officer stationed along the route of a parade has been ordered by his superior to allow no cars to cross the route while the parade is in progress. An ambulance driver on an emergency run attempts to drive his ambulance across the route while the parade is passing.
Under these circumstances, the officer should

    A. ask the driver to wait while the officer contacts his superior and obtains a decision
    B. stop the parade long enough to permit the ambulance to cross the street
    C. direct the ambulance driver to the shortest detour available which will add at least ten minutes to the run
    D. hold up the ambulance in accordance with the superior's order
    E. . advise the driver to telephone the hospital and notify his superior that he is being delayed by the parade

5.____

6. A woman has her husband arrested for severely beating their five-year-old son. A crowd of angry neighbors has gathered around the husband.
In making the arrest, the arresting officer should

    A. treat the husband like any other person accused of breaking the law
    B. deal with the husband sympathetically since the man may be mentally ill
    C. handle him harshly since his crime is a despicable one
    D. treat him roughly only if he shows no remorse for his actions
    E. let him be *roughed up* a bit by neighbors so long as he is not injured severely

6.____

7. An officer notices two students engaged in a fistfight in front of a high school. Three or four students have gathered around the fighting youngsters.
Of the following actions, the one the officer should take FIRST is to

    A. summon assistance before attending to the fight
    B. forcibly disperse the onlooking students and then attend to the belligerents
    C. try to separate the two belligerents without hurting either
    D. fire a shot into the air to warn the onlookers and the belligerents to disperse
    E. use his nightstick on the two belligerents to stop the fight

7.____

8. An officer who responded at 2 A.M. to a radio call that a burglary had been committed in an apartment heard the sound of clashing tools coming from the adjoining apartment. For the officer to investigate the noise would be

    A. *undesirable;* he may not search without a warrant
    B. *desirable;* the thief may be found
    C. *undesirable;* unusual noises in apartments are common
    D. *desirable;* the victim would tend to be impressed by the concern shown
    E. *undesirable;* the thief may be armed

8.____

9. An off-duty officer in civilian clothes is riding in the rear of a bus. He notices two teen-age boys tampering with the rear emergency door.
The MOST appropriate action for him to take is to

    A. watch the boys closely but take no action unless they actually open the emergency door
    B. report the boys' actions to the bus operator and let the bus operator take whatever action he deems best
    C. signal the bus operator to stop, show the boys his badge, and then order them off the bus
    D. show the boys his badge, order them to stop their actions, and take down their names and addresses
    E. tell the boys to discontinue their tampering, pointing out the dangers to life that their actions may create

9.____

10. At 3:00 A.M., while on his tour of duty, an officer notices a traffic light at an intersection is not operating. There is little traffic at night at this intersection.
Under these circumstances, the MOST appropriate action for the officer to take is to

    A. report this matter to his superior at the end of his tour of duty
    B. station himself at the intersection to direct traffic until the appearance of daylight reduces the hazard of a collision
    C. report this matter immediately to his precinct
    D. post a sign at the intersection stating that the traffic light is not operating
    E. ignore the situation since nothing can be done at this time and the patrolman on the day shift can make the necessary report

10.____

Questions 11-15.

DIRECTIONS: Questions 11 through 15 are to be answered on the basis of the following Police Department rule.

A description of persons or property wanted by the Police Department, which is to be given to the police force through the medium of a general alarm, if not distinctive, is of no value.

11. Mrs. R. Jones reported the theft of a valuable brooch from her apartment. The brooch was of gold and consisted of a very large emerald surrounded by 50 small diamonds. The one of the following additional pieces of information which would be MOST helpful to you in identifying the brooch is that

11.____

A. the value of the brooch is $50,000
B. there are 48 small diamonds and 2 slightly larger diamonds
C. the emerald is carved in the form of a woman's head
D. the brooch is made of gold with a slightly green cast
E. the brooch is circular with the emerald in the center and the diamond around it

12. Assume that you have stopped a 1993 Dodge four-door sedan which you suspect is a   12._____
car which had been reported as stolen the day before.
The one of the following items of information which would be of GREATEST value in
determining whether this is the stolen car is that the

    A. stolen car's license number was QA 2356; this car's license number is U 21375
    B. stolen car's engine number was AB 6231; this car's engine number is CS 2315
    C. windshield of the stolen car was not cracked; this car's windshield is cracked
    D. stolen car had no dents; this car has numerous dents
    E. stolen car had white-walled tires; this car does not have white-walled tires

13. Assume that you are questioning a woman who, you suspect, is wanted by the Depart-   13._____
ment.
Of the characteristics listed below, the one which would be of GREATEST value in
determining whether this is the wanted person is

    A. Age: about 30; Height: 5'8"; Weight: 160 lbs.
    B. Eyes: blue; Hair: blonde; Complexion: fair
    C. that she frequently drinks to excess
    D. Scars: two thin, half-moon scars just on right cheek bone and below eye
    E. that when last seen she was wearing a dark, grey wool dress and was accompa-
nied by the prizefighter John Day

14. You are watching a great number of people leave the sports arena after a boxing match.   14._____
Of the characteristics listed below, the one which would be of GREATEST value to you
in spotting a man wanted by the Department is

    A. Height: 5'3"; Weight: 200 lbs.
    B. Eyes: brown; Hair: black wavy; Complexion: sallow
    C. that he frequents bars and grills and customarily associates with females
    D. Scars: thin 1/2" scar on left upper lip; Tattoos: on right forearm - *Pinto*
    E. Mustache: when last seen August 1997, he wore a small black mustache

15. Assume that on a hot summer day you are stationed on the grass of the south bank of a   15._____
busy parkway looking at eastbound traffic for a light blue 1991. Ford two-door sedan.
If traffic is very heavy, the one of the following additional pieces of information which
would be MOST helpful to you in identifying the car is that

    A. all chrome is missing from the left side of the car
    B. there is a bullethole in the left front window
    C. motor number is 22674 AH
    D. the front bumper is missing
    E. the paint on the right side of the car is somewhat faded

16. While you are on patrol, you notice that the lone occupant of a car parked at the top of a long, steep hill is a boy about 7 years old. The boy is playing with the steering wheel and other controls.
The FIRST action for you to take is to

    A. make sure that the car is safely parked
    B. test the car's emergency brake to make sure it will hold
    C. drive the car to the bottom of the hill and park it there
    D. test the car's controls to make sure that the boy has not changed anything
    E. order the boy to leave the car for his own safety

16._____

17. The proprietor of a tavern summons an officer and turns over to him a loaded revolver that was found in one of the tavern's booths.
Of the following, the LEAST appropriate action for the officer to take is to

    A. close off the booth from use by other patrons
    B. determine exactly when the revolver was found
    C. obtain the names or descriptions of the persons who occupied the booth before the revolver was found
    D. question the proprietor very closely concerning the matter
    E. unload the gun and place it in an inside pocket

17._____

18. *The traditional method of training an officer - equipping him and putting him on the street with an experienced man - is no longer adequate.*
The one of the following which is the MOST probable reason for this change in view-point is that

    A. officers are no longer simply guardians of the peace but each one is a specialist
    B. the kind of recruit that the Police Department gets has changed
    C. the former belief that *the best way to learn is to do* is no longer accepted
    D. there has been a great change in police problems and methods
    E. more money has been made available for training purposes

18._____

19. An officer overhears a businessman complain that his sales of tires had fallen off sharply because a new competitor has suddenly appeared in his territory and is under-selling him at unbelievably low prices. The officer recalls that a large shipment of tires had been reported stolen a short time ago.
It is ADVISABLE for the officer to

    A. forget the matter as it is probably a coincidence
    B. tell the businessman to report the new competitor to the Better Business Bureau for unfair practices
    C. check to see if there is any connection between the two sets of circumstances
    D. inform the businessman about the robbery and ask him if he thinks that there is a connection
    E. arrest the owner of the new store as he is obviously involved in the robbery

19._____

20. While patrolling his post in a section of the county late Saturday night, an officer notices a well-dressed man break a car window with a rock, open a front door, and enter. He is followed into the car by a woman companion. Of the following, the MOST essential action for the officer to take is to

    20.___

    A. point his gun at the man, enter the car, and order the man to drive to the station house to explain his action
    B. approach the car and ask the man why it was necessary to break the car window
    C. take down the license number of the car and note the description of both the man and the woman in the event that the car is later reported as stolen
    D. *bawl the man out* for endangering himself by breaking the window
    E. request proof of ownership of the car from the man

21. *Juveniles who rob do not usually use the money they obtain in this manner for essentials but rather to indulge in spending to impress others.*
This observation indicates that clues leading to the apprehension of juvenile delinquents may be found by noting

    21.___

    A. family requirements and needs
    B. the recreation habits of young people
    C. which young people have a tendency to commit robbery
    D. the relationships which exist in criminal gangs between criminals who commit crimes to satisfy essential needs and those who do not
    E. what objects are taken in robberies

22. A storekeeper complains to an officer that his store window has been broken by a gang of neighborhood hoodlums. The officer tells the storekeeper to notify headquarters.
This action is

    22.___

    A. *desirable;* the storekeeper will be able to tell the proper official his story firsthand
    B. *undesirable;* the problem is so minor that there is no need to bother headquarters
    C. *desirable;* the storekeeper will be more confident if his case is handled by a sergeant or lieutenant
    D. *undesirable;* buckpassing of this type makes for inefficiency and poor public relations
    E. *desirable;* investigation of the case would take the officer away from his post for too long a period

23. *In order to reduce the amount of contradictory testimony, the witnesses to a crime should be allowed to discuss, as a group, what had happened before they are questioned.*
The procedure suggested is

    23.___

    A. *bad;* a witness is less likely to commit himself if other witnesses to the event are present
    B. *good;* the need to sift stories will be considerably reduced
    C. *bad;* a witness is less likely to blurt out the truth if other witnesses are present to give him moral backing
    D. *good;* witnesses will be more apt to recall exactly what happened
    E. *bad;* the views of the strongest personalities may be obtained rather than the truth

24. An officer positively recognizes a man on a busy street as one wanted for passing   24.____
worthless checks.
Of the following, the MOST appropriate action for the officer to take is to

    A. approach and then arrest the man
    B. follow the man until a place is reached where there are few people; then take out
       his gun and arrest the man
    C. immediately take out his gun, stop the man, and search him
    D. follow the man until he stops long enough for the patrolman to summon aid from
       his precinct
    E. follow the man as he may lead the way to associates

25. It is generally agreed that criminal tendencies are present in every person.   25.____
A basic difference, however, between the normal person and the criminal is that the

    A. normal person, sometimes, commits trivial crimes but the criminal commits crimes
       of a major nature
    B. criminal is unable to understand the possible results of antisocial acts he commits
    C. normal person is able to control his antisocial tendencies and direct his activity in
       socially approved channels
    D. criminal believes that he is not different from the person who does not commit
       crimes
    E. normal person believes that he is not different from the person who commits
       crimes

26. It has been claimed that a person who commits a crime sometimes has an unconscious   26.____
wish to be punished, which is caused by strong unconscious feelings of guilt.
The one of the following actions by a criminal which may be partly due to an unconscious desire for punishment is

    A. claiming that he doesn't know anything about the crime when he is questioned by
       the police
    B. running away from the state where he committed the crime
    C. revisiting the place where he committed the crime
    D. his care not to leave any clues at the scene of the crime
    E. accusing someone else when he is captured by the police

27. *Experience has shown that many crimes have been planned in prison.*   27.____
From this finding, it is REASONABLE to assume that

    A. the principal motive for the commission of first crimes is the wish to take revenge
       on society
    B. some criminals may be influenced to continue their careers of crime because they
       associate with other criminals
    C. the real motives for the commission of most crimes originate in punishment for
       criminal acts
    D. fear of imprisonment will make a criminal who has been in jail plan his second
       crime more carefully
    E. the criminal mind is sharpened by maturity

28. *Any change in insurance coverage immediately prior to a fire should be considered. Strange as it may seem, most such changes made by convicted arsonists are made to a smaller amount.*
The MOST probable reason for such changes is that the arsonist

    A. usually is not a rational person
    B. decided to set the fire after the change was made
    C. did not have enough money to pay for the full amount
    D. reduced the insurance to the amount he expected to be lost in the fire
    E. was trying to divert suspicion

28._____

29. Suppose that you are an officer whose tour of duty extends from 12 Midnight to 8:00 A.M. While on the first round of your tour, you notice that the nightlight in the front of a small candy store is out. In the past, the proprietor has always left the light on. The door to the store is locked.
Of the following, the MOST appropriate action for you to take FIRST is to

    A. use your flashlight to light the store interior so that you may inspect it for unusual conditions
    B. continue on your beat since the light probably burned out
    C. break open the door lock so that you may conduct a thorough search of the store
    D. call the storekeeper to notify him that the nightlight is out
    E. call your precinct and report this unusual condition

29._____

30. *A criminal becomes either a thief, an assailant, or a sexual offender, never an all-around criminal.*
Of the following, an IMPORTANT reason for these basic differences in criminal behavior is probably that

    A. to be an all-around criminal requires more intelligence than the average criminal has
    B. crime syndicates have gained control over certain branches of crime and have made it difficult for a beginner to break in
    C. criminal acts are an expression of the criminal's whole personality
    D. all-around crime is not as profitable as specialization in crime
    E. most crimes are committed on the spur of the moment and without previous thought

30._____

31. A young man who was arrested for smashing a store window and stealing a portable radio was asked why he did it. He answered, *Well, I wanted a radio and I just took it.*
If this answer is characteristic of the behavior of the young criminal, it is MOST reasonable to believe that

    A. the young criminal has a well-organized personality
    B. he sizes up each new situation in terms of his past experiences
    C. his decision to commit a crime is made after careful consideration of its possible effect on his future
    D. his temptation to commit a crime is an isolated situation, having, in his mind, little relation to his life as a whole
    E. he hesitates to commit a crime unless he thinks he can get away with it

31._____

32. When the bodies of two women were found stabbed in an inner room of an apartment, it   32._____
was first believed that it was a case of mutual homicide.
Of the following clues found at the scene, the one which indicates that it was more
likely a case of murder by a third party is the fact that

    A. the door to the apartment was found locked
    B. there were bloodstains on the outer door of the apartment
    C. there was a switchblade knife in each body
    D. no money could be found in the room where the bodies were
    E. both women were fully clothed

33. A radio crime program dramatizing a different police case every week showed the cap-   33._____
ture or death of the criminal and ended with the slogan *Crime Does Not Pay*. It was found
that a gang of teen-age boys listened to this program every week in order to see what
mistake was made by the criminal, and then duplicated the crime, trying to avoid the
same mistake.
This case illustrates that

    A. all criminal minds work the same way
    B. attempts to keep young people out of crime by frightening them into obeying the
law are not always successful
    C. it is not possible to commit the perfect crime unless care is taken
    D. radio crime programs should not be permitted as they lead to an increase in the
number of unsolved crimes
    E. most criminals learn from their own mistakes

34. While on patrol at 2 A.M., you notice a man and a woman walking down the street talking   34._____
together in low tones. They do not see you as you are standing in the shadow. The pair
stop in front of a large apartment house. The man takes a bunch of keys from his pocket
and tries several before he finds one which will open the door. While he is doing this, the
woman taps her foot impatiently.
At this point, as the two are entering the apartment house, you should

    A. notify precinct headquarters of the incident
    B. permit them to enter but follow close behind them to see what they do
    C. ignore the incident and continue on your patrol
    D. force them to show their identification papers
    E. arrest them on suspicion of illegal entry

35. The one of the following which is the probable reason for restricting parking to alternate   35._____
sides of some streets on successive days is that, without this restriction, the parked cars
make it difficult for the

    A. Police Department to direct traffic
    B. Department of Water Supply, Gas and Electricity to service hydrants
    C. Traffic Department to plan the flow of traffic
    D. Sanitation Department to clear the streets
    E. Fire Department to put out fires

36. Looking through the window of a jewelry store, an officer sees a man take a watch   36.____
from the counter and drop it into his pocket while the jeweler is busy talking to someone
else. The man looks around the store and then walks out.
The officer should

    A.   follow the man to see what he does with the watch as thieves of this type usually
work in pairs
    B.   ignore the incident; if the man were performing an illegal act, the jeweler would
have called for help
    C.   arrest the man, take him to the stationhouse, and then return to obtain the jeweler's
statement
    D.   ignore the incident; if the man were a thief, the jeweler would not have left the
watches unattended
    E.   stop the man and bring him back into the shop so that both he and the jeweler can
be questioned

37. *It is quite possible to set up a general procedure which will result in the rehabilitation of*   37.____
all juvenile delinquents.
This statement is, in general,

    A.   *correct;* the major causes of all juvenile delinquency are improper home life and a
general lack of morals; cure these and there will be no problem of juvenile delinquency
    B.   *not correct;* juvenile delinquency results from the generally lower moral climate;
therefore, rehabilitation is not possible until the world climate changes
    C.   *correct;* if juvenile delinquents are severely punished, rehabilitation will follow
    D.   *not correct;* each case of juvenile delinquency is different and for most effective
treatment must be handled on an individual basis
    E.   *correct;* if the proper general procedure is set up, it always can be applied

38. An officer observes a young man who is obviously very excited, walking unusually   38.____
fast, and repeatedly halting to look behind him. Upon stopping the young man, the officer
finds that he is carrying a gun and has just held up a liquor store a few blocks away.
This incident illustrates that

    A.   circumstances that are not suspicious in themselves frequently provide clues for
the solution of crimes
    B.   an experienced officer can pick the criminal type out of a crowd by alert obser-
vation
    C.   action is always to be preferred to thought
    D.   an officer should investigate suspicious circumstances
    E.   an officer who stops to think may sometimes fail to get his man

39. *When making arrests, the officer should treat all suspects in the same manner.*   39.____
This suggested rule is

    A.   *undesirable;* the specific problems presented should govern the officer's
actions
    B.   *desirable;* this is the only democratic solution to the problem
    C.   *undesirable;* officers should not be expected to abide by rules as criminals do
not
    D.   *desirable;* only by setting up fixed and rigid rules can patrolmen know what is
expected of them
    E.   *undesirable;* persons who are only suspected are not criminals and should not be
treated as such

40. *One of the most difficult questions in a crime prevention program is to decide how many men are needed to police a particular area. There have been a number of attempts to invent a simple formula, but none has no far been successful.*
    Of the following reasons for this, the MOST probable is that

    A. men, not formulas, patrol beats
    B. many factors are involved whose relative importance has not been determined
    C. there is no information on which to base such a formula
    D. such a formula, even if it were accurate, would be of little use as it would be too theoretical
    E. police problems in no two areas in the city are alike in any way

40._____

Questions 41-43.

DIRECTIONS: Questions 41 through 43 are to be answered on the basis of the following paragraph.

Modern police science may be said to have three phases. The first phase embraces the identification of living and dead persons. The second embraces the field work carried out by specially trained detectives at the scene of the crime. The third embraces methods used in the police laboratory to examine and analyze clues and traces discovered in the course of the investigation. While modern police science has had a striking influence on detective work and will surely further enhance its effectiveness, the time-honored methods, that is, knowledge of methods used by criminals, patience, tact, industry, thoroughness and imagination, will always be requisites for successful detective work.

41. According to the above paragraph, we may expect modern police science to

    A. help detective work more and more
    B. become more and more scientific
    C. depend less and less on the time-honored methods
    D. bring together the many different approaches to detective work
    E. play a less important role in detective work

41._____

42. According to the above paragraph, a knowledge of the procedures used by criminals is

    A. solely an element of the modern police science approach to detective work
    B. related to the identification of persons
    C. not related to detective field work
    D. related to methods used in the police laboratory
    E. an element of the traditional approach to detective work

42._____

43. Modern police science and practical detective work, according to the above paragraph,

    A. when used together can only lead to confusion
    B. are based on distinctly different theories of detective work
    C. have had strikingly different influences on detective work
    D. should both be used for successful detective work
    E. lead usually to similar results

43._____

Questions 44-47.

DIRECTIONS: Questions 44 through 47 are to be answered on the basis of the following paragraph.

A member of the force shall render reasonable aid to a sick or injured person. He shall summon an ambulance, if necessary, by telephoning the communications bureau of the borough, who shall notify the precinct concerned. If possible, he shall wait in full view of the arriving ambulance and take necessary action to direct the responding doctor or attendant to the patient without delay. If the ambulance does not arrive in twenty minutes, he shall send in a second call. However, if the sick person is in his or her own home, a member of the force, before summoning an ambulance, will ascertain whether such person is willing to be taken to a hospital for treatment.

44. According to the above paragraph, if an officer wants to get an ambulance for a sick person, he should telephone   44.___

    A. the precinct concerned
    B. only if the sick person is in his home
    C. the nearest hospital
    D. only if the sick person is not in his home
    E. the borough communications bureau

45. According to the above paragraph, if an officer telephones for an ambulance and none arrives within twenty minutes, he should   45.___

    A. ask the injured person if he is willing to be taken to a hospital
    B. call the borough communications bureau
    C. call the precinct concerned
    D. attempt to give the injured person such assistance as he may need
    E. call the nearest hospital

46. An officer is called to help a woman who has fallen in her own home and has apparently broken her leg.   46.___
According to the above paragraph, he should

    A. ask her if she wants to go to a hospital
    B. try to set her leg if it is necessary
    C. call for an ambulance at once
    D. attempt to get a doctor as quickly as possible
    E. not attempt to help the woman in any way before competent medical aid arrives

47. A man falls from a window into the backyard of an apartment house. Assume that you are an officer and that you are called to assist this man.   47.___
According to the above paragraph, after you have called for an ambulance and comforted the injured man as much as you can, you should

    A. wait in front of the house for the ambulance
    B. ask the injured man if he wishes to go to the hospital for treatment
    C. remain with the injured man until the ambulance arrives
    D. send a bystander to direct the nearest doctor to the patient
    E. not ask the man to explain how the accident happened

Questions 48-50.

DIRECTIONS: Questions 48 through 50 are to be answered on the basis of the following paragraph.

What is required is a program that will protect our citizens and their property from criminal and antisocial acts, will effectively restrain and reform juvenile delinquents, and will prevent the further development of antisocial behavior. Discipline and punishment of offenders must necessarily play an important part in any such program. Serious offenders cannot be mollycoddled merely because they are under twenty-one. Restraint and punishment necessarily follow serious antisocial acts. But punishment, if it is to be effective, must be a planned part of a more comprehensive program of treating delinquency.

48.   The one of the following goals NOT included among those listed above is to   48.____

    A.   stop young people from defacing public property
    B.   keep homes from being broken into
    C.   develop an intra-city boys' baseball league
    D.   change juvenile delinquents into useful citizens
    E.   prevent young people from developing antisocial behavior patterns

49.   According to the above paragraph, punishment is   49.____

    A.   not satisfactory in any program dealing with juvenile delinquents
    B.   the most effective means by which young vandals and hooligans can be reformed
    C.   not used sufficiently when dealing with serious offenders who are under twenty-one
    D.   of value in reducing juvenile delinquency only if it is part of a complete program
    E.   most effective when it does not relate to specific antisocial acts

50.   With respect to serious offenders who are under twenty-one, the above paragraph suggests that they   50.____

    A.   be mollycoddled
    B.   be dealt with as part of a comprehensive program to punish mature criminals
    C.   should be punished
    D.   be prevented, by brute force if necessary, from performing antisocial acts
    E.   be treated as delinquent children who require more love than punishment

Questions 51-54.

DIRECTIONS: Questions 51 through 54 are to be answered on the basis of the following paragraph.

In all cases of homicide, members of the police department who investigate will make every effort to obtain statements from dying persons. Such statements are of the greatest importance to the District Attorney. In many cases, there may be a failure to solve the crime if they are not taken. The principal element to be considered in taking the declaration of a dying person is his mental attitude. In order to be admissible in evidence, the person must have no hope of recovery. The patient will be fully interrogated on that point before a statement is taken.

51. In cases of homicide, according to the above paragraph, members of the police force will   51.____

    A. try to change the mental attitude of the dying person
    B. attempt to obtain a statement from the dying person
    C. not give the information they obtain directly to the District Attorney
    D. be careful not to injure the dying person unnecessarily
    E. prevent unauthorized persons from taking dying declarations

52. The mental attitude of the person making the dying statement is of great importance   52.____
because it can determine, according to the above paragraph, whether the

    A. victim should be interrogated in the presence of witnesses
    B. victim will be willing to make a statement of any kind
    C. victim has been forced to make the statement
    D. statement will tell the District Attorney who committed the crime
    E. statement can be used as evidence

53. District Attorneys find that statements of a dying person are important, according to the   53.____
above paragraph, because

    A. it may be that the victim will recover and then refuse to testify
    B. they are important elements in determining the mental attitude of the victim
    C. they present a point of view
    D. it may be impossible to punish the criminal without such a statement
    E. dead men tell no tales

54. A well-known gangster is found dying from a bullet wound.   54.____
The officer first on the scene, in the presence of witnesses, tells the man that he is
going to die and asks,
Who shot you? The gangster says, *Jones shot me, but he hasn't killed me. I'll live to
get him.* He then falls back dead.
According to the above paragraph, this statement is

    A. *admissible* in evidence; the man was obviously speaking the truth
    B. *not admissible* in evidence; the man obviously did not believe that he was dying
    C. *admissible* in evidence; there were witnesses to the statement
    D. *not admissible* in evidence; the victim did not sign any statement and the evidence
       is merely hearsay
    E. *admissible* in evidence; there was no time to interrogate the victim

Questions 55-57.

DIRECTIONS: Questions 55 through 57 are to be answered on the basis of the following
paragraph.

*The factors contributing to crime and delinquency are varied and complex. The home
and its immediate environment have been found to be crucial in determining the behavior patterns of the individual, and criminality can frequently be traced to faulty family relationships
and a bad neighborhood. But in the search for a clearer understanding of the underlying
causes of delinquent and criminal behavior, the total environment must be taken into consideration.*

55. According to the above paragraph, family relationships   55._____

    A. tend to become faulty in bad neighborhoods
    B. are important in determining the actions of honest people as well as criminals
    C. are the only important element in the understanding of causes of delinquency
    D. are determined by the total environment
    E. of criminals are understandable only in terms of the behavior patterns of the individuals concerned

56. According to the above paragraph, the causes of crime and delinquency are   56._____

    A. not simple   B. not meaningless
    C. meaningless   D. simple
    E. always understandable

57. According to the above paragraph, faulty family relationships frequently are   57._____

    A. responsible for varied and complex results
    B. caused by differences
    C. caused when one or both parents have a criminal behavior pattern
    D. independent of the total environment
    E. the cause of criminal acts

Questions 58-60.

DIRECTIONS: Questions 58 through 60 are to be answered on the basis of the following paragraph.

A change in the specific problems which confront the police and in the methods for dealing with them has taken place in the last few decades. The automobile is a two-way symbol of this change in policing. It menaces every city with a complicated traffic problem and has speeded up the process of committing a crime and making a getaway, but at the same time has increased the effectiveness of police operations. However, the major concern of police departments continues to be the antisocial or criminal actions and behavior of human beings.

58. On the basis of the above paragraph, it can be stated that for the most part in the past   58._____
few decades the specific problems of a police force

    A. have changed but the general problems have not
    B. as well as the general problems have changed
    C. have remained the same but the general problems have changed
    D. as well as the general problems have remained the same
    E. have caused changes in the general problems

59. According to the above paragraph, advances in science and industry have, in general,   59._____
made the police

    A. operations less effective from the overall point of view
    B. operations more effective from the overall point of view
    C. abandon older methods of solving police problems
    D. concern themselves more with the antisocial acts of human beings
    E. concern themselves less with the antisocial acts of human beings

60. The automobile is a *two-way symbol,* according to the above paragraph, because its use   60.____

    A. has speeded up getting to, and away from, the scene of a crime
    B. both helps and hurts police operations
    C. introduces a new antisocial act - traffic violation -and does away with criminals like horse thieves
    D. both increases and decreases speed by introducing traffic problems
    E. helps people get to the city but prevents them from moving once they are there

Questions 61-80.

DIRECTIONS: In each of Questions 61 through 80, select the lettered word or phrase which means MOST NEARLY the same as, or the opposite of, the first word in the row.

61. vindictive   61.____

    A. centrifugal   B. forgiving   C. molten
    D. tedious   E. vivacious

62. scope   62.____

    A. compact   B. detriment   C. facsimile
    D. potable   E. range

63. hinder   63.____

    A. amplify   B. aver   C. method
    D. observe   E. retard

64. irate   64.____

    A. adhere   B. angry   C. authentic
    D. peremptory   E. vacillate

65. apathy   65.____

    A. accessory   B. availability   C. fervor
    D. pacify   E. stride

66. lucrative   66.____

    A. effective   B. imperfect   C. injurious
    D. timely   E. worthless

67. diversity   67.____

    A. convection   B. slip   C. temerity
    D. uniformity   E. viscosity   F.

68. overt   68.____

    A. laugh   B. lighter   C. orifice
    D. quay   E. sly

69. sporadic   69.____

    A. divide   B. incumbrance   C. livid
    D. occasional   E. original

70. rescind

    A. annul   B. deride   C. extol
    D. indulge   E. insist

70.____

71. augment

    A. alter   B. decrease   C. obey
    D. perceive   E. supersede

71.____

72. autonomous

    A. careless   B. conceptual   C. constant
    D. defamatory E. independent

72.____

73. transcript

    A. copy   B. report   C. sentence
    D. termination E. verdict

73.____

74. discordant

    A. astride   B. comprised   C. effusive
    D. harmonious E. slick

74.____

75. distend

    A. constrict   B. direct   C. redeem
    D. silence   E. submerge

75.____

76. emanate

    A. bridge   B. coherency   C. conquer
    D. degrade   E. flow

76.____

77. exultant

    A. easily upset   B. in bad taste
    C. in high spirits   D. subject to moods
    E. very much over-priced

77.____

78. prevaricate

    A. hesitate   B. increase   C. lie
    D. procrastinate E. reject

78.____

79. cognizant

    A. obvious   B. search   C. stupid
    D. suspicious   E. unaware

79.____

80. credible

    A. daring   B. helpful   C. surreptitious
    D. unbelievable E. uncontrollable

80.____

81. Assume that a parking space for six cars is to be outlined with white paint. The total area   81.____
to be outlined is 24 feet by 40 feet, and the space for each car, also marked off by white
lines, is to be 8 feet by 20 feet.
The total length of white lines to be painted is MOST NEARLY _____ feet.

   A. 64   B. 128   C. 156
   D. 184   E. 232

82. A police car is ordered to report to the scene of a crime 5 miles away.   82.____
If the car travels at an average rate of 40 miles per hour, the length of time it will take to
reach its destination is MOST NEARLY _____ minutes.

   A. 3   B. 7   C. 10
   D. 13   E. 16

83. A block has metered parking for 19 cars from 7 A.M. to 9 P.M. at a charge of 10 cents per   83.____
hour.
Assuming that each car that is parked remains for a full hour and that on an average
for each hour of parking there is a vacancy of five minutes for each meter, the amount
of revenue from the meters for a day will be MOST NEARLY

   A. $10   B. $15   C. $20
   D. $25   E. $30

84. The standard formula for the stopping distance of a car with all four wheels locked is   84.____

$$S = \frac{V \text{ times } V}{30\,W}$$

where S is the stopping distance in feet, V the speed of the car in miles per hour at the
moment the brakes are applied, and W is a number which depends on the friction
between the tires and the road. If the speed of a car is 50 miles per hour and W is
equal to 5/3, the stopping distance will be MOST NEARLY _____ feet.

   A. 30   B. 40   C. 50
   D. 60   E. 70

85. The radiator of a police car contains 20 quarts of a mixture consisting of 80% water and   85.____
20% anti-freeze compound. Assume that you have been ordered to draw off some of the
mixture and add pure anti-freeze compound until the mixture is 75% water and 25% anti-
freeze compound.
The number of quarts of the mixture which should be removed is MOST NEARLY

   A. 2   B. 3   C. 4
   D. 5   E. 6

Questions 86-90.

DIRECTIONS: Questions 86 through 90 are to be answered on the basis of the following table

FATAL HIGHWAY ACCIDENTS

	Drivers Over 18 Years of Age			Drivers 18 Years of Age & Under		
	Auto	Other Vehicles	Total	Auto	Other Vehicles	Total
January	43	0	43	4	0	4
February	52	0	52	10	0	10
March	36	0	36	8	0	8
April	50	0	50	17	0	17
May	40	2	42	5	0	5
June	26	0	26	8	0	8
July	29	0	29	6	0	6
August	29	1	30	3	0	3
September	36	0	36	4	0	4
October	45	1	46	2	1	3
November	54	1	55	3	0	3
December	66	1	67	6	0	6
TOTALS	506	6	512	76	1	77

86. The average number of fatal auto accidents per month involving drivers older than sixteen was MOST NEARLY

    A. 42   B. 43   C. 44
    D. 45   E. 46

86.____

87. The TOTAL number of fatal highway accidents was

    A. 506   B. 512   C. 562
    D. 582   E. 589

87.____

88. The month during which the LOWEST number of fatal highway accidents occurred was

    A. March   B. June   C. July
    D. August   E. September

88.____

89. Of the total number of fatal highway accidents involving drivers older than 18, the percentage of accidents which took place during December is MOST NEARLY

    A. 10   B. 13   C. 16
    D. 19   E. 22

89.____

90. The GREATEST percentage drop in fatal highway accidents occurred from

    A. February to March   B. April to May
    C. June to July   D. July to August
    E. August to September

90.____

KEY (CORRECT ANSWERS)

1.	A	21.	B	41.	A	61.	B	81.	E
2.	C	22.	D	42.	E	62.	E	82.	B
3.	B	23.	E	43.	D	63.	E	83.	D
4.	E	24.	A	44.	E	64.	B	84.	C
5.	B	25.	C	45.	B	65.	C	85.	A
6.	A	26.	C	46.	A	66.	E	86.	A
7.	C	27.	B	47.	A	67.	D	87.	E
8.	B	28.	E	48.	C	68.	E	88.	D
9.	E	29.	A	49.	D	69.	D	89.	B
10.	C	30.	C	50.	C	70.	A	90.	B
11.	C	31.	D	51.	B	71.	B		
12.	B	32.	B	52.	E	72.	E		
13.	D	33.	B	53.	D	73.	A		
14.	A	34.	C	54.	B	74.	D		
15.	D	35.	D	55.	B	75.	A		
16.	A	36.	E	56.	A	76.	E		
17.	E	37.	D	57.	E	77.	C		
18.	D	38.	D	58.	A	78.	C		
19.	C	39.	A	59.	B	79.	E		
20.	E	40.	B	60.	B	80.	D		

PERSONALITY/AUTOBIOGRAPHICAL INVENTORY
EXAMINATION SECTION
TEST 1

DIRECTIONS: Each question or incomplete statement is followed by several suggested answers or completions. Select the one that BEST answers the question or completes the statement. *PRINT THE LETTER OF THE CORRECT ANSWER IN THE SPACE AT THE RIGHT.*

1. While a senior in high school, I was absent   1._____

    A. never   B. seldom
    C. frequently   D. more than 10 days
    E. only when I felt bored

2. While in high school, I failed classes   2._____

    A. never   B. once
    C. twice   D. more than twice
    E. at least four times

3. During class discussions in my high school classes, I usually   3._____

    A. listened without participating
    B. participated as much as possible
    C. listened until I had something to add to the discussion
    D. disagreed with others simply for the sake of argument
    E. laughed at stupid ideas

4. My high school grade point average (on a 4.0 scale) was   4._____

    A. 2.0 or lower   B. 2.1 to 2.5   C. 2.6 to 3.0
    D. 3.1 to 3.5   E. 3.6 to 4.0

5. As a high school student, I completed my assignments   5._____

    A. as close to the due date as I could manage
    B. whenever the teacher gave me an extension
    C. frequently
    D. on time
    E. when they were interesting

6. While in high school, I participated in   6._____

    A. athletic and nonathletic extracurricular activities
    B. athletic extracurricular activities
    C. nonathletic extracurricular activities
    D. no extracurricular activities
    E. mandatory after-school programs

7. In high school, I made the honor roll   7._____

    A. several times   B. once
    C. more than once   D. twice
    E. I can't remember if I made the honor roll

8. Upon graduation from high school, I received   8._____

    A. academic and nonacademic honors
    B. academic honors
    C. nonacademic honors
    D. no honors
    E. I can't remember if I received honors

9. While attending high school, I worked at a paid job or as a volunteer   9._____

    A. never
    B. every so often
    C. 5 to 10 hours a month
    D. more than 10 hours a month
    E. more than 15 hours a month

10. During my senior year of high school, I skipped school   10._____

    A. whenever I could   B. once a week
    C. several times a week   D. not at all
    E. when I got bored

11. I was suspended from high school   11._____

    A. not at all   B. once or twice
    C. once or twice, for fighting   D. several times
    E. more times than I can remember

12. During high school, my fellow students and teachers considered me   12._____

    A. above average
    B. below average
    C. average
    D. underachieving
    E. underachieving and prone to fighting

13. The ability to _____ is most important to a Police Officer.   13._____

    A. draw his/her gun quickly
    B. see over great distances and difficult terrain
    C. verbally and physically intimidate criminals
    D. communicate effectively in circumstances which can be dangerous
    E. hear over great distances

14. I began planning for college   14._____

    A. when my parents told me to
    B. when I entered high school
    C. during my junior year
    D. during my senior year
    E. when I signed up for my SAT (or other standardized) exam

15. An effective leader is someone who

    15._____

    A.   inspires confidence in his/her followers
    B.   inspires fear in his/her followers
    C.   tells subordinates exactly what they should do
    D.   creates an environment in which subordinates feel insecure about their job security and performance
    E.   makes as few decisions as possible

16. I prepared myself for college by

    16._____

    A.   learning how to get extensions on major assignments
    B.   working as many hours as possible at my after-school job
    C.   spending as much time with my friends as possible
    D.   getting good grades and participating in extracurricular activities
    E.   watching television shows about college kids

17. I paid for college by

    17._____

    A.   supplementing my parents contributions with my own earnings
    B.   relying on scholarships, loans, and my own earnings
    C.   relying on my parents and student loans
    D.   relying on my parents to pay my tuition, room and board
    E.   relying on sources not listed here

18. While a college student, I spent my summers and holiday breaks

    18._____

    A.   in summer or remedial classes
    B.   traveling
    C.   working
    D.   relaxing
    E.   spending time with my friends

19. My final college grade point average (on a 4.0 scale) was

    19._____

    A.   3.8 to 4.0   B.   3.5 to 3.8   C.   3.0 to 3.5
    D.   2.5 to 3.0   E.   2.0 to 2.5

20. As a college student, I cut classes

    20._____

    A.   frequently   B.   when I didn't like them
    C.   sometimes   D.   rarely
    E.   when I needed the sleep

21. In college, I received academic honors

    21._____

    A.   not at all   B.   once
    C.   twice   D.   several times
    E.   I can't remember if I received academic honors

22. While in college, I declared a major

    22._____

    A.   during my first year   B.   during my sophomore year
    C.   during my junior year   D.   during my senior year
    E.   several times

23. While on patrol as a Police Officer, you spot someone attempting to flee the scene of a crime. Your first reaction is to

    A. draw your weapon
    B. observe the person until he or she completes the fleeing
    C. identify yourself as a Police Officer
    D. fire your weapon over the person's head in order to scare him or her
    E. call immediately for backup

23.____

24. As a college student, I failed _____ classes.

    A. no   B. two
    C. three   D. four
    E. more than four

24.____

25. Friends describe me as

    A. introverted   B. hot-tempered
    C. unpredictable   D. quiet
    E. easygoing

25.____

KEY (CORRECT ANSWERS)

PLEASE NOTE: The answers listed are the best answers. However, you are to answer the exam honestly. Your personal answer may differ from the *best* answers.

1.	A	11.	A
2.	A	12.	A
3.	C	13.	D
4.	E	14.	B
5.	D	15.	A
6.	A	16.	D
7.	A	17.	B
8.	A	18.	C
9.	E	19.	A
10.	D	20.	D

21.	D
22.	A
23.	C
24.	A
25.	E

TEST 2

DIRECTIONS: Each question or incomplete statement is followed by several suggested answers or completions. Select the one that BEST answers the question or completes the statement. *PRINT THE LETTER OF THE CORRECT ANSWER IN THE SPACE AT THE RIGHT.*

1. As a Police Officer, you apprehend three men whom you believe are in the country illegally. However, none of the men speaks English, and you don't speak their language. Your reaction should be to

    A. draw your weapon so that they understand the seriousness of the situation
    B. take them into custody, where they will have access to a translator
    C. attempt to communicate through hand gestures and shouting
    D. call for a translator to come and meet you at your location
    E. pretend you understand their language and apprehend them

1._____

2. During my college classes, I preferred to

    A. remain silent during class discussions
    B. do other homework during class discussions
    C. participate frequently in class discussions
    D. argue with others as much as possible
    E. laugh at the stupid opinions of others

2._____

3. As a Police Officer, you are chasing a small group of people who are running away from the scene of a crime. During your pursuit, one member of the group is left behind. You see that she is injured and in need of medical attention. Your reaction is to

    A. fire your weapon at the group members to get them to stop
    B. cease pursuit of the group members and take the woman into custody
    C. continue pursuit of the group members, leaving the woman behind since acting ill is a common trick
    D. radio for backup to stay with the woman while medical help arrives while you continue pursuit of the group members
    E. radio for backup to continue pursuit of the group members while you stay with the woman and wait for medical help to arrive

3._____

4. As a college student, I was placed on academic probation

    A. not at all   B. once
    C. twice   D. three times
    E. more than three times

4._____

5. At work, being a team player means to

    A. compromise your ideals and beliefs
    B. compensate for the incompetence of others
    C. count on others to compensate for my inexperience
    D. cooperate with others to get a project finished
    E. rely on others to get the job done

5._____

6. As a Police Officer, you confront someone you believe has just committed a crime. After   6._____
identifying yourself, you notice the suspect holding something that looks like a knife. Your
FIRST reaction should be to

    A. draw your weapon and fire
    B. call immediately for backup
    C. keep your weapon drawn until you get the suspect into a position that is controllable
    D. ask the suspect if he is armed
    E. talk to the suspect without drawing your weapon

7. My friends from college remember me primarily as a(n)   7._____

    A. person who loved to party
    B. ambitious student
    C. athlete
    D. joker
    E. fighter

8. My college experience is memorable primarily because of   8._____

    A. the friends I made
    B. the sorority/fraternity I was able to join
    C. the social activities I participated in
    D. my academic achievements
    E. the money I spent

9. A friend who is applying for a job asks you to help him pass the mandatory drug test by   9._____
substituting a sample of your urine for his. You should

    A. help him by supplying the sample
    B. help him by supplying the sample and insisting he seek drug counseling
    C. supply the sample, but tell him that this is the only time you'll help in this way
    D. call the police
    E. refuse

10. As a college student, I handed in my assignments   10._____

    A. when they were due
    B. whenever I could get an extension
    C. when they were interesting
    D. when my friends reminded me to
    E. when I was able to

11. At work you are accused of a minor infraction which you didn't commit. Your first reaction   11._____
is to

    A. call a lawyer
    B. speak to your supervisor about the mistake
    C. call the police
    D. yell at the person who did commit the infraction
    E. accept the consequences regardless of your guilt or innocence

12. While on patrol, you are surprised by a large group of disorderly teenage gang members.   12._____
You are greatly outnumbered.
As a Police Officer, your first reaction is to

    A. draw your weapon and identify yourself
    B. get back into your vehicle and wait for help to arrive
    C. call for backup
    D. pretend you are part of a large group of police in the area
    E. identify yourself and get the group members into a controllable position

13. As a college student, I began to prepare for final exams   13._____

    A. the night before taking them
    B. when the professor handed out the review sheets
    C. several weeks before taking them
    D. when my friends began to prepare for their exams
    E. the morning of the exam

14. As a Police Officer in the field, you confront a small group of people you believe to be   14._____
wanted criminals. Your most important consideration during this exchange should be

    A. apprehension of criminals
    B. safety of county citizens in nearby towns
    C. safety of the criminals
    D. number of criminals you must apprehend in order to receive a commendation
    E. the amount of respect the criminals show to you and your position

15. At work, I am known as   15._____

    A. popular   B. quiet   C. intense
    D. easygoing   E. dedicated

16. The most important quality in a coworker is   16._____

    A. friendliness   B. cleanliness
    C. a good sense of humor   D. dependability
    E. good listening skills

17. In the past year, I have stayed home from work   17._____

    A. frequently
    B. only when I felt depressed
    C. rarely
    D. only when I felt overwhelmed
    E. only to run important errands

18. As a Police Officer, the best way to collect information from a suspect during an interview   18._____
is to

    A. physically intimidate the suspect
    B. verbally intimidate the suspect
    C. threaten the suspect's family and/or friends with criminal prosecution
    D. encourage a conversation with the suspect
    E. sit in silence until the suspect begins speaking

19. For me, the best thing about college was the   19._____

    A. chance to strengthen my friendships and develop new ones
    B. chance to test my abilities and develop new ones
    C. number of extracurricular activities and clubs
    D. chance to socialize
    E. chance to try several different majors

20. As an employee, my weakest skill is   20._____

    A. controlling my temper
    B. my organizational ability
    C. my ability to effectively understand directions
    D. my ability to effectively manage others
    E. my ability to communicate my thoughts in writing

21. As a Police Officer, my greatest strength would be   21._____

    A. my sense of loyalty   B. my organizational ability
    C. punctuality   D. dedication
    E. my ability to intimidate others

22. As a Police Officer, you find a group of suspicious youths gathered around a truck which   22._____
is on fire. Your first reaction is to

    A. call the fire department
    B. arrest them all for destruction of property
    C. draw your weapon and begin questioning them
    D. return to your vehicle and wait for the fire department
    E. instruct the group to remain while you return to your vehicle and request backup

23. If asked by my company to learn a new job-related skill, my reaction would be to   23._____

    A. ask for a raise
    B. ask for overtime pay
    C. question the necessity of the skill
    D. cooperate with some reluctance
    E. cooperate with enthusiasm

24. When I disagree with others, I tend to   24._____

    A. listen quietly despite my disagreement
    B. laugh openly at the person I disagree with
    C. ask the person to explain their views before I respond
    D. leave the conversation before my anger gets the best of me
    E. point out exactly why the person is wrong

25. When I find myself in a situation which is confusing or unclear, my reaction is to   25._____

    A. pretend I am not confused
    B. remain calm and, if necessary, ask someone else for clarification
    C. grow frustrated and angry
    D. walk away from the situation
    E. immediately insist that someone explain things to me

KEY (CORRECT ANSWERS)

PLEASE NOTE: The answers listed are the best answers. However, you are to answer the exam honestly. Your personal answer may differ from the *best* answers.

1. B
2. C
3. E
4. A
5. D

6. C
7. B
8. D
9. E
10. A

11. B
12. E
13. C
14. A
15. E

16. D
17. C
18. D
19. B
20. E

21. D
22. A
23. E
24. C
25. B

TEST 3

DIRECTIONS: Each question or incomplete statement is followed by several suggested answers or completions. Select the one that BEST answers the question or completes the statement. *PRINT THE LETTER OF THE CORRECT ANSWER IN THE SPACE AT THE RIGHT.*

1. While on patrol as a Police Officer, you find a dead body lying in the open. Hiding a few feet away, behind some rocks, you find a suspicious person who is holding items which seem to have been taken from the dead body, including a pair of shoes and some jewelry.
   You should

   A. apprehend the suspect and bring him to the station for further questioning
   B. arrest the suspect for murder and robbery
   C. arrest the suspect for murder
   D. subdue the suspect with force and check the area for his accomplices
   E. subdue the suspect with force and call for backup to check the area for his accomplices

   1.____

2. If you were placed in a supervisory position, which of the following abilities would you consider to be most important to your job performance?

   A. Stubbornness
   B. The ability to hear all sides of a story before making a decision
   C. Kindness
   D. The ability to make and stick to a decision
   E. Patience

   2.____

3. What is your highest level of education?

   A. Less than a high school diploma
   B. A high school diploma or equivalency
   C. A graduate of community college
   D. A graduate of a four-year accredited college
   E. A degree from graduate school

   3.____

4. When asked to supervise other workers, your approach should be to

   A. ask for management wages since you're doing management work
   B. give the workers direction and supervise every aspect of the process
   C. give the workers direction and then allow them to do the job
   D. hand the workers their job specifications
   E. do the work yourself, since you're uncomfortable supervising others

   4.____

5. Which of the following best describes you?

   A. Need little or no supervision
   B. Resent too much supervision
   C. Require as much supervision as my peers
   D. Require slightly more supervision than my peers
   E. Require close supervision

   5.____

6. You accept a job which requires an ability to perform several tasks at once. What is the best way to handle such a position?   6._____

    A. With strong organizational skills and a close attention to detail
    B. By delegating the work to someone with strong organizational skills
    C. Staying focused on one task at a time, no matter what happens
    D. Working on one task at a time until each task is successfully completed
    E. Asking my supervisor to help me

7. As a Police Officer, you take a suspected perpetrator into custody. After returning to the field, you notice that your gun is missing. You should   7._____

    A. retrace your steps to see if you dropped it somewhere
    B. report the loss immediately
    C. ask your partner to borrow his or her gun
    D. pretend that nothing's happened
    E. rely on your hands for defense and protection

8. Which of the following best describes your behavior when you disagree with someone? You   8._____

    A. state your own point of view as quickly and loudly as you can
    B. listen quietly and keep your opinions to yourself
    C. listen to the other person's perspective and then carefully point out all the flaws in their logic
    D. list all of the ignorant people who agree with the opposing point of view
    E. listen to the other person's perspective and then explain your own perspective

9. As a new Police Officer, you make several mistakes during your first week of work. You react by   9._____

    A. learning from your mistakes and moving on
    B. resigning
    C. blaming it on your supervisor
    D. refusing to talk about it
    E. blaming yourself

10. My ability to communicate effectively with others is _____ average.   10._____

    A. below   B. about   C. above   D. far above   E. far below

11. In which of the following areas are you most highly skilled?   11._____

    A. Written communication
    B. Oral communication
    C. Ability to think quickly in difficult situations
    D. Ability to work with a broad diversity of people and personalities
    E. Organizational skills

12. As a Police Officer, you are assigned to work with a partner whom you dislike. You should   12._____

    A. immediately report the problem to your supervisor
    B. ask your partner not to speak to you during working hours
    C. tell your colleagues about your differences
    D. tell your partner why you dislike him/her
    E. work with your partner regardless of your personal feelings

13. During high school, what was your most common after-school activity?   13._____

    A. Remaining after school to participate in various clubs and organizations (such as band, sports, etc.)
    B. Remaining after school to make up for missed classes
    C. Remaining after school as punishment (detention, etc.)
    D. Going straight to an after-school job
    E. Spending the afternoon at home or with friends

14. During high school, in which of the following subjects did you receive the highest grades?   14._____

    A. English, History, Social Studies
    B. Math, Science
    C. Vocational classes
    D. My grades were consistent in all subjects
    E. Classes I liked

15. When faced with an overwhelming number of duties at work, your reaction is to   15._____

    A. do all of the work yourself, no matter what the cost
    B. delegate some responsibilities to capable colleagues
    C. immediately ask your supervisor for help
    D. put off as much work as possible until you can get to it
    E. take some time off to relax and clear your mind

16. As a Police Officer, your supervisor informs you that a prisoner whom you arrested has accused you of beating him. You know you are innocent. You react by   16._____

    A. quitting your job
    B. hiring a lawyer
    C. challenging your supervisor to prove the charges against you
    D. calmly telling your supervisor what really happened and presenting evidence to support your position
    E. insisting that you be allowed to speak alone to the prisoner

17. Which of the following best describes your desk at your current or most recent job?   17._____

    A. Messy and disorganized
    B. Neat and organized
    C. Messy but organized
    D. Neat but disorganized
    E. Messy

18. The _____ BEST describes your reasons for wanting to become a Police Officer*   18._____

    A. ability to carry and use a weapon
    B. excitement and challenges of the career
    C. excellent salary and benefits package
    D. chance to tell other people what to do
    E. chance to help people find a better life

19. As a Police Officer in the field, you are approached by a man who is frantic but unable to speak English. After several minutes of trying to communicate, you realize that the man is asking you to come with him in order to help someone who has been hurt. You should   19._____

A. ignore him, since it might be a trap
B. call for backup
C. immediately offer to help the man
D. return to your vehicle and wait for the man to leave
E. radio your position and situation to another officer, then go with the man to offer help

20. When asked to take on extra responsibility at work, in order to help out a coworker who is overwhelmed, your response is to

20.____

A. ask for overtime pay
B. complain to your supervisor that you are being taken advantage of
C. help the coworker to the best of your ability
D. ask the coworker to come back some other time
E. give the coworker some advice on how to get his/her job done

21. At my last job, I was promoted

21.____

A. not at all   B. once
C. twice   D. three times
E. more than three times

22. As a Police Officer, you discover the body of a person whom you suspect to be a gang member. You also suspect that there are several other gang members hiding in the nearby vicinity.
Your first reaction should be to

22.____

A. begin a search of the nearby area for the other gang members
B. return to your vehicle and call for backup
C. return to your vehicle with the body of the person you found
D. check whether the person you found is dead or alive
E. draw your weapon and identify yourself

23. You are faced with an overwhelming deadline at work. Your reaction is to

23.____

A. procrastinate until the last minute
B. procrastinate until someone notices you need some help
C. notify your supervisor that you can't complete the work on your own
D. work in silence without asking any questions
E. arrange your schedule so that you can get the work done before the deadline

24. When you feel yourself under deadline pressures at work, your response is to

24.____

A. make sure you keep to a schedule which allows you to complete the work on time
B. wait until just before the deadline to complete the work
C. ask someone else to do the work
D. grow so obsessive about the work that your coworkers feel compelled to help you
E. ask your supervisor immediately for help

25. Which of the following best describes your appearance at your current or most recent position?

25.____

A. Well-groomed, neat, and clean   B. Unkempt, but dressed neatly
C. Messy and dirty clothing   D. Unshaven and untidy
E. Clean-shaven, but sloppily dressed

KEY (CORRECT ANSWERS)

PLEASE NOTE: The answers listed are the best answers. However, you are to answer the exam honestly. Your personal answers may differ from the *best* answers.

1.	A		11.	C
2.	D		12.	E
3.	E		13.	A
4.	C		14.	D
5.	A		15.	B
6.	A		16.	D
7.	B		17.	B
8.	E		18.	B
9.	A		19.	E
10.	C		20.	C

21.	C
22.	D
23.	E
24.	A
25.	A

TEST 4

DIRECTIONS: Each question or incomplete statement is followed by several suggested answers or completions. Select the one that BEST answers the question or completes the statement. *PRINT THE LETTER OF THE CORRECT ANSWER IN THE SPACE AT THE RIGHT.*

1. Which of the following best describes the way you react to making a difficult decision?   1.____

    A. Consult with the people you're closest to before making the decision
    B. Make the decision entirely on your own
    C. Consult only with those people whom your decision will affect
    D. Consult with everyone you know, in an effort to make a decision that will please everyone
    E. Forget about the decision until you have to make it

2. If placed in a supervisory role, which of the following characteristics would you rely on   2.____
most heavily when dealing with the employees you supervise?

    A. Kindness   B. Cheeriness   C. Honesty
    D. Hostility   E. Aloofness

3. As a Police Officer, you are pursuing a suspect when he turns and pulls something out of   3.____
his jacket that looks like a gun. You should

    A. run away and call for backup
    B. assure the man that you mean him no harm
    C. draw your gun and order the man to stop and drop his weapon
    D. draw your gun and fire a warning shot
    E. draw your gun and fire immediately

4. In addition to English, in which of the following languages are you also fluent?   4.____

    A. Spanish   B. French   C. Italian
    D. German   E. Other

5. When confronted with gossip at work, your typical reaction is to   5.____

    A. participate
    B. listen without participating
    C. notify your supervisor
    D. excuse yourself from the discussion
    E. confront your coworkers about their problem

6. In the past two years, how many jobs have you held?   6.____

    A. None   B. One   C. Two
    D. Three   E. More than three

7. In your current or most recent job, your favorite part of the job is the part which involves   7.____

    A. telling other people what they're doing wrong
    B. supervising others
    C. working without supervision to finish a project
    D. written communication
    E. oral communication

8. Your supervisor asks you about a colleague who is applying for a position which you also   8.____
   want. You react by

   A. commenting honestly on the person's work performance
   B. enhancing the person's negative traits
   C. informing your supervisor about your colleague's personal problems
   D. telling your supervisor that you would be better in the position
   E. refusing to comment

9. As a Police Officer, you confiscate some contraband which was being imported by an   9.____
   illegal alien who is now in your custody. Your partner asks you not to turn the contraband
   in to your supervisor.
   Your response is to

   A. inform your supervisor of your partner's request immediately
   B. tell your partner you feel uncomfortable with his request
   C. pretend you didn't hear your partner's request
   D. tell your supervisor and all your colleagues about your partner's request
   E. give the contraband to your partner and let him handle it

10. Which of the following best describes your responsibilities in your last job?   10.____

    A. Entirely supervisory
    B. Much supervisory responsibility
    C. Equal amounts of supervisory and nonsupervisory responsibility
    D. Some supervisory responsibilities
    E. No supervisory responsibilities

11. How much written communication did your previous or most recent job require of you?   11.____

    A. A great deal of written communication
    B. Some written communication
    C. I don't remember
    D. A small amount of written communication
    E. No written communication

12. In the past two years, how many times have you been fired from a job?   12.____

    A. None   B. Once   C. Twice   D. Three times
    E. More than three times

13. How much time have you spent working for volunteer organizations in the past year?   13.____

    A. 10 to 20 hours per week   B. 5 to 10 hours per week
    C. 3 to 5 hours per week   D. 1 to 3 hours per week
    E. I have spent no time volunteering in the past year

14. Your efforts at volunteer work usually revolve around which of the following types of orga-   14.____
    nizations?

    A. Religious
    B. Community-based organizations working to improve the community
    C. Charity organizations working on behalf of the poor
    D. Charity organizations working on behalf of the infirm or handicapped
    E. Other

15. Which of the following best describes your professional history?   15.____
    Promoted at

    A.   a much faster rate than coworkers
    B.   a slightly faster rate than coworkers
    C.   the same rate as coworkers
    D.   a slightly slower rate than coworkers
    E.   a much slower rate than coworkers

16. Which of the following qualities do you most appreciate in a coworker?   16.____

    A.   Friendliness   B.   Dependability
    C.   Good looks   D.   Silence
    E.   Forgiveness

17. When you disagree with a supervisor's instructions or opinion about how to complete a   17.____
    project, your reaction is to

    A.   inform your supervisor that you refuse to complete the project according to his or
         her instructions
    B.   inform your colleagues of your supervisor's incompetence
    C.   accept your supervisor's instructions in silence
    D.   voice your concerns and then complete the project according to your own instincts
    E.   voice your concerns and then complete the project according to your supervisor's
         instructions

18. Which of the following best describes your reaction to close supervision and specific   18.____
    direction from your supervisors?
    You

    A.   listen carefully to the directions, and then figure out a way to do the job more effec-
         tively
    B.   complete the job according to the given specifications
    C.   show some initiative by doing the job your way
    D.   ask someone else to do the job for you
    E.   listen carefully to the directions, and then figure out a better way to do the job
         which will save more money

19. How should a Police Officer handle a situation in which he or she is offered a bribe not to   19.____
    issue a traffic ticket?

    A.   Pretend the bribe was never offered
    B.   Accept the money as evidence and release the person
    C.   Draw your weapon and call for backup
    D.   Refuse the bribe and then arrest the person
    E.   Accept the bribe and then arrest the person

20. At work, you are faced with a difficult decision. You react by   20.____

    A.   seeking advice from your colleagues
    B.   following your own path regardless of the consequences
    C.   asking your supervisor what you should do
    D.   keeping the difficulties to yourself
    E.   working for a solution which will please everyone

21. If asked to work with a person whom you dislike, your response would be   21._____

     A.   to ask your supervisor to allow you to work with someone else
     B.   to ask your coworker to transfer to another department or project
     C.   talk to your coworker about the proper way to behave at work
     D.   pretend the coworker is your best friend for the sake of your job
     E.   to set aside your personal differences in order to complete the job

22. As a supervisor, which of the following incentives would you use to motivate your   22._____
employees?

     A.   Fear of losing their jobs
     B.   Fear of their supervisors
     C.   Allowing employees to provide their input on a number of policies
     D.   Encouraging employees to file secret reports regarding colleagues' transgressions
     E.   All of the above

23. A fellow Police Officer, with whom you enjoy a close friendship, has a substance-abuse   23._____
problem which has gone undetected. You suspect the problem may be affecting his job.
You would

     A.   ask the Police Officer if the problem is affecting his job performance
     B.   warn the Police Officer that he must seek counseling or you will report him
     C.   wait a few weeks to see whether the officer's problem really is affecting his job
     D.   discuss it with your supervisor
     E.   wait for the supervisor to discover the problem

24. In the past two months, you have missed work   24._____

     A.   zero times   B.   once
     C.   twice   D.   three times
     E.   more than three times

25. As a Police Officer, you are pursuing a group of robbers when you discover two small   25._____
children who have been abandoned near a railroad crossing. You should

     A.   tell the children to stay put while you continue your pursuit
     B.   lock the children in your vehicle and continue your pursuit
     C.   stay with the children and radio for help in the pursuit of the robbers
     D.   use the children to set a trap for the robbers
     E.   ignore the children and continue your pursuit

KEY (CORRECT ANSWERS)

PLEASE NOTE: The answers listed are the best answers. However, you are to answer the exam honestly. Your personal answer may differ from the *best* answers.

1.	A		11.	B
2.	C		12.	A
3.	C		13.	C
4.	A		14.	B
5.	D		15.	A
6.	B		16.	B
7.	C		17.	E
8.	A		18.	B
9.	A		19.	D
10.	D		20.	A

21.	E
22.	C
23.	D
24.	A
25.	C

SAMPLE QUESTIONS

BIOGRAPHICAL INVENTORY

The questions included in the Biographical Inventory ask for information about you and your background. These kinds of questions are often asked during an oral interview. For years, employers have been using interviews to relate personal history, preferences, and attitudes to job success. This Biographical Inventory attempts to do the same and includes questions which have been shown to be related to job success. It has been found that successful employees tend to select some answers more often than other answers, while less successful employees tend to select different answers. The questions in the Biographical Inventory do not have a single correct answer. Every choice is given some credit. More credit is given for answers selected more often by successful employees.

These Biographical Inventory questions are presented for illustrative purposes only. The answers have not been linked to the answers of successful employees; therefore, we cannot designate any "correct" answer(s).

DIRECTIONS: You may only mark ONE response to each question. It is possible that none of the answers applies well to you. However, one of the answers will surely be true (or less inaccurate) for you than others. In such a case, mark that answer. Answer each question honestly. The credit that is assigned to each response on the actual test is based upon how successful employees described themselves when honestly responding to the questions. *PRINT THE LETTER OF THE CORRECT ANSWER IN THE SPACE AT THE RIGHT.*

1.   Generally, in your work assignments, would you prefer   1.____
     A. to work on one thing at a time
     B. to work on a couple of things at a time
     C. to work on many things at the same time

2.   In the course of a week, which of the following gives you the GREATEST   2.____
     satisfaction?
     A. Being told you have done a good job.
     B. Helping other people to solve their problems.
     C. Coming up with a new or unique way to handle a situation.
     D. Having free time to devote to personal interests.

EVALUATING INFORMATION AND EVIDENCE
EXAMINATION SECTION
TEST 1

DIRECTIONS: Each question or incomplete statement is followed by several suggested answers or completions. Select the one that BEST answers the question or completes the statement. *PRINT THE LETTER OF THE CORRECT ANSWER IN THE SPACE AT THE RIGHT.*

Questions 1-4.

DIRECTIONS: Questions 1 to 4 measure your ability (1) to determine whether statements from witnesses say essentially the same thing and (2) to determine the evidence needed to make it reasonably certain that a particular conclusion is true.

To do well in this part of the test, you do NOT have to have a working knowledge of police procedures and techniques or to have any more familiarity with crimes and criminal behavior than that acquired from reading newspapers, listening to radio, or watching TV. To do well in this part, you must read carefully and reason closely. Sloppy reading or sloppy reasoning will lead to a low score.

1. In which of the following do the two statements made say essentially the same thing in two different ways?
    I.   All members of the pro-x group are free from persecution. No person that is persecuted is a member of the pro-x group.
    II. Some responsible employees of the police department are not supervisors. Some police department supervisors are not responsible employees.
The CORRECT answer is:

    A. I *only*
    B. II *only*
    C. Both I and II
    D. Neither I nor II

1.____

2. In which of the following do the two statements made say essentially the same thing in two different ways?
    I.   All Nassau County police officers weigh less than 225 pounds.
    II. No police officer weighs more than 225 pounds.
        No police officer is an alcoholic. No alcoholic is a police officer.
The CORRECT answer is:

    A. I *only*
    B. II *only*
    C. Both I and II
    D. Neither I nor II

2.____

3. Summary of Evidence Collected to Date: All pimps in the precinct own pink-colored cars and carry knives.
Prematurely Drawn Conclusion: Any person in the precinct who carries a knife is a pimp.
Which one of the following additional pieces of evidence, if any, would make it *reasonably certain* that the conclusion drawn is TRUE?

    A. Each person who carries a knife owns a pink-colored car.
    B. All persons who own pink-colored cars pimp.

3.____

C.   No one who carries a knife has a vocation other than pimping.
D.   None of these

4.   Summary of Evidence Collected to Date: 4._____
     1.   Some of the robbery suspects have served time as convicted felons.
     2.   Some of the robbery suspects are female.
     Prematurely Drawn Conclusion: Some of the female suspects have never served time
     as convicted felons.
     Which one of the following additional pieces of evidence, if any, would make it *reason-ably certain* that the conclusion drawn is TRUE?

     A.   The number of female suspects is the same as the number of robbery suspects
          who have served time as convicted felons.
     B.   The number of female suspects is smaller than the number of convicted felons.
     C.   The number of suspects that have served time is smaller than the number of sus-
          pects that have been convicted of a felony.
     D.   None of these

Questions 5-8.

DIRECTIONS: Questions 5 to 8 measure your ability to orient yourself within a given section
              of a town, neighborhood, or particular area. Each of the questions describes a
              starting point and a destination. Assume that you are driving a patrol car in the
              area shown on the map accompanying the questions. Use the map as a basis
              for choosing the shortest way to get from one point to another without breaking
              the law.

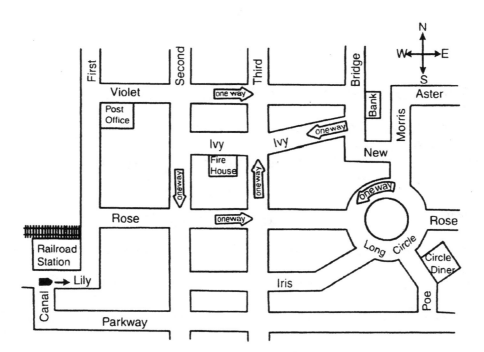

A street marked *one way* is one-way for the full length, even when there are breaks or jogs in
the street. EXCEPTION: A street that does not have the same name over the full length.

5. A patrol car at the train station is sent to the bank to investigate a robbery. The SHORT-EST way to get there without breaking any traffic laws is to go

    5.____

  A. east on Lily, north on First, east on Rose, north on Third, and east on Ivy to bank
  B. east on Lily, north on First, east on Violet, and south on Bridge to bank
  C. south on Canal, east on Parkway, north on Poe, around Long Circle to Morris, west on New, and north on Bridge to bank
  D. south on Canal, east on Parkway, north on Third, and east on Ivy to bank

6. At the bank, the patrol car receives a call to hurry to the post office. The SHORTEST way to get there without breaking any traffic laws is to go

    6.____

  A. west on Ivy, south on Second, west on Rose, and north on First to post office
  B. west on Ivy, south on Second, west on Rose, and south on First to post office
  C. south on Bridge, east on New, south on Morris, around Long Circle, south on Poe, west on Parkway, north on Canal, east on Lily, and north on First to post office
  D. north on Bridge, west on Violet, and south on First to post office.

7. On leaving the post office, the police officers decide to go to the Circle Diner. The SHORTEST way to get there without breaking any traffic laws is to go

    7.____

  A. south on First, left on Rose, right on Second, left on Parkway, and right on Poe to diner
  B. south on First, left on Rose, around Long Circle, and right on Poe to diner
  C. south on First, left on Rose, right on Second, right on Iris, around Long Circle, and left on Poe to diner
  D. west on Violet, right on Bridge, right on New, right on Morris, around Long Circle, and left on Poe to diner

8. During lunch break, a fire siren sounds and the police officers rush to their patrol car and head for the fire-house. The SHORTEST way to get there without breaking any traffic laws is to go

    8.____

  A. north on Poe, around Long Circle, west on Iris, north on Third, and west on Ivy to firehouse
  B. north on Poe, around Long Circle, north on Morris, west on New, north on Bridge, and west on Ivy to firehouse
  C. north on Poe, around Long Circle, west on Rose, north on Third, and west on Ivy to firehouse
  D. south on Poe, west on Parkway, north on Third, and east on Ivy to firehouse

Questions 9-13.

DIRECTIONS: Questions 9 to 13 measure your ability to understand written descriptions of events. Each question presents you with a description of an accident, a crime, or an event and asks you which of four drawings BEST represent it.

In the drawings, the following symbols are used (these symbols and their meanings will be repeated in the test):

A moving vehicle is represented by this symbol: (front) ⊲ (rear)

A parked vehicle is represented by this symbol: (front) ◀ (rear)

A pedestrian or a bicyclist is represented by this symbol: •

The path and direction of travel of a vehicle or pedestrian is indicated by a solid line: —→

EXCEPTION: The path and direction of travel of each vehicle or person directly involved in a collision from the point of impact is indicated by a dotted line: - - →

9. A driver pulling out from between two parked cars on Magic is struck by a vehicle heading east which turns left onto Maple and flees.
Which of the following depicts the accident?

9.____

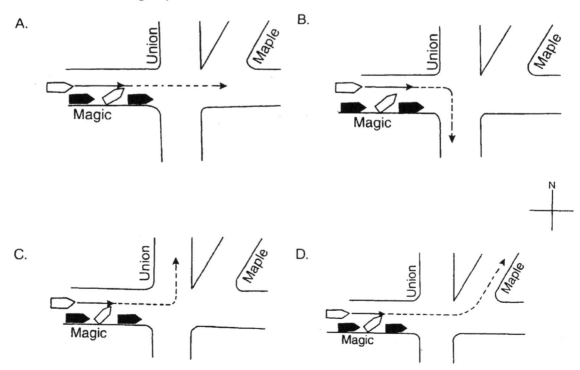

10. As Mr. Jones is driving south on Side. St., he falls asleep at the wheel. His car goes out   10.____
of control and sideswipes an oncoming car, goes through an intersection, and hits a
pedestrian on the southeast corner of Main Street.
Which of the following depicts the accident?

A.
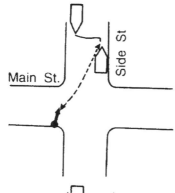

B.
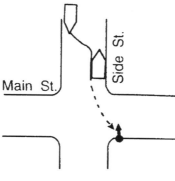

C.
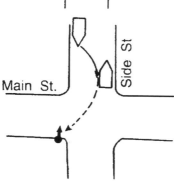

D.
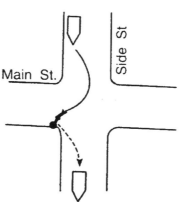

11. A car traveling south on Baltic skids through a red light at the intersection of Baltic and   11.____
Atlantic, sideswipes a car stopped for a light in the northbound lane, skids 180 degrees,
and stops on the west sidewalk of Baltic.
Which of the following depicts the accident?

A.
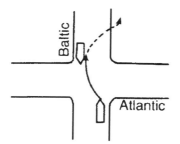

B.

C.
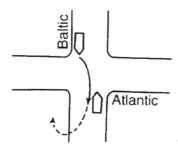

D.
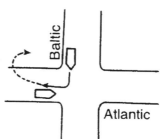

12. When found, the right front end of an automobile was smashed and bent around a post, and the hood was buckled.
Which of the following cars on a service lot is the car described?

12.____

A.

B.

C.

D.

13. An open floor safe with its door bent out of shape was found at the scene. It was empty. An electric drill and several envelopes and papers were found on the floor near the safe. Which of the following shows the scene described?

13.____

A.

B.

C.

D.

Questions 14-16.

DIRECTIONS: In Questions 14 to 16, you are to pick the word or phrase CLOSEST in meaning to the word or phrase printed in capital letters.

14. HAZARDOUS

14.____

    A. uncertain   B. threatening   C. difficult   D. dangerous

15. NEGLIGENT

15.____

    A. careless   B. fearless   C. ruthless   D. useless

16. PROVOKE

16.____

    A. accuse   B. arouse   C. insist   D. suspend

144

Questions 17-20.

DIRECTIONS: Questions 17 to 20 measure your ability to do arithmetic related to police work.
Each question presents a separate arithmetic problem to be solved.

17. To the nearest hour, how long can a specialized police vehicle with a 40-gallon fuel tank
be on the road before heading for a service facility, assuming that the vehicle consumes
8 gallons per hour and must head for a service facility when there are only 8 gallons in
the tank?

    A.   3   B.   4   C.   5   D.   None of these

17.____

18. A man with a history of vagrancy was found dead under a bridge with the following U.S.
currency in a band around his belly:

          7   $5   bills
          3 $10 bills
        11 $20 bills
          9 $50 bills
         4 $100 bills

What is the total amount of the money that was found in the band?

    A. $1,015   B. $1,135   C. $2,710   D.   None of these

18.____

19. X is 110 dimes.
Y is 1,111 pennies.
Which of the following statements about the values of X and Y above is TRUE?

    A.   X is greater than Y.
    B.   Y is greater than X.
    C.   X equals Y.
    D.   The relationship of X to Y cannot be determined from the information given.

19.____

20. Which of the following individuals drinking hard liquor in a bar was 21 years old at the
time of the incident?

    A.   One born August 26, 1989 - Date of incident is March 17, 2010
    B.   One born January 6, 1989 - Date of incident is New Year's Eve 2009
    C.   One born 3/17/89 - Date of incident is 2/14/10
    D.   None of these

20.____

KEY (CORRECT ANSWERS)

1.	A		11.	C
2.	B		12.	D
3.	C		13.	B
4.	D		14.	D
5.	B		15.	A
6.	C		16.	B
7.	B		17.	B
8.	B		18.	B
9.	D		19.	B
10.	B		20.	D

EVALUATING INFORMATION AND EVIDENCE

EXAMINATION SECTION
TEST 1

DIRECTIONS: Each question or incomplete statement is followed by several suggested answers or completions. Select the one that BEST answers the question or completes the statement. *PRINT THE LETTER OF THE CORRECT ANSWER IN THE SPACE AT THE RIGHT.*

Questions 1 -9

Questions 1 through 9 measure your ability to (1) determine whether statements from witnesses say essentially the same thing and (2) determine the evidence needed to make it reasonably certain that a particular conclusion is true.

1. Which of the following pairs of statements say essentially the same thing in two different ways?
   I. The only time the machine's red light is on is when the door is locked.
      If the machine's door is locked, the red light is on.
   II. Some gray-jacketed cables are connected to the blower.
      If a cable is connected to the blower, it must be gray-jacketed.

   A. I only
   B. I and II
   C. II only
   D. Neither I nor II

1.____

2. Which of the following pairs of statements say essentially the same thing in two different ways?
   I. If you live on Maple Street, your child is in the Valley District.
      If your child is in the Valley District, you must live on Maple Street.
   II. All the Smith children are brown-eyed.
      If a child is brown-eyed, it is not one of the Smith children

   A. I only
   B. I and II
   C. II only
   D. Neither I nor II

2.____

3. Which of the following pairs of statements say essentially the same thing in two different ways?
   I. If it's Monday, Mrs. James will be here.
      Mrs. James is here every Monday.
   II. Most people in the Drama Club do not have stage fright, but everyone in the Drama Club wants to be noticed.
      Some people in the Drama Club have stage fright and want to be noticed.

   A. I only
   B. I and II
   C. II only
   D. Neither I nor II

3.____

4. Which of the following pairs of statements say essentially the same thing in two different ways?
   I. If you are older than 65, you will get a senior's discount.
      Either you will get a senior's discount, or you are not older than 65.
   II. Every cadet in Officer Johnson's class has passed the firearms safety course.
      No cadet that has failed the firearms safety course is in Officer Johnson's class.

   A. I only
   B. I and II
   C. II only
   D. Neither I nor II

4.____

5. Summary of Evidence Collected to Date:
   Most people in the Greenlawn housing project do not have criminal records.
   Prematurely Drawn Conclusion: Some people in Greenlawn who have been crime victims have criminal records themselves.
   Which of the following pieces of evidence, if any, would make it *reasonably certain* that the conclusion drawn is true?

   A. Some of those who live in the Greenlawn project have been arrested or convicted of "victimless" crimes
   B. Most people in Greenlawn have been the victims of crime
   C. Everyone in Greenlawn has been the victim of crime
   D. None of these

5.____

6. Summary of Evidence Collected to Date:
   Every drug dealer in the Oak Lawn neighborhood wears blue and carries a Glock.
   Prematurely Drawn Conclusion: A person in the Oak Lawn neighborhood who carries a Glock is a drug dealer.
   Which of the following pieces of evidence, if any, would make it *reasonably certain* that the conclusion drawn is true?

   A. In the Oak Lawn neighborhood, only drug dealers wear blue
   B. Drug dealers in Oak Lawn only carry Glocks when they're dealing drugs
   C. In the Oak Lawn neighborhood, only drug dealers carry Glocks
   D. None of these

6.____

7. Summary of Evidence Collected to Date:
   I. Dr. Jones is older than Dr. Gupta.
   II. Dr. Gupta and Dr. Unruh were born on the same day.
   Prematurely Drawn Conclusion: Dr. Gupta does not work in the emergency room.
   Which of the following pieces of evidence, if any, would make it *reasonably certain* that the conclusion drawn is true?

   A. Dr. Jones is older than Dr. Unruh
   B. Dr. Jones works in the emergency room
   C. Every doctor in the emergency room is older then Dr. Unruh
   D. None of these

7.____

8. <u>Summary of Evidence Collected to Date:</u>
      I. On the street, a "dose" of a certain drug contains four "drams."
     II. A person can trade three "rolls" of a drug for a "plunk."
<u>Prematurely Drawn Conclusion:</u> A plunk is the most valuable amount of the drug on the street.
Which of the following pieces of evidence, if any, would make it *reasonably certain* that the conclusion drawn is true?

8.____

   A. A person can trade five doses for two rolls
   B. A dram contains two rolls
   C. A roll is larger than a dram
   D. None of these

9. <u>Summary of Evidence Collected to Date:</u>
Sam is a good writer and editor.
<u>Prematurely Drawn Conclusion:</u> Sam is qualified for the job.
Which of the following pieces of evidence, if any, would make it *reasonably certain* that the conclusion drawn is true?

9.____

   A. The job calls for good writing and editing skills
   B. A person who is not a good editor could still apply for the job on the strength of his/her writing skills
   C. If Sam applies for the job, he must be both a good writer and editor
   D. None of these

Questions 10-14

Questions 10 through 14 refer to Map #7 and measure your ability to orient yourself within a given section of town, neighborhood or particular area. Each of the questions describes a starting point and a destination. Assume that you are driving a car in the area shown on the map accompanying the questions. Use the map as a basis for the shortest way to get from one point to another without breaking the law.

On the map, a street marked by arrows, or by arrows and the words "One Way," indicates one-way travel, and should be assumed to be one-way for the entire length, even when there are breaks or jogs in the street. EXCEPTION: A street that does not have the same name over the full length.

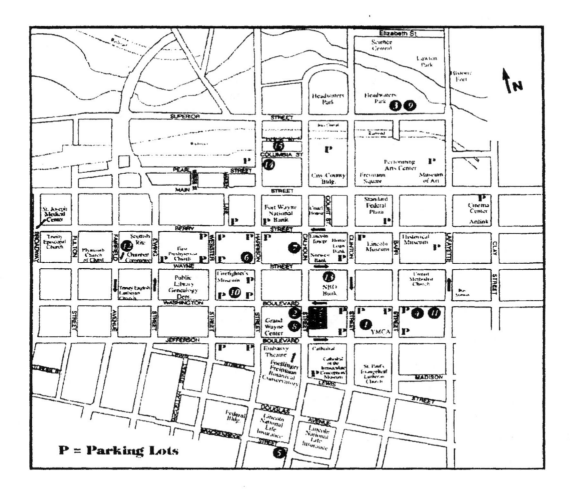

Map #7

10. The shortest legal way from Trinity Episcopal Church to Science Central is   10._____

     A. east on Berry, north on Clinton, east on Elizabeth
     B. east on Berry, north on Lafayette, west on Elizabeth
     C. north on Fulton, east on Main, north on Lafayette, west on Elizabeth
     D. north on Fulton, east on Main, north on Calhoun

11. The shortest legal way from the Grand Wayne Center to the Museum of Art is   11._____

     A. north on Harrison, east on Superior, south on Lafayette
     B. east on Washington Blvd., north on Lafayette
     C. east on Jefferson Blvd., north on Clinton, east on Main
     D. east on Jefferson Blvd., north on Lafayette

12. The shortest legal way from the Embassy Theatre to the City/County Building is   12._____

     A. west on Jefferson Blvd., north on Ewing, east on Main
     B. east on Jefferson Blvd., north on Lafayette, west on Main
     C. east on Jefferson Blvd., north on Clinton
     D. north on Harrison, east on Main

13. The shortest legal way from the YMCA to the Firefighter's Museum is   13._____

    A.   west on Jefferson Blvd., north on Webster
    B.   north on Barr, west on Washington Blvd., north on Webster
    C.   north on Barr, west on Wayne
    D.   north on Barr, west on Berry, south on Webster

14. The shortest legal way from the Historic Fort to Freimann Square is   14._____

    A.   north on Lafayette, west on Elizabeth, south on Clinton
    B.   north on Lafayette, west on Elizabeth, west/south on Calhoun, east on Main
    C.   south on Lafayette, west on Main
    D.   south on Lafayette, west on Superior, south on Clinton

Questions 15-19

Questions 15 through 19 refer to Figure #7, on the following page, and measure your ability to understand written descriptions of events. Each question presents a description of an accident or event and asks you which of the five drawings in Figure #7 BEST represents it.

In the drawings, the following symbols are used:

Moving vehicle: Non-moving vehicle:

Pedestrian or bicyclist:

The path and direction of travel of a vehicle or pedestrian is indicated by a solid line.

The path and direction of travel of each vehicle or pedestrian directly involved in a collision from the point of impact is indicated by a dotted line.

In the space at the right, print the letter of the drawing that best fits the descriptions written below:

15. A driver headed northeast on Cary strikes a car in the intersection and is diverted north, where he collides with the rear of a car that is traveling north on Park. The northbound car is knocked into the rear of another car that is traveling north ahead of it.   15._____

16. A driver headed northeast on Cary strikes a car in the intersection and is diverted north, where he collides head-on with a car stopped at a traffic light in the southbound lane on Park.   16._____

17. A driver headed northeast on Cary strikes a car in the intersection and is diverted east, where he collides head-on with a car stopped at a traffic light in the westbound lane on Roble.   17._____

18. A driver headed east on Roble collides with the left front of a car that is turning right from Knox onto Roble. The driver swerves right after the collision and collides head-on with another car headed north on Park.   18._____

19. A driver headed northeast on Cary strikes a car in the intersection and is diverted north, where he collides with the rear of a car parked in the northbound lane on Park.   19._____

FIGURE #7

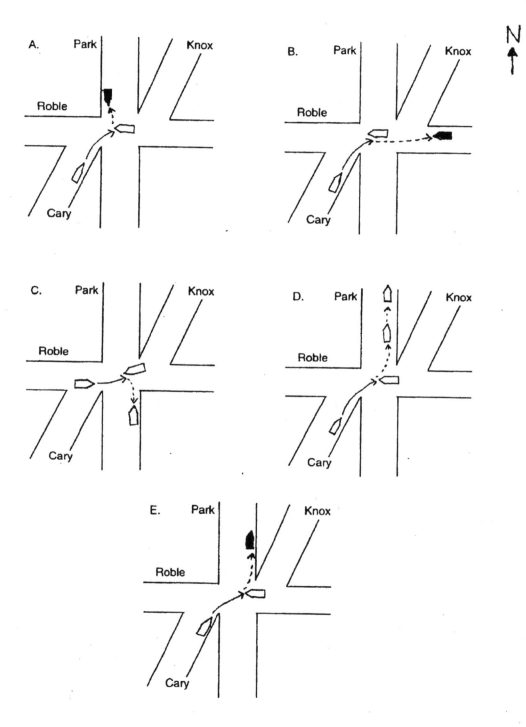

Questions 20-22

In questions 20 through 22, choose the word or phrase CLOSEST in meaning to the word or phrase printed in capital letters.

20. JURISDICTION 20._____

    A. authority
    B. decision
    C. judgment
    D. argument

21. PROXY 21._____

    A. neighbor
    B. agent
    C. enforcer
    D. impostor

22. LARCENY 22._____

    A. theft
    B. assault
    C. deceit
    D. gentleness

Questions 23-25

Questions 23 through 25 measure your ability to do fieldwork-related arithmetic. Each question presents a separate arithmetic problem for you to solve.

23. Mr. Long has 14 employees. He has four more male employees than female employees. 23._____
How many female employees does he have?

    A. 4   B. 5   C. 9   D. 10

24. A box of latex gloves costs $18. A crate has 12 boxes, each of which contains 48 gloves. 24._____
How much does a crate of latex gloves cost?

    A. $216   B. $328   C. $576   D. $864

25. In a single week, the Department of Parking collected 540 quarters, 623 dimes and 146 25._____
nickels from its parking meters. What was the total revenue collected from the meters during the week?

    A. $135.00   B. $154.00   C. $204.60   D. $270.30

KEY (CORRECT ANSWERS)

1.	A		11.	D
2.	D		12.	D
3.	B		13.	B
4.	B		14.	A
5.	C		15.	D
6.	C		16.	A
7.	C		17.	B
8.	A		18.	C
9.	A		19.	E
10.	C		20.	A

21.	B
22.	A
23.	B
24.	A
25.	C

———

SOLUTIONS (QUESTIONS 1 - 9)

P implies Q = original statement

Not Q implies not P = contrapositive of the original statement. A statement and its contrapositive are logically equivalent.

Q implies P = converse of the original statement.

Not P implies not Q = inverse of the original statement. The converse and inverse of an original statement are logically equivalent.

P implies Q = Not P or Q.

#1. The correct answer is **A**. For item I, the equivalent of the first statement would be "If the red light is on, the door is locked." This is the converse of the second statement, so it is not equivalent to the first statement. For item II, the first statement does not guarantee that all cables that are connected to the blower must be gray-jacketed. There may very well be other cables that are connected to the blower that are not gray-jacketed. Equally possible, some gray-jacketed cables are not necessarily connected to the blower.

#2. The correct answer is **D**. For item I, the second statement is the converse of the first statement, so it is not logically equivalent. For item II, the equivalent of the first statement is "If a child is not brown-eyed, then it is not one of the Smith children." Thus, statement II as it stands is not equivalent to statement I.

#3 The correct answer is **B**. For item I, Mrs. James is here every Monday, so we conclude that if it is Monday, she is here. (She may be here on other days as well.) For item II, we can conclude that there are some people in the Drama club who do have stage fright. Since everyone in the Drama Club wants to be noticed, this would include those who have stage fright.

#4. The correct answer is **B**. For item I, these two statements represent " P implies Q" and "Not P or Q," where P = Older than 65 and Q = Get a senior discount. These are equivalent statements. For item II, these statements are contrapositives of each other and so must be equivalent. (P = Cadet in Johnson's class and Q = Passes the safety course.)

#5. The correct answer is **C**. If everyone in the housing project has been a victim of crime and most of these people do not have a criminal record, we can conclude that some of them do have a criminal record. Thus, we have the situation that some of the people who live in this housing project are both a victim of crime as well as a perpetrator of crime.

#6. The correct answer is **C**. This choice can be written as "In this neighborhood, if a person carries a Glock, he is a drug dealer. This would lead directly to the drawn conclusion.

#7. The correct answer is **C**. We know that every doctor in the emergency room is older than Dr. Unruh; it is not possible for Dr. Gupta to be working in the emergency room since he is the same age as Dr. Unruh.

#8. The correct answer is **A**. From statement I, a dose is worth more than a dram. If 5 doses is equal to 2 rolls, than a roll is worth more than a dose. So of these three, a roll is worth the most.

Finally, statement II tells us that a plunk is worth more than a roll. This means that a plunk is worth the most among all four of these categories.

#9. The correct answer is **A**. Sam has the qualifications of being a good writer and editor, which is exactly what is needed for the job. Therefore, Sam is qualified for this job.

TEST 2

DIRECTIONS: Each question or incomplete statement is followed by several suggested answers or completions. Select the one that BEST answers the question or completes the statement. *PRINT THE LETTER OF THE CORRECT ANSWER IN THE SPACE AT THE RIGHT.*

Questions 1-9

Questions 1 through 9 measure your ability to (1) determine whether statements from witnesses say essentially the same thing and (2) determine the evidence needed to make it reasonably certain that a particular conclusion is true.

To do well on this part of the test, you do NOT have to have a working knowledge of police procedures and techniques. Nor do you have to have any more familiarity with criminals and criminal behavior than that acquired from reading newspapers, listening to radio or watching TV. To do well in this part, you must read and reason carefully.

1. Which of the following pairs of statements say essentially the same thing in two different ways?   1.____
   I.   If the garbage is collected today, it is definitely Wednesday.
        The garbage is collected every Wednesday.
   II. Nobody has no answer to the question.
        Everybody has at least one answer to the question.

   A.   I only
   B.   I and II
   C.   II only
   D.   Neither I nor II

2. Which of the following pairs of statements say essentially the same thing in two different ways?   2.____
   I.   If it rains, the streets will be wet.
        If the streets are wet, it has rained.
   II. All of the Duluth Five are immune from prosecution.
        No member of the Duluth Five can be prosecuted.

   A.   I only
   B.   I and II
   C.   II only
   D.   Neither I nor II

3. Which of the following pairs of statements say essentially the same thing in two different ways?   3.____
   I.   Ms. Friar will accept her promotion if and only if she is offered a 10% raise.
        For Ms. Friar to accept her promotion, it is necessary that she be offered a 10% raise.
   II. If the hydraulic lines are flushed, it is definitely inspection day.
        The hydraulic lines are flushed only on inspection days.

   A.   I only
   B.   I and II
   C.   II only
   D.   Neither I nor II

157

4. Which of the following pairs of statements say essentially the same thing in two different   4._____
   ways?

    I.   If you are tall you will get onto the basketball team.
        Unless you are tall you will not get onto the basketball team.
    II. That raven is black.
        If that bird is black, it's a raven.

    A. I only
    B. I and II
    C. II only
    D. Neither I nor II

5. <u>Summary of Evidence Collected to Date:</u>   5._____
   Every member of the Rotary Club is retired.
   <u>Prematurely Drawn Conclusion:</u> At least some people in the planning commission are
   retired.
   Which of the following pieces of evidence, if any, would make it *reasonably certain* that
   the conclusion drawn is true?

    A. Retirement is a condition for membership in the Rotary Club
    B. Every member of the planning commission has been in the Rotary Club at one
        time
    C. Every member of the Rotary Club is also on the planning commission
    D. None of these

6. <u>Summary of Evidence Collected to Date:</u>   6._____
   Some of the SWAT team snipers have poor aim.
   <u>Prematurely Drawn Conclusion:</u> The snipers on the SWAT team with the worst aim
   also have 20/20 vision.
   Which of the following pieces of evidence, if any, would make it *reasonably certain* that
   the conclusion drawn is true?

    A. Some of the SWAT team snipers have 20/20 vision
    B. Every sniper on the SWAT team has 20/20 vision
    C. Some snipers on the SWAT team wear corrective lenses
    D. None of these

7. <u>Summary of Evidence Collected to Date:</u>   7._____
   The only time Garson hears voices is on a day when he doesn't take his medication.
   <u>Prematurely Drawn Conclusion:</u> On Fridays, Garson never hears voices.
   Which of the following pieces of evidence, if any, would make it *reasonably certain* that
   the conclusion drawn is true?

    A. Garson is supposed to take his medication every day
    B. Garson usually undergoes shock therapy on Fridays
    C. Garson usually takes his medication and undergoes shock therapy on Fridays
    D. None of these

8. <u>Summary of Evidence Collected to Date</u>:
Among the three maintenance workersFrank, Lily and JeanFrank is not the tallest.
<u>Prematurely Drawn Conclusion:</u> Lily is the tallest.
Which of the following pieces of evidence, if any, would make it *reasonably certain* that the conclusion drawn is true?

8.____

   A.   Jean is not the tallest
   B.   Frank is the shortest
   C.   Jean is the shortest
   D.   None of these

9. <u>Summary of Evidence Collected to Date</u>:
Doctor Lyons went to the cafeteria for lunch today and did not eat dessert.
<u>Prematurely Drawn Conclusion:</u> The cafeteria did not serve dessert.
Which of the following pieces of evidence, if any, would make it *reasonably certain* that the conclusion drawn is true?

9.____

   A.   Dr. Lyons never eats dessert
   B.   When the cafeteria serves dessert, Dr. Lyons always eats it
   C.   The cafeteria rarely serves dessert when Dr. Lyons eats there
   D.   None of these

Questions 10-14

Questions 10 through 14 refer to Map #8 and measure your ability to orient yourself within a given section of town, neighborhood or particular area. Each of the questions describes a starting point and a destination. Assume that you are driving a car in the area shown on the map accompanying the questions. Use the map as a basis for the shortest way to get from one point to another without breaking the law.

On the map, a street marked by arrows, or by arrows and the words "One Way," indicates one-way travel, and should be assumed to be one-way for the entire length, even when there are breaks or jogs in the street. EXCEPTION: A street that does not have the same name over the full length.

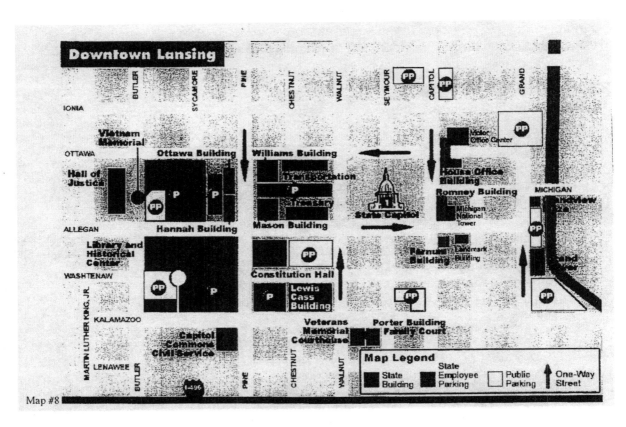

Map #8

10. The shortest legal way from the Library and Historical Center to Grandview Plaza is   10.____

    A.   south on Butler, east on Kalamazoo, north on Grand
    B.   east on Allegan, north on Grand
    C.   north on Butler, east on Ionia, south on Grand
    D.   north on Martin Luther King, Jr., east on Ottawa, south on Pine, east on Allegan, north on Grand

11. The shortest legal way from the Victor Office Center to the Mason Building is   11.____

    A.   west on Ottawa, south on Pine
    B.   south on Capitol, west on Allegan, north on Pine
    C.   south on Capitol, west on Washtenaw, north on Walnut, west on Allegan
    D.   west on Ottawa, north on Seymour, west on Ionia, south on Pine

12. The shortest legal way from the Treasury to the Hall of Justice is   12.____

    A.   north on Walnut, west on Ottawa, south on Martin Luther King, Jr.
    B.   west on Allegan
    C.   east on Allegan, north on Grand, west on Ottawa, south on Martin Luther King, Jr.
    D.   south on Walnut, west on Kalamazoo, north on Martin Luther King, Jr.

13. The shortest legal way from the Veterans Memorial Courthouse to the House Office   13._____
    Building is

    A. north on Walnut, east on Ottawa
    B. east on Kalamazoo, north on Capitol
    C. east on Kalamazoo, north on Grand, west on Ottawa
    D. north on Walnut, east on Allegan, north on Capitol

14. The shortest legal way from Grand Tower to Constitution Hall is   14._____

    A. west on Washtenaw
    B. north on Grand, west on Allegan, south on Pine
    C. north on Grand, west on Ottawa, south on Pine
    D. south on Grand, west on Kalamazoo, north on Pine

Questions 15-19

Questions 15 through 19 refer to Figure #8, on the following page, and measure your ability to
understand written descriptions of events. Each question presents a description of an accident
or event and asks you which of the five drawings in Figure #8 BEST represents it.

In the drawings, the following symbols are used:

Moving vehicle: ⬭   Non-moving vehicle: ⬛

Pedestrian or bicyclist: ●

The path and direction of travel of a vehicle or pedestrian is indicated by a solid line.
The path and direction of travel of each vehicle or pedestrian directly involved in a collision from
the point of impact is indicated by a dotted line.
In the space at the right, print the letter of the drawing that best fits the descriptions written
below:

15. A driver headed west on Holly runs a red light and turns left. He sideswipes a car headed   15._____
    south in the intersection, and then flees south on Bay. The southbound car is diverted
    into the rear end of a car parked in the southbound lane on Bay.

16. A driver headed east on Holly runs a red light. Another driver headed south through the   16._____
    intersection slams on her brakes just in time to avoid a serious collision. The eastbound
    driver glances off the front of the southbound car and continues east, where he collides
    with a car parked in the eastbound lane on Holly.

17. A driver headed east on Holly runs a red light. She strikes the left front of a westbound   17._____
    car that is turning left from Holly onto Bay, and then veers left and strikes the rear end of
    a car parked in the northbound lane on Bay.

18. A driver headed north on Bay strikes the right front of a car heading south in the intersec-   18._____
    tion of Bay and Holly. After the collision, the driver veers left and collides with the rear
    end of a car parked in the westbound lane of Holly. The southbound car veers left and
    collides with the rear end of a car in the eastbound lane on Holly.

19. A driver headed north on Bay strikes the left front of a car heading south in the intersection of Bay and Holly. After the collision, the driver continues north and collides with the rear end of a car parked in the northbound lane. The southbound car continues south and collides with the rear end of a car in the southbound lane.

19._____

FIGURE #8

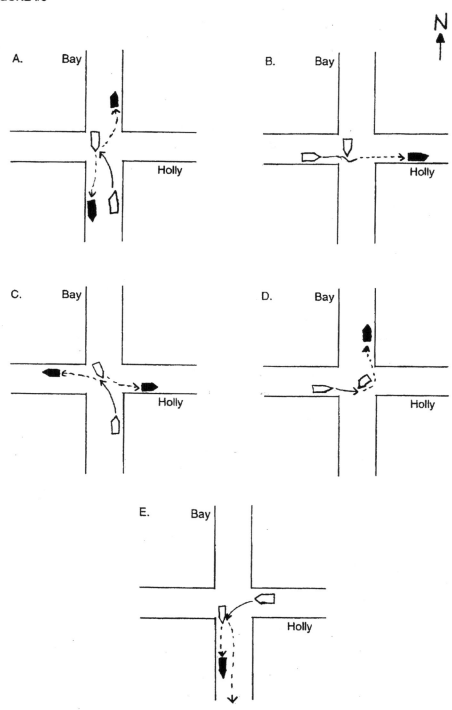

Questions 20-22

In questions 20 through 22, choose the word or phrase CLOSEST in meaning to the word or phrase printed in capital letters.

20. LIABLE

    A. sensitive
    B. dishonest
    C. responsible
    D. valid

20._____

21. CLAIM

    A. debt
    B. period
    C. denial
    D. banishment

21._____

22. ADMISSIBLE

    A. false
    B. conclusive
    C. acceptable
    D. indisputable

22._____

Questions 23-25

Questions 23 through 25 measure your ability to do fieldwork-related arithmetic. Each question presents a separate arithmetic problem for you to solve.

23. Three departments divide an $800 payment. Department 1 takes $270, and Department 2 takes $150 more than Department 3. How much does Department 2 take?

    A. $150   B. $190   C. $340   D. $490

23._____

24. Detective Smalley cleared 100 murder cases in five years. Each year he cleared six more than he cleared in the previous year. How many cases did he clear during the first year?

    A. 6   B. 8   C. 12   D. 18

24._____

25. The purchasing agent bought three binders for $2 each, four reams of copier paper for $3 each and five packs of black pens for $7 each. How much did the agent spend?

    A. $12.00   B. $25.20   C. $53.00   D. $72.00

25._____

KEY (CORRECT ANSWERS)

1.	C		11.	A
2.	C		12.	A
3.	B		13.	C
4.	D		14.	A
5.	C		15.	E
6.	B		16.	B
7.	D		17.	D
8.	C		18.	C
9.	B		19.	A
10.	B		20.	C

21.	A
22.	C
23.	C
24.	B
25.	C

SOLUTIONS (QUESTIONS 1 – 9)

P implies Q = original statement

Not Q implies not P = contrapositive of the original statement. A statement and its contrapositive are logically equivalent.

Q implies P = converse of the original statement.

Not P implies not Q = inverse of the original statement. The converse and inverse of an original statement are logically equivalent.

P implies Q = Not P or Q.

#1. The correct answer is **B**. For item I, we can conclude that it is Wednesday if and only if the garbage is collected. For item II, the phrase "nobody has no" is equivalent to 'everybody has at least one."

#2. The correct answer is **C**. For item I, each statement is the converse of the other. Thus, they are not equivalent. For item II, each statement says that each member of the Duluth Five is immune from prosecution.

#3. The correct answer is **B**. For item I, accepting a promotion is a necessary and sufficient condition for receiving a 10% raise. For item II, we have the P implies Q condition, where P = hydraulic lines are flushed and Q = it is an inspection day.

#4. The correct answer is **D**. For item I, each statement is the converse of the other (so they not equivalent). For item II, the first statement simply states that a particular raven is black. The second statement says that all black birds are ravens. They are not equivalent.

#5. The correct answer is **C**. The two scenarios are (a) a Rotary Club member is a subset of the set of all retirees, which is a subset of all planning commission members or (b) a Rotary Club member is a subset of all planning commission members, which is a subset of all retirees. In either case, each member of the Rotary Club is also a member of the planning commission.

#6. The correct answer is **B**. We know that some SWAT sniper members have poor aim. If we also know that all snipers on the SWAT team also have 20/20 vision, then we conclude that any sniper (including those with the worst aim) must have 20/20 vision.

#7. The correct answer is **D**. The only way that Garson will not hear voices is if he takes his medication. The premature conclusion can only be correct if he takes his medication every Friday. None of choices A, B, or C mentions this specifically.

#8. The correct answer is **A**. If Frank is not the tallest and Jean is not the tallest, then the conclusion that Lily is the tallest is correct. This is a reasonable conclusion, unless all three are the same height (very unlikely).

#9. The correct answer is **B**. We are given that Dr. Lyons went to the cafeteria for lunch and that he did not have dessert. If Dr. Lyons always eats dessert when it is served in the cafeteria, we can conclude that the cafeteria did not serve dessert.

EVALUATING INFORMATION AND EVIDENCE

EXAMINATION SECTION
TEST 1

DIRECTIONS: Each question or incomplete statement is followed by several suggested answers or completions. Select the one that BEST answers the question or completes the statement. *PRINT THE LETTER OF THE CORRECT ANSWER IN THE SPACE AT THE RIGHT.*

Questions 1-9

Questions 1 through 9 measure your ability to (1) determine whether statements from witnesses say essentially the same thing and (2) determine the evidence needed to make it reasonably certain that a particular conclusion is true.

1. Which of the following pairs of statements say essentially the same thing in two different ways?
    1.____

    I. If you get your feet wet, you will catch a cold.
        If you catch a cold, you must have gotten your feet wet.
    II. If I am nominated, I will run for office.
        I will run for office only if I am nominated.

    A. I only
    B. I and II
    C. II only
    D. Neither I nor II

2. Which of the following pairs of statements say essentially the same thing in two different ways?
    2.____

    I. The enzyme Rhopsin cannot be present if the bacterium Trilox is absent.
        Rhopsin and Trilox always appear together.
    II. A member of PENSA has an IQ of at least 175.
        A person with an IQ of less than 175 is not a member of PENSA.

    A. I only
    B. I and II
    C. II only
    D. Neither I nor II

3. Which of the following pairs of statements say essentially the same thing in two different ways?
    3.____

    I. None of Finer High School's sophomores will be going to the prom.
        No student at Finer High School who is going to the prom is a sophomore.
    II. If you have 20/20 vision, you may carry a firearm.
        You may not carry a firearm unless you have 20/20 vision.

    A. I only
    B. I and II
    C. II only
    D. Neither I nor II

4. Which of the following pairs of statements say essentially the same thing in two different ways?   4.____

    I. If the family doesn't pay the ransom, they will never see their son again.
       It is necessary for the family to pay the ransom in order for them to see their son again.
    II. If it is raining, I am carrying an umbrella.
       If I am carrying an umbrella, it is raining.

    A. I only
    B. I and II
    C. II only
    D. Neither I nor II

5. Summary of Evidence Collected to Date: 5.____
In the county's maternity wards, over the past year, only one baby was born who did not share a birthday with any other baby.
Prematurely Drawn Conclusion: At least one baby was born on the same day as another baby in the county's maternity wards.
Which of the following pieces of evidence, if any, would make it *reasonably certain* that the conclusion drawn is true?

    A. More than 365 babies were born in the county's maternity wards over the past year
    B. No pairs of twins were born over the past year in the county's maternity wards
    C. More than one baby was born in the county's maternity wards over the past year
    D. None of these

6. Summary of Evidence Collected to Date: 6.____
Every claims adjustor for MetroLife drives only a Ford sedan when on the job.
Prematurely Drawn Conclusion: A person who works for MetroLife and drives a Ford sedan is a claims adjustor.
Which of the following pieces of evidence, if any, would make it *reasonably certain* that the conclusion drawn is true?

    A. Most people who work for MetroLife are claims adjustors
    B. Some people who work for MetroLife are not claims adjustors
    C. Most people who work for MetroLife drive Ford sedans
    D. None of these

7. Summary of Evidence Collected to Date: 7.____
Mason will speak to Zisk if Zisk will speak to Ronaldson.
Prematurely Drawn Conclusion: Jones will not speak to Zisk if Zisk will speak to Ronaldson
Which of the following pieces of evidence, if any, would make it *reasonably certain* that the conclusion drawn is true?

    A. If Zisk will speak to Mason, then Ronaldson will not speak to Jones
    B. If Mason will speak to Zisk, then Jones will not speak to Zisk
    C. If Ronaldson will speak to Jones, then Jones will speak to Ronaldson
    D. None of these

8. <u>Summary of Evidence Collected to Date:</u>   8._____
   No blue lights on the machine are indicators for the belt drive status.
   <u>Prematurely Drawn Conclusion:</u> Some of the lights on the lower panel are not indicators for the belt drive status.
   Which of the following pieces of evidence, if any, would make it *reasonably certain* that the conclusion drawn is true?

   A. No lights on the machine's lower panel are blue
   B. An indicator light for the machine's belt drive status is either green or red
   C. Some lights on the machine's lower panel are blue
   D. None of these

9. <u>Summary of Evidence Collected to Date:</u>   9._____
   Of the four Sweeney sisters, two are married, three have brown eyes, and three are doctors.
   <u>Prematurely Drawn Conclusion:</u> Two of the Sweeney sisters are brown-eyed, married doctors.
   Which of the following pieces of evidence, if any, would make it *reasonably certain* that the conclusion drawn is true?

   A. The sister who does not have brown eyes is married
   B. The sister who does not have brown eyes is not a doctor, and one who is not married is not a doctor
   C. Every Sweeney sister with brown eyes is a doctor
   D. None of these

Questions 10-14

Questions 10 through 14 refer to Map #5 and measure your ability to orient yourself within a given section of town, neighborhood or particular area. Each of the questions describes a starting point and a destination. Assume that you are driving a car in the area shown on the map accompanying the questions. Use the map as a basis for the shortest way to get from one point to another without breaking the law.

On the map, a street marked by arrows, or by arrows and the words "One Way," indicates one-way travel, and should be assumed to be one-way for the entire length, even when there are breaks or jogs in the street. EXCEPTION: A street that does not have the same name over the full length.

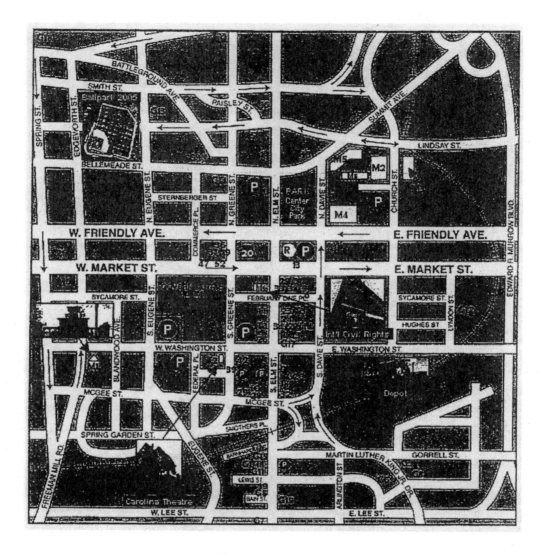

Map #5

10. The shortest legal way from the depot to Center City Park is   10._____

    A.   north on Church, west on Market, north on Elm
    B.   east on Washington, north on Edward R. Murrow Blvd., west on Friendly Ave.
    C.   west on Washington, north on Greene, east on Market, north on Davie
    D.   north on Church, west on Friendly Ave.

11. The shortest legal way from the Governmental Plaza to the ballpark is   11._____

    A.   west on Market, north on Edgeworth
    B.   west on Market, north on Eugene
    C.   north on Greene, west on Lindsay
    D.   north on Commerce Place, west on Bellemeade

12. The shortest legal way from the International Civil Rights Building to the building marked "M3" on the map is 12.____

  A. east on February One Place, north on Davie, east on Friendly Ave., north on Church
  B. south on Elm, west on Washington, north on Greene, east on Market, north on Church
  C. north on Elm, east on Market, north on Church
  D. north on Elm, east on Lindsay, south on Church

13. The shortest legal way from the ballpark to the Carolina Theatre is 13.____

  A. east on Lindsay, south on Greene
  B. south on Edgeworth, east on Friendly Ave., south on Greene
  C. east on Bellemeade, south on Elm, west on Washington
  D. south on Eugene, east on Washington

14. A car traveling north or south on Church Street may NOT go 14.____

  A. west onto Friendly Ave.
  B. west onto Lindsay
  C. east onto Market
  D. west onto Smith

Questions 15-19

Questions 15 through 19 refer to Figure #5, on the following page, and measure your ability to understand written descriptions of events. Each question presents a description of an accident or event and asks you which of the five drawings in Figure #5 BEST represents it.

In the drawings, the following symbols are used:

Moving vehicle: Non-moving vehicle:

Pedestrian or bicyclist:

The path and direction of travel of a vehicle or pedestrian is indicated by a solid line.

The path and direction of travel of each vehicle or pedestrian directly involved in a collision from the point of impact is indicated by a dotted line.

In the space at the right, print the letter of the drawing that best fits the descriptions written below:

15. A driver heading south on Ohio runs a red light and strikes the front of a car headed west on Grand. He glances off and leaves the roadway at the southwest corner of Grand and Ohio. 15.____

16. A driver heading east on Grand drifts into the oncoming lane as it travels through the intersection of Grand and Ohio, and strikes an oncoming car head-on. 16.____

17. A driver heading **east** on Grand veers into the **oncoming** lane, sideswipes a **westbound** car and overcorrects as he swerves back into his lane. He leaves the roadway **near** the southeast corner of Grand and Ohio.

17._____

18. A driver heading **east** on Grand strikes the **front** of a car that is traveling north on Ohio and has run a red light. After striking the front of the northbound car, the driver veers **left** and leaves the roadway at the northeast corner of Grand and Ohio.

18._____

19. A driver heading **east** on Grand is traveling above the speed limit and clips the rear end of another eastbound car. The driver then veers to the left and leaves the roadway at the northeast corner of Grand and Ohio.

19._____

FIGURE #5

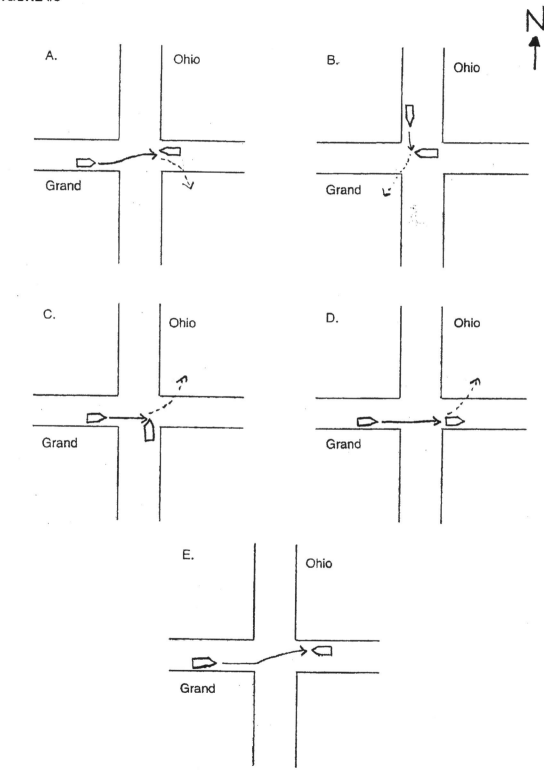

Questions 20-22

In questions 20 through 22, choose the word or phrase CLOSEST in meaning to the word or phrase printed in capital letters.

20. PETITION
   A. appeal
   B. law
   C. oath
   D. opposition

20.____

21. MALPRACTICE
   A. commission
   B. mayhem
   C. error
   D. misconduct

21.____

22. EXONERATE
   A. incriminate
   B. accuse
   C. lengthen
   D. acquit

22.____

Questions 23-25

Questions 23 through 25 measure your ability to do fieldwork-related arithmetic. Each question presents a separate arithmetic problem for you to solve.

23. Officers Lane and Bryant visited another city as part of an investigation. Because each is from a different precinct, they agree to split all expenses. With her credit card, Lane paid $70 for food and $150 for lodging. Bryant wrote checks for gas ($50) and entertainment ($40).
How much does Bryant owe Lane?

   A. $65   B. $90   C. $155   D. $210

23.____

24. In a remote mountain pass, two search-and-rescue teams, one from Silverton and one from Durango, combine to look for a family that disappeared in a recent snowstorm. The combined team is composed of 20 members. Which of the following statements could NOT be true?

   A. The Durango team has a dozen members
   B. The Silverton team has only one member
   C. The Durango team has two more members than the Silverton team
   D. The Silverton team has one more member than the Durango team

24.____

25. Three people in the department share a vehicle for a period of one year. The average number of miles traveled per month by each person is 150. How many miles will be added to the car's odometer at the end of the year?

   A. 1,800   B. 2,400   C. 3,600   D. 5,400

25.____

KEY (CORRECT ANSWERS)

1.	D		11.	D
2.	C		12.	C
3.	A		13.	D
4.	A		14.	D
5.	A		15.	B
6.	D		16.	E
7.	B		17.	A
8.	C		18.	C
9.	B		19.	D
10.	D		20.	A

21. D
22. D
23. A
24. D
25. D

SOLUTIONS TO QUESTIONS 1-9

P implies Q = original statement

Not Q implies not P = contrapositive of the original statement. A statement and its contrapositive are logically equivalent.

Q implies P = converse of the original statement.

Not P implies not Q = inverse of the original statement. The converse and inverse of an original statement are logically equivalent.

P implies Q = Not P or Q.

#1. The correct answer is **D**. In items I and II, each statement is the converses of the other. A converse of a statement is not equivalent to its original statement.

#2. The correct answer is **C**. In item I, the first statement is equivalent to "If Trilox is absent, then Rhopsin is also absent." But this does <u>not</u> imply that if Trilox is present, so too must Rhopsin be present. In item II, each statement is the contrapositive of the other. Thus, they are equivalent.

#3. The correct answer is **A**. In item I, the first statement tells us that if a student is a sophomore, he/she will not go to the prom. The second statement is equivalent to "If a student does attend the prom, he/she is not a sophomore." This is the contrapositive of the first statement, (so it is equivalent to it).

#4. The correct answer is **A**. In item I, the second statement can be written as "If the family sees their son again, then they must have paid the ransom." This is the contrapositive of the first statement. In item II, these statements are converses of each other; thus, they are not equivalent.

#5. The correct answer is **A**. If more than 365 babies were born in the county in one year, then at least two babies must share the same birthday.

#6. The correct answer is **A**. Given that most people who work for MetroLife are claims adjustors, plus the fact that all claims adjustors drive only a Ford sedan, it is a reasonable conclusion that any person who drives a Ford sedan and works for MetroLife is a claims adjustor.

#7. The correct answer is **B**. Jones will not speak to Zisk if Zisk will speak to Ronaldson, which <u>will</u> happen if Mason will speak to Zisk.

#8. The correct answer is **C**. We are given that blue lights are never an indicator for the drive belt status. If some of the lights on the lower panel of the machine are blue, then it is reasonable to conclude that some of the lights on the lower panel are not indicators for the drive belt status.

#9. The correct answer is **D**. It is possible to have the following situation: Sister 1 is not married, does not have brown eyes, and is a doctor; each of sisters 2 and 3 is married, has brown eyes and is a doctor; sister 4 is not married, has brown eyes, and is not a doctor. None of choices A, B, or C would lead to the situation as described above.

TEST 2

DIRECTIONS: Each question or incomplete statement is followed by several suggested answers or completions. Select the one that BEST answers the question or completes the statement. *PRINT THE LETTER OF THE CORRECT ANSWER IN THE SPACE AT THE RIGHT.*

Questions 1-9

Questions 1 through 9 measure your ability to (1) determine whether statements from witnesses say essentially the same thing and (2) determine the evidence needed to make it reasonably certain that a particular conclusion is true.

To do well on this part of the test, you do NOT have to have a working knowledge of police procedures and techniques. Nor do you have to have any more familiarity with criminals and criminal behavior than that acquired from reading newspapers, listening to radio or watching TV. To do well in this part, you must read and reason carefully.

1. Which of the following pairs of statements say essentially the same thing in two different ways?

    I. If there is life on Mars, we should fund NASA.
        Either there is life on Mars, or we should not fund NASA.

    II. All Eagle Scouts are teenage boys.
        All teenage boys are Eagle Scouts.

  A. I only
  B. I and II
  C. II only
  D. Neither I nor II

1.____

2. Which of the following pairs of statements say essentially the same thing in two different ways?

    I. If that notebook is missing its front cover, it definitely belongs to Carter.
        Carter's notebook is the only one missing its front cover.

    II. If it's hot, the pool is open.
        The pool is open if it's hot.

  A. I only
  B. I and II
  C. II only
  D. Neither I nor II

2.____

3. Which of the following pairs of statements say essentially the same thing in two different ways?

    I. Nobody who works at the mill is without benefits.
        Everyone who works at the mill has benefits.

    II. We will fund the program only if at least 100 people sign the petition.
        Either we will fund the program or at least 100 people will sign the petition.

  A. I only
  B. I and II
  C. II only
  D. Neither I nor II

3.____

4. Which of the following pairs of statements say essentially the same thing in two different ways?   4.____

    I. If the new parts arrive, Mr. Luther's request has been answered.
        Mr. Luther requested new parts to arrive.
    II. The machine's test cycle will not run unless the operation cycle is not running.
        The machine's test cycle must be running in order for the operation cycle to run.

    A. I only
    B. I and II
    C. II only
    D. Neither I nor II

5. Summary of Evidence Collected to Date: 5.____

    I. To become a member of the East Side Crips, a kid must be either "jumped in" or steal a squad car without getting caught.
    II. Sid, a kid on the East Side, was caught stealing a squad car.

Prematurely Drawn Conclusion: Sid did not become a member of the East Side Crips.
Which of the following pieces of evidence, if any, would make it *reasonably certain* that the conclusion drawn is true?

    A. "Jumping in" is not allowed in prison
    B. Sid was not "jumped in"
    C. Sid's stealing the squad car had nothing to do with wanting to join the East Side Crips
    D. None of these

6. Summary of Evidence Collected to Date: 6.____

    I. Jones, a Precinct 8 officer, has more arrests than Smith.
    II. Smith and Watson have exactly the same number of arrests.

Prematurely Drawn Conclusion: Watson is not a Precinct 8 officer.
Which of the following pieces of evidence, if any, would make it *reasonably certain* that the conclusion drawn is true?

    A. All the officers in Precinct 8 have more arrests than Watson
    B. All the officers in Precinct 8 have fewer arrests than Watson
    C. Watson has fewer arrests than Jones
    D. None of these

7. Summary of Evidence Collected to Date: 7.____

    I. Twenty one-dollar bills are divided among Frances, Kerry and Brian.
    II. If Kerry gives her dollar bills to Frances, then Frances will have more money than Brian.

Prematurely Drawn Conclusion: Frances has twelve dollars.
Which of the following pieces of evidence, if any, would make it *reasonably certain* that the conclusion drawn is true?

    A. If Brian gives his dollars to Kerry, then Kerry will have more money than Frances
    B. Brian has two dollars
    C. If Kerry gives her dollars to Brian, Brian will still have less money than Frances
    D. None of these

8. <u>Summary of Evidence Collected to Date:</u>   8._____
      I.   The street sweepers will be here at noon today.
     II. Residents on the west side of the street should move their cars before noon.
<u>Prematurely Drawn Conclusion:</u> Today is Wednesday.
Which of the following pieces of evidence, if any, would make it *reasonably certain* that the conclusion drawn is true?

   A.   The street sweepers never sweep the east side of the street on Wednesday
   B.   The street sweepers arrive at noon every other day
   C.   There is no parking allowed on the west side of the street on Wednesday
   D.   None of these

9. <u>Summary of Evidence Collected to Date:</u>   9._____
The only time the warning light comes on is when there is a power surge.
<u>Prematurely Drawn Conclusion:</u> The warning light does not come on if the air conditioner is not running.
Which of the following pieces of evidence, if any, would make it *reasonably certain* that the conclusion drawn is true?

   A.   The air conditioner does not turn on if the warning light is on
   B.   Sometimes a power surge is caused by the dishwasher
   C.   There is only a power surge when the air conditioner turns on
   D.   None of these

Questions 10-14

Questions 10 through 14 refer to Map #6 and measure your ability to orient yourself within a given section of town, neighborhood or particular area. Each of the questions describes a starting point and a destination. Assume that you are driving a car in the area shown on the map accompanying the questions. Use the map as a basis for the shortest way to get from one point to another without breaking the law.

On the map, a street marked by arrows, or by arrows and the words "One Way," indicates one-way travel, and should be assumed to be one-way for the entire length, even when there are breaks or jogs in the street. EXCEPTION: A street that does not have the same name over the full length.

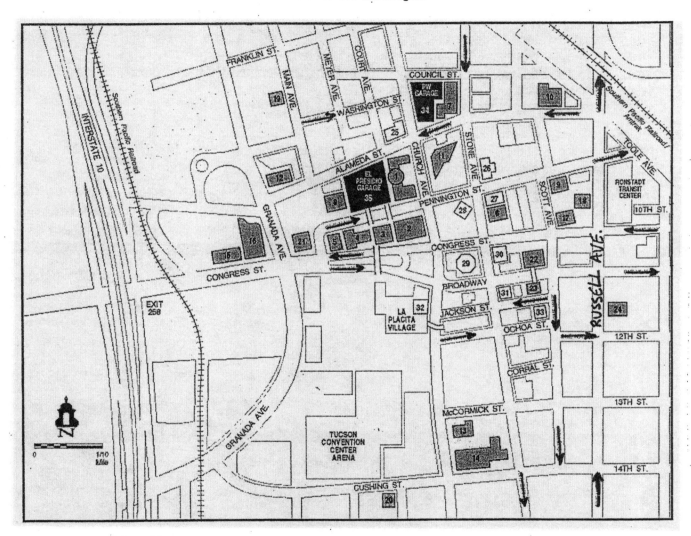

Map #6

PIMA COUNTY	*CITY OF TUCSON*
1 Old Courthouse	8 City Hall
2 Superior Court Building	9 City Hall Annex
3 Administration Building	10 Alameda Plaza City Court Building
4 Health and Welfare Building	11 Public Library - Main Branch
5 Mechanical Building	12 Tucson Water Building
6 Legal Services Building	13 Fire Department Headquarters
7 County/City Public Works Center	14 Police Department Building

10. The shortest legal way from the Public Library to the Alameda Plaza City Court Building is   10.____

    A. north on Stone Ave., east on Alameda
    B. south on Stone Ave., east on Congress, north on Russell Ave., west on Alameda
    C. south on Stone Ave., east on Pennington, north on Russell Ave., west on Alameda
    D. south on Church Ave., east on Pennington, north on Russell Ave., west on Alameda

11. The shortest legal way from City Hall to the Police Department is   11.____

    A. east on Congress, south on Scott Ave., west on 14th
    B. east on Pennington, south on Stone Ave.
    C. east on Congress, south on Stone Ave.
    D. east on Pennington, south on Church Ave.

12. The shortest legal way from the Tucson Water Building to the Legal Service Building is   12.____

    A. south on Granada Ave., east on Congress, north to east on Pennington, south on Stone Ave.
    B. east on Alameda, south on Church Ave., east on Pennington, south on Stone Ave.
    C. north on Granada Ave., east on Washington, south on Church Ave., east on Pennington, south on Stone Ave.
    D. south on Granada Ave., east on Cushing, north on Stone Ave.

13. The shortest legal way from the Tucson Convention Center Arena to the City Hall Annex is   13.____

    A. west on Cushing, north on Granada Ave., east on Congress, east on Broadway, north on Scott Ave.
    B. east on Cushing, north on Church Ave., east on Pennington
    C. east on Cushing, north on Russell Ave., west on Pennington
    D. east on Cushing, north on Stone Ave., east on Pennington

14. The shortest legal way from the Ronstadt Transit Center to the Fire Department is   14.____

    A. west on Pennington, south on Stone Ave., west on McCormick
    B. west on Congress, south on Russell Ave., west on 13th
    C. west on Congress, south on Church Ave.
    D. west on Pennington, south on Church Ave.

Questions 15-19

Questions 15 through 19 refer to Figure #6, on the following page, and measure your ability to understand written descriptions of events. Each question presents a description of an accident or event and asks you which of the five drawings in Figure #6 BEST represents it.

In the drawings, the following symbols are used:

Moving vehicle: ⬠   Non-moving vehicle: ◆

Pedestrian or bicyclist: ●

The path and direction of travel of a vehicle or pedestrian is indicated by a solid line.

The path and direction of travel of each vehicle or pedestrian directly involved in a collision from the point of impact is indicated by a dotted line.

In the space at the right, print the letter of the drawing that best fits the descriptions written below:

15. A bicyclist heading southwest on Rose travels into the intersection, sideswipes a car that is heading east on Page, and veers right, leaving the roadway at the northwest corner of Page and Mill.   15.____

16. A driver traveling north on Mill swerves right to avoid a bicyclist that is traveling southwest on Rose. The driver strikes the rear end of a car parked on Rose. The bicyclist continues through the intersection and travels west on Page.   16.____

17. A bicyclist heading southwest on Rose travels into the intersection, sideswipes a car that is heading east on Page, and veers right, striking the rear end of a car parked in the westbound lane on Page.   17.____

18. A driver traveling east on Page swerves left to avoid a bicyclist that is traveling southwest on Rose. The driver strikes the rear end of a car parked on Mill. The bicyclist continues through the intersection and travels west on Page.   18.____

19. A bicyclist heading southwest on Rose enters the intersection and sideswipes a car that is swerving left to avoid her. The bicyclist veers left and collides with a car parked in the southbound lane on Mill. The driver of the car veers left and collides with a car parked in the northbound lane on Mill.   19.____

FIGURE #6

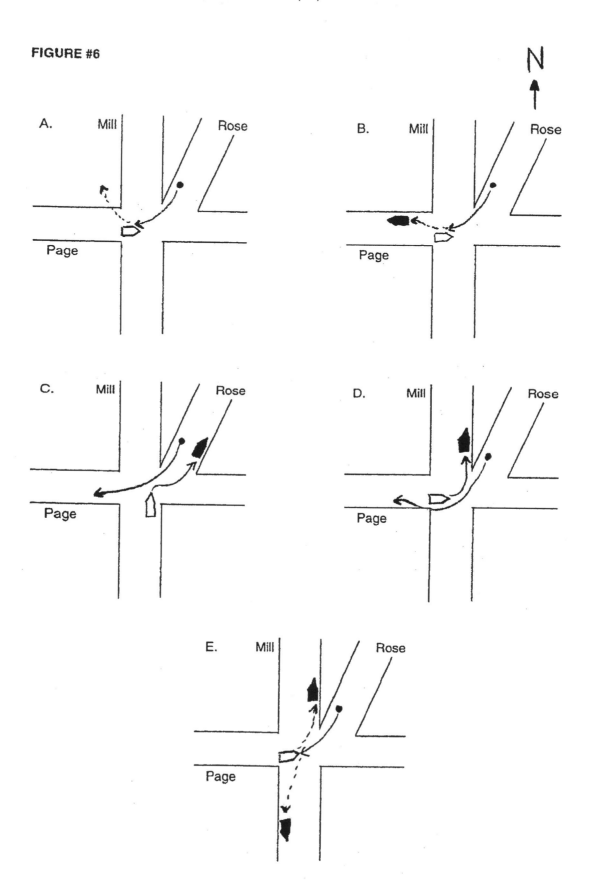

Questions 20-22

In questions 20 through 22, choose the word or phrase CLOSEST in meaning to the word or phrase printed in capital letters.

20. WAIVE

    A. cease
    B. surrender
    C. prevent
    D. die

20._____

21. DEPOSITION

    A. settlement
    B. deterioration
    C. testimony
    D. character

21._____

22. IMMUNITY

    A. exposure
    B. accusation
    C. protection
    D. exchange

22._____

Questions 23-25

Questions 23 through 25 measure your ability to do fieldwork-related arithmetic. Each question presents a separate arithmetic problem for you to solve.

23. Dean, a claims investigator, is reading a 445-page case record in his spare time at work. He has already read 157 pages. If Dean reads 24 pages a day, he should finish reading the rest of the record in _____ days.

    A. 7   B. 12   C. 19   D. 24

23._____

24. The Fire Department owns four cars. The Department of Sanitation owns twice as many cars as the Fire Department. The Department of Parks and Recreation owns one fewer car than the Department of Sanitation. The Department of Parks and Recreation is buying new tires for each of its cars. Each tire costs $100. How much is the Department of Parks and Recreation going to spend on tires?

    A. $400   B. $2,800   C. $3,200   D. $4,900

24._____

25. A dance hall is about 5,000 square feet. The local ordinance does not allow more than 50 people per every 100 square feet of commercial space. The maximum occupancy of the hall is

    A. 500   B. 2,500   C. 5,000   D. 25,000

25._____

KEY (CORRECT ANSWERS)

1.	D		11.	D
2.	B		12.	A
3.	A		13.	B
4.	A		14.	C
5.	B		15.	A
6.	D		16.	C
7.	D		17.	B
8.	D		18.	D
9.	C		19.	E
10.	C		20.	B

21.	C
22.	C
23.	B
24.	B
25.	B

SOLUTIONS TO QUESTIONS 1-9

P implies Q = original statement

Not Q implies not P = contrapositive of the original statement. A statement and its contrapositive are logically equivalent.

Q implies P = converse of the original statement.

Not P implies not Q = inverse of the original statement. The converse and inverse of an original statement are logically equivalent.

P implies Q = Not P or Q.

#1. The correct answer is **D**. For item I, the second statement should be "Either there is no life on Mars or we should fund NASA" in order to be logically equivalent to the first statement. For item II, the statements are converses of each other; thus they are not equivalent.

#2. The correct answer is **B**. In item I, this is an example of P implies Q and Q implies P. In this case, P = the notebook is missing its cover and Q = the notebook belongs to Carter. In item II, the ordering of the words is changed, but the If P then Q is exactly the same. P = it is hot and Q = the pool is open.

#3. The correct answer is **A**. For item I, if nobody is without benefits, then everybody has benefits. For item II, the second equivalent statement should be "either we will not fund the program or at least 100 people will sign the petition."

#4. The answer is **D**. For item I, the first statement is an implication, whereas the second statement mentions only one part of the implication (new parts are requested) and says nothing about the other part. For item II, the first statement is equivalent to "if the operating cycle is not running, then the test cycle will run." The second statement is equivalent to "if the operating cycle is running, then the test cycle will run." So, these statements in item II are not equivalent.

#5. The correct answer is **B**. Since Sid did not steal a car and avoid getting caught, the only other way he could become a Crips member would be "jumped in." Choice B tells us that Sid was not "jumped in," so we conclude that he did not become a member of the Crips.

#6. The correct answer is **D**. Since Smith and Watson have the same number of arrests, Watson must have fewer arrests than Jones. This means that each of choices A and B is impossible. Choice C would also not reveal whether or not Watson is a Precinct 8 officer.

#7. The correct answer is **D**. Exact dollar amounts still cannot be ascertained by using any of the other choices.

#8. The correct answer is **A**. The street sweepers never sweep on the east side of the street on Wednesday; however, they will be here at noon today. This implies that they will sweep on the west side of the street. Since the residents should move their cars before noon, we can conclude that today is Wednesday.

#9. The correct answer is **C**. We start with W implies P, where W = warning light comes on and P = power surge. Choice C would read as P implies A, where A = air conditioning is running. Combining these statements leads to W implies A. The conclusion can be read as: Not A implies Not W, which is equivalent to W implies A.

Evaluating Conclusions in Light of Known Facts

EXAMINATION SECTION
TEST 1

DIRECTIONS: Each question or incomplete statement is followed by several suggested answers or completions. Select the one that BEST answers the question or completes the statement. *PRINT THE LETTER OF THE CORRECT ANSWER IN THE SPACE AT THE RIGHT.*

Questions 1-9.

DIRECTIONS: In questions 1-9, you will read a set of facts and a conclusion drawn from them. The conclusion may be valid or invalid, based on the facts—it's your task to determine the validity of the conclusion.

For each question, select the letter before the statement that BEST expresses the relationship between the given facts and the conclusion that has been drawn from them. Your choices are:
A. The facts prove the conclusion
B. The facts disprove the conclusion; or
C. The facts neither prove nor disprove the conclusion.

1. FACTS: If the supervisor retires, James, the assistant supervisor, will not be transferred to another department. James will be promoted to supervisor if he is not transferred. The supervisor retired.

    CONCLUSION: James will be promoted to supervisor.

    A. The facts prove the conclusion.
    B. The facts disprove the conclusion.
    C. The facts neither prove nor disprove the conclusion.

1.____

2. FACTS: In the town of Luray, every player on the softball team works at Luray National Bank. In addition, every player on the Luray softball team wears glasses.

    CONCLUSION: At least some of the people who work at Luray National Bank wear glasses.

    A. The facts prove the conclusion.
    B. The facts disprove the conclusion.
    C. The facts neither prove nor disprove the conclusion.

2.____

3. FACTS: The only time Henry and June go out to dinner is on an evening when they have childbirth classes. Their childbirth classes meet on Tuesdays and Thursdays.

    CONCLUSION: Henry and June never go out to dinner on Friday or Saturday.

    A. The facts prove the conclusion.
    B. The facts disprove the conclusion.
    C. The facts neither prove nor disprove the conclusion.

3.____

4.   FACTS: Every player on the field hockey team has at least one bruise. Everyone on the
      field hockey team also has scarred knees.

4.____

CONCLUSION: Most people with both bruises and scarred knees are field hockey
players.

    A.   The facts prove the conclusion.
    B.   The facts disprove the conclusion.
    C.   The facts neither prove nor disprove the conclusion.

5.   FACTS: In the chess tournament, Lance will win his match against Jane if Jane wins her
      match against Mathias. If Lance wins his match against Jane, Christine will not win her
      match against Jane.

5.____

CONCLUSION: Christine will not win her match against Jane if Jane wins her match
against Mathias.

    A.   The facts prove the conclusion.
    B.   The facts disprove the conclusion.
    C.   The facts neither prove nor disprove the conclusion.

6.   FACTS: No green lights on the machine are indicators for the belt drive status. Not all of
      the lights on the machine's upper panel are green. Some lights on the machine's lower
      panel are green.

6.____

CONCLUSION: The green lights on the machine's lower panel may be indicators for
the belt drive status.

    A.   The facts prove the conclusion.
    B.   The facts disprove the conclusion.
    C.   The facts neither prove nor disprove the conclusion.

7.   FACTS: At a small, one-room country school, there are eight students: Amy, Ben, Carla,
      Dan, Elliot, Francine, Greg, and Hannah. Each student is in either the 6th, 7th, or 8th
      grade. Either two or three students are in each grade. Amy, Dan, and Francine are all in
      different grades. Ben and Elliot are both in the 7th grade. Hannah and Carl are in the
      same grade.

7.____

CONCLUSION: Exactly three students are in the 7th grade.

    A.   The facts prove the conclusion.
    B.   The facts disprove the conclusion.
    C.   The facts neither prove nor disprove the conclusion.

8.   FACTS: Two married couples are having lunch together. Two of the four people are Ger-
      man and two are Russian, but in each couple the nationality of a spouse is not necessar-
      ily the same as the other's. One person in the group is a teacher, the other a lawyer, one
      an engineer, and the other a writer. The teacher is a Russian man. The writer is Russian,
      and her husband is an engineer. One of the people, Mr. Stern, is German.

8.____

CONCLUSION: Mr. Stern's wife is a writer.

A. The facts prove the conclusion.
B. The facts disprove the conclusion.
C. The facts neither prove nor disprove the conclusion.

9. FACTS: The flume ride at the county fair is open only to children who are at least 36 inches tall. Lisa is 30 inches tall. John is shorter than Henry, but more than 10 inches taller than Lisa.

    CONCLUSION: Lisa is the only one who can't ride the flume ride.

A. The facts prove the conclusion.
B. The facts disprove the conclusion.
C. The facts neither prove nor disprove the conclusion.

9.____

Questions 10-17.

DIRECTIONS: Questions 10-17 are based on the following reading passage. It is not your knowledge of the particular topic that is being tested, but your ability to reason based on what you have read. The passage is likely to detail several proposed courses of action and factors affecting these proposals. The reading passage is followed by a conclusion or outcome based on the facts in the passage, or a description of a decision taken regarding the situation. The conclusion is followed by a number of statements that have a possible connection to the conclusion. For each statement, you are to determine whether:

A. The statement proves the conclusion.
B. The statement supports the conclusion but does not prove it.
C. The statement disproves the conclusion.
D. The statement weakens the conclusion but does not disprove it.
E. The statement has no relevance to the conclusion.

Remember that the conclusion after the passage is to be accepted as the outcome of what actually happened, and that you are being asked to evaluate the impact each statement would have had on the conclusion.

PASSAGE:

The Grand Army of Foreign Wars, a national veteran's organization, is struggling to maintain its National Home, where the widowed spouses and orphans of deceased members are housed together in a small village-like community. The Home is open to spouses and children who are bereaved for any reason, regardless of whether the member's death was related to military service, but a new global conflict has led to a dramatic surge in the number of members' deaths: many veterans who re-enlisted for the conflict have been killed in action.

The Grand Army of Foreign Wars is considering several options for handling the increased number of applications for housing at the National Home, which has been traditionally supported by membership dues. At its national convention, it will choose only one of the following:

The first idea is a one-time $50 tax on all members, above and beyond the dues they pay already. Since the organization has more than a million members, this tax should be sufficient for the construction and maintenance of new housing for applicants on the existing grounds of the National Home. The idea is opposed, however, by some older members who live on fixed incomes. These members object in principle to the taxation of Grand Army members. The Grand Army has never imposed a tax on its members.

The second idea is to launch a national fund-raising drive and public relations campaign that will attract donations for the National Home. Several national celebrities are members of the organization, and other celebrities could be attracted to the cause. Many Grand Army members are wary of this approach, however: in the past, the net receipts of some fund-raising efforts have been relatively insignificant, given the costs of staging them.

A third approach, suggested by many of the younger members, is to have new applicants share some of the costs of construction and maintenance. The spouses and children would pay an up-front "enrollment" fee, based on a sliding scale proportionate to their income and assets, and then a monthly fee adjusted similarly to contribute to maintenance costs. Many older members are strongly opposed to this idea, as it is in direct contradiction to the principles on which the organization was founded more than a century ago.

The fourth option is simply to maintain the status quo, focus the organization's efforts on supporting the families who already live at the National Home, and wait to accept new applicants based on attrition.

CONCLUSION: At its annual national convention, the Grand Army of Foreign Wars votes to impose a one-time tax of $10 on each member for the purpose of expanding and supporting the National Home to welcome a larger number of applicants. The tax is considered to be the solution most likely to produce the funds needed to accommodate the growing number of applicants.

10. Actuarial studies have shown that because the Grand Army's membership consists mostly of older veterans from earlier wars, the organization's membership will suffer a precipitous decline in numbers in about five years.

10.____

    A.
    B.
    C.
    D.
    E.

11. After passage of the funding measure, a splinter group of older members appeals for the "sliding scale" provision to be applied to the tax, so that some members may be allowed to contribute less based on their income.

11.____

    A.
    B.
    C.
    D.
    E.

12. The original charter of the Grand Army of Foreign Wars specifically states that the organization will not levy any taxes or duties on its members beyond its modest annual dues. It takes a super-majority of attending delegates at the national convention to make alterations to the charter.

A.
B.
C.
D.
E.

13. Six months before Grand Army of Foreign Wars' national convention, the Internal Revenue Service rules that because it is an organization that engages in political lobbying, the Grand Army must no longer enjoy its own federal tax-exempt status.

13

A.
B.
C.
D.
E.

14. Two months before the national convention, Dirk Rockwell, arguably the country's most famous film actor, announces in a nationally televised interview that he has been saddened to learn of the plight of the National Home, and that he is going to make it his own personal crusade to see that it is able to house and support a greater number of widowed spouses and orphans in the future.

A.
B.
C.
D.
E.

15. The Grand Army's final estimate is that the cost of expanding the National Home to accommodate the increased number of applicants will be about $61 million.

A.
B.
C.
D.
E.

16. Just before the national convention, the federal Department of Veterans Affairs announces steep cuts in the benefits package that is currently offered to the widowed spouses and orphans of veterans.

A.
B.
C.
D.

17. After the national convention, the Grand Army of Foreign Wars begins charging a modest   17.____
    "start-up" fee to all families who apply for residence at the national home.

    A.
    B.
    C.
    D.
    E.

Questions 18-25.

DIRECTIONS: Questions 18-25 each provide four factual statements and a conclusion based
               on these statements. After reading the entire question, you will decide
               whether:
               A.   The conclusion is proved by statements 1-4;
               B.   The conclusion is disproved by statements 1-4; or
               C.   The facts are not sufficient to prove or disprove the conclusion.

18. FACTUAL STATEMENTS: 18.____

    1. In the Field Day high jump competition, Martha jumped higher than Frank.
    2. Carl jumped higher than Ignacio.
    3. Ignacio jumped higher than Frank.
    4. Dan jumped higher than Carl.

    CONCLUSION: Frank finished last in the high jump competition.

    A.   The conclusion is proved by statements 1-4.
    B.   The conclusion is disproved by statements 1-4.
    C.   The facts are not sufficient to prove or disprove the conclusion.

19. FACTUAL STATEMENTS: 19.____

    1. The door to the hammer mill chamber is locked if light 6 is red.
    2. The door to the hammer mill chamber is locked only when the mill is operating.
    3. If the mill is not operating, light 6 is blue.
    4. Light 6 is blue.

    CONCLUSION: The door to the hammer mill chamber is locked.

    A.   The conclusion is proved by statements 1-4.
    B.   The conclusion is disproved by statements 1-4.
    C.   The facts are not sufficient to prove or disprove the conclusion.

20. FACTUAL STATEMENTS:

    1. Ziegfried, the lion tamer at the circus, has demanded ten additional minutes of performance time during each show.
    2. If Ziegfried is allowed his ten additional minutes per show, he will attempt to teach Kimba the tiger to shoot a basketball.
    3. If Kimba learns how to shoot a basketball, then Ziegfried was not given his ten additional minutes.
    4. Ziegfried was given his ten additional minutes.

CONCLUSION: Despite Ziegfried's efforts, Kimba did not learn how to shoot a basketball.

    A. The conclusion is proved by statements 1-4.
    B. The conclusion is disproved by statements 1-4.
    C. The facts are not sufficient to prove or disprove the conclusion.

21. FACTUAL STATEMENTS:

    1. If Stan goes to counseling, Sara won't divorce him.
    2. If Sara divorces Stan, she'll move back to Texas.
    3. If Sara doesn't divorce Stan, Irene will be disappointed.
    4. Stan goes to counseling.

CONCLUSION: Irene will be disappointed.

    A. The conclusion is proved by statements 1-4.
    B. The conclusion is disproved by statements 1-4.
    C. The facts are not sufficient to prove or disprove the conclusion.

22. FACTUAL STATEMENTS:

    1. If Delia is promoted to district manager, Claudia will have to be promoted to team leader.
    2. Delia will be promoted to district manager unless she misses her fourth-quarter sales quota.
    3. If Claudia is promoted to team leader, Thomas will be promoted to assistant team leader.
    4. Delia meets her fourth-quarter sales quota.

CONCLUSION: Thomas is promoted to assistant team leader.

    A. The conclusion is proved by statements 1-4.
    B. The conclusion is disproved by statements 1-4.
    C. The facts are not sufficient to prove or disprove the conclusion.

23. FACTUAL STATEMENTS:

    23.____

    1. Clone D is identical to Clone B.
    2. Clone B is not identical to Clone A.
    3. Clone D is not identical to Clone C.
    4. Clone E is not identical to the clones that are identical to Clone B.

    CONCLUSION: Clone E is identical to Clone D.

    A. The conclusion is proved by statements 1-4.
    B. The conclusion is disproved by statements 1-4.
    C. The facts are not sufficient to prove or disprove the conclusion.

24. FACTUAL STATEMENTS:

    24.____

    1. In the Stafford Tower, each floor is occupied by a single business.
    2. Big G Staffing is on a floor between CyberGraphics and MainEvent.
    3. Gasco is on the floor directly below CyberGraphics and three floors above Treehorn Audio.
    4. MainEvent is five floors below EZ Tax and four floors below Treehorn Audio.

    CONCLUSION: EZ Tax is on a floor between Gasco and MainEvent.

    A. The conclusion is proved by statements 1-4.
    B. The conclusion is disproved by statements 1-4.
    C. The facts are not sufficient to prove or disprove the conclusion.

25. FACTUAL STATEMENTS:

    25.____

    1. Only county roads lead to Nicodemus.
    2. All the roads from Hill City to Graham County are federal highways.
    3. Some of the roads from Plainville lead to Nicodemus.
    4. Some of the roads running from Hill City lead to Strong City.

    CONCLUSION: Some of the roads from Plainville are county roads.

    A. The conclusion is proved by statements 1-4.
    B. The conclusion is disproved by statements 1-4.
    C. The facts are not sufficient to prove or disprove the conclusion.

KEY (CORRECT ANSWERS)

1.	A		11.	A
2.	A		12.	D
3.	A		13.	E
4.	C		14.	D
5.	A		15.	B
6.	B		16.	B
7.	A		17.	C
8.	A		18.	A
9.	A		19.	B
10.	E		20.	A

21.	A
22.	A
23.	B
24.	A
25.	A

SOLUTIONS TO PROBLEMS

1) (A) Given statement 3, we deduce that James will not be transferred to another department. By statement 2, we can conclude that James will be promoted.

2) (A) Since every player on the softball team wears glasses, these individuals compose some of the people who work at the bank. Although not every person who works at the bank plays softball, those bank employees who do play softball wear glasses.

3) (A) If Henry and June go out to dinner, we conclude that it must be on Tuesday or Thursday, which are the only two days when they have childbirth classes. This implies that if it is not Tuesday or Thursday, then this couple does not go out to dinner.

4) (C) We can only conclude that if a person plays on the field hockey team, then he or she has both bruises and scarred knees. But there are probably a great number of people who have both bruises and scarred knees but do not play on the field hockey team. The given conclusion can neither be proven or disproven.

5) (A) From statement 1, if Jane beats Mathias, then Lance will beat Jane. Using statement 2, we can then conclude that Christine will not win her match against Jane.

6) (B) Statement 1 tells us that no green light can be an indicator of the belt drive status. Thus, the given conclusion must be false.

7) (A) We already know that Ben and Elliot are in the 7th grade. Even though Hannah and Carl are in the same grade, it cannot be the 7th grade because we would then have at least four students in this 7th grade. This would contradict the third statement, which states that either two or three students are in each grade. Since Amy, Dan, and Francine are in different grades, exactly one of them must be in the 7th grade. Thus, Ben, Elliot and exactly one of Amy, Dan, and Francine are the three students in the 7th grade.

8) (A) One man is a teacher, who is Russian. We know that the writer is female and is Russian. Since her husband is an engineer, he cannot be the Russian teacher. Thus, her husband is of German descent, namely Mr. Stern. This means that Mr. Stern's wife is the writer. Note that one couple consists of a male Russian teacher and a female German lawyer. The other couple consists of a male German engineer and a female Russian writer.

9) (A) Since John is more than 10 inches taller than Lisa, his height is at least 46 inches. Also, John is shorter than Henry, so Henry's height must be greater than 46 inches. Thus, Lisa is the only one whose height is less than 36 inches. Therefore, she is the only one who is not allowed on the flume ride.

18) (A) Dan jumped higher than Carl, who jumped higher than Ignacio, who jumped higher than Frank. Since Martha jumped higher than Frank, every person jumped higher than Frank. Thus, Frank finished last.

19) (B) If the light is red, then the door is locked. If the door is locked, then the mill is operating. Reversing the logical sequence of these statements, if the mill is not operating, then the door is not locked, which means that the light is blue. Thus, the given conclusion is disproved.

20) (A) Using the contrapositive of statement 3, if Ziegfried was given his ten additional minutes, then Kimba did not learn how to shoot a basketball. Since statement 4 is factual, the conclusion is proved.

21) (A) From statements 4 and 1, we conclude that Sara doesn't divorce Stan. Then statement 3 reveals that Irene will be disappointed. Thus the conclusion is proved.

22) (A) Statement 2 can be rewritten as "Delia is promoted to district manager or she misses her sales quota." Furthermore, this statement is equivalent to "If Delia makes her sales quota, then she is promoted to district manager." From statement 1, we conclude that Claudia is promoted to team leader. Finally, by statement 3, Thomas is promoted to assistant team leader. The conclusion is proved.

23) (B) By statement 4, Clone E is not identical to any clones identical to clone B. Statement 1 tells us that clones B and D are identical. Therefore, clone E cannot be identical to clone D. The conclusion is disproved.

24) (A) Based on all four statements, CyberGraphics is somewhere below Main Event. Gasco is one floor below CyberGraphics. EZ Tax is two floors below Gasco. Treehorn Audio is one floor below EZ Tax. Main Event is four floors below Treehorn Audio. Thus, EZ Tax is two floors below Gasco and five floors above Main Event. The conclusion is proved.

25) (A) From statement 3, we know that some of the roads from Plainville lead to Nicodemus. But statement 1 tells us that only county roads lead to Nicodemus. Therefore, some of the roads from Plainville must be county roads. The conclusion is proved.

TEST 2

DIRECTIONS: Each question or incomplete statement is followed by several suggested answers or completions. Select the one that BEST answers the question or completes the statement. *PRINT THE LETTER OF THE CORRECT ANSWER IN THE SPACE AT THE RIGHT.*

Questions 1-9.

DIRECTIONS: In questions 1-9, you will read a set of facts and a conclusion drawn from them. The conclusion may be valid or invalid, based on the facts-it's your task to determine the validity of the conclusion.

For each question, select the letter before the statement that BEST expresses the relationship between the given facts and the conclusion that has been drawn from them. Your choices are:
A. The facts prove the conclusion
B. The facts disprove the conclusion; or
C. The facts neither prove nor disprove the conclusion.

1. FACTS: Some employees in the testing department are statisticians. Most of the statisticians who work in the testing department are projection specialists. Tom Wilks works in the testing department.

   CONCLUSION: Tom Wilks is a statistician.

   A. The facts prove the conclusion.
   B. The facts disprove the conclusion.
   C. The facts neither prove nor disprove the conclusion.

   1._____

2. FACTS: Ten coins are split among Hank, Lawrence, and Gail. If Lawrence gives his coins to Hank, then Hank will have more coins than Gail. If Gail gives her coins to Lawrence, then Lawrence will have more coins than Hank.

   CONCLUSION: Hank has six coins.

   A. The facts prove the conclusion.
   B. The facts disprove the conclusion.
   C. The facts neither prove nor disprove the conclusion.

   2._____

3. FACTS: Nobody loves everybody. Janet loves Ken. Ken loves everybody who loves Janet.

   CONCLUSION: Everybody loves Janet.

   A. The facts prove the conclusion.
   B. The facts disprove the conclusion.
   C. The facts neither prove nor disprove the conclusion.

   3._____

4. FACTS: Most of the Torres family lives in East Los Angeles. Many people in East Los Angeles celebrate Cinco de Mayo. Joe is a member of the Torres family.

4.____

CONCLUSION: Joe lives in East Los Angeles.

   A. The facts prove the conclusion.
   B. The facts disprove the conclusion.
   C. The facts neither prove nor disprove the conclusion.

5. FACTS: Five professionals each occupy one story of a five-story office building. Dr. Kane's office is above Dr. Assad's. Dr. Johnson's office is between Dr. Kane's and Dr. Conlon's. Dr. Steen's office is between Dr. Conlon's and Dr. Assad's. Dr. Johnson is on the fourth story.

5.____

CONCLUSION: Dr. Kane occupies the top story.

   A. The facts prove the conclusion.
   B. The facts disprove the conclusion.
   C. The facts neither prove nor disprove the conclusion.

6. FACTS: To be eligible for membership in the Yukon Society, a person must be able to either tunnel through a snowbank while wearing only a T-shirt and shorts, or hold his breath for two minutes under water that is 50° F. Ray can only hold his breath for a minute and a half.

6.____

CONCLUSION: Ray can still become a member of the Yukon Society by tunneling through a snowbank while wearing a T-shirt and shorts.

   A. The facts prove the conclusion.
   B. The facts disprove the conclusion.
   C. The facts neither prove nor disprove the conclusion.

7. FACTS: A mark is worth five plunks. You can exchange four sharps for a tinplot. It takes eight marks to buy a sharp.

7.____

CONCLUSION: A sharp is the most valuable.

   A. The facts prove the conclusion.
   B. The facts disprove the conclusion.
   C. The facts neither prove nor disprove the conclusion.

8. FACTS: There are gibbons, as well as lemurs, who like to play in the trees at the monkey house. All those who like to play in the trees at the monkey house are fed lettuce and bananas.

8.____

CONCLUSION: Lemurs and gibbons are types of monkeys.

   A. The facts prove the conclusion.
   B. The facts disprove the conclusion.
   C. The facts neither prove nor disprove the conclusion.

9. FACTS: None of the Blackfoot tribes is a Salishan Indian tribe. Sal-ishan Indians came   9._____
from the northern Pacific Coast. All Salishan Indians live east of the Continental Divide.

CONCLUSION: No Blackfoot tribes live east of the Continental Divide.

   A. The facts prove the conclusion.
   B. The facts disprove the conclusion.
   C. The facts neither prove nor disprove the conclusion.

Questions 10-17.

DIRECTIONS: Questions 10-17 are based on the following reading passage. It is not your
              knowledge of the particular topic that is being tested, but your ability to reason
              based on what you have read. The passage is likely to detail several proposed
              courses of action and factors affecting these proposals. The reading passage
              is followed by a conclusion or outcome based on the facts in the passage, or a
              description of a decision taken regarding the situation. The conclusion is fol-
              lowed by a number of statements that have a possible connection to the con-
              clusion. For each statement, you are to determine whether:

   A. The statement proves the conclusion.
   B. The statement supports the conclusion but does not prove it.
   C. The statement disproves the conclusion.
   D. The statement weakens the conclusion but does not disprove it.
   E. The statement has no relevance to the conclusion.

Remember that the conclusion after the passage is to be accepted as the outcome of
what actually happened, and that you are being asked to evaluate the impact each statement would have had on the conclusion.

PASSAGE:

On August 12, Beverly Willey reported that she was in the elevator late on the previous
evening after leaving her office on the 16th floor of a large office building. In her report,
she states that a man got on the elevator at the 11th floor, pulled her off the elevator,
assaulted her, and stole her purse. Ms. Willey reported that she had seen the man in the
elevators and hallways of the building before. She believes that the man works in the
building. Her description of him is as follows: he is tall, unshaven, with wavy brown hair
and a scar on his left cheek. He walks with a pronounced limp, often dragging his left foot
behind his right.

CONCLUSION: After Beverly Willey makes her report, the police arrest a 43-year-man,
Barton Black, and charge him with her assault.

10. Barton Black is a former Marine who served in Vietnam, where he sustained shrapnel   10._____
wounds to the left side of his face and suffered nerve damage in his left leg.

   A.
   B.
   C.
   D.
   E.

11. When they arrived at his residence to question him, detectives were greeted at the door by Barton Black, who was tall and clean-shaven.

    A.
    B.
    C.
    D.
    E.

11.____

12. Barton Black was booked into the county jail several days after Beverly Willey's assault.

    A.
    B.
    C.
    D.
    E.

12.____

13. Upon further investigation, detectives discover that Beverly Willey does not work at the office building.

    A.
    B.
    C.
    D.
    E.

13.____

14. Upon further investigation, detectives discover that Barton Black does not work at the office building.

    A.
    B.
    C.
    D.
    E.

14.____

15. In the spring of the following year, Barton Black is convicted of assaulting Beverly Willey on August 11.

    A.
    B.
    C.
    D.
    E.

15.____

16. During their investigation of the assault, detectives determine that Beverly Willey was assaulted on the 12th floor of the office building.

    A.
    B.
    C.
    D.
    E.

16.____

17. The day after Beverly Willey's assault, Barton Black fled the area and was never seen   17.____
again.

    A.
    B.
    C.
    D.
    E.

Questions 18-25.

DIRECTIONS: Questions 18-25 each provide four factual statements and a conclusion based on these statements. After reading the entire question, you will decide whether:

    A.   The conclusion is proved by statements 1-4;
    B.   The conclusion is disproved by statements 1-4; or
    C.   The facts are not sufficient to prove or disprove the conclusion.

18. FACTUAL STATEMENTS: 18.____

1. Among five spice jars on the shelf, the sage is to the right of the parsley.
2. The pepper is to the left of the basil.
3. The nutmeg is between the sage and the pepper.
4. The pepper is the second spice from the left.

CONCLUSION: The sage is the farthest to the right.

    A.   The conclusion is proved by statements 1-4.
    B.   The conclusion is disproved by statements 1-4.
    C.   The facts are not sufficient to prove or disprove the conclusion.

19. FACTUAL STATEMENTS: 19.____

1. Gear X rotates in a clockwise direction if Switch C is in the OFF position
2. Gear X will rotate in a counter-clockwise direction if Switch C is ON.
3. If Gear X is rotating in a clockwise direction, then Gear Y will not be rotating at all.
4. Switch C is ON.

CONCLUSION: Gear X is rotating in a counter-clockwise direction.

    A.   The conclusion is proved by statements 1-4.
    B.   The conclusion is disproved by statements 1-4.
    C.   The facts are not sufficient to prove or disprove the conclusion.

20. FACTUAL STATEMENTS:
    1. Lane will leave for the Toronto meeting today only if Terence, Rourke, and Jackson all file their marketing reports by the end of the work day.
    2. Rourke will file her report on time only if Ganz submits last quarter's data.
    3. If Terence attends the security meeting, he will attend it with Jackson, and they will not file their marketing reports by the end of the work day.
    4. Ganz submits last quarter's data to Rourke.

    CONCLUSION: Lane will leave for the Toronto meeting today.

    A. The conclusion is proved by statements 1-4.
    B. The conclusion is disproved by statements 1-4.
    C. The facts are not sufficient to prove or disprove the conclusion.

20

21. FACTUAL STATEMENTS:

    1. Bob is in second place in the Boston Marathon.
    2. Gregory is winning the Boston Marathon.
    3. There are four miles to go in the race, and Bob is gaining on Gregory at the rate of 100 yards every minute.
    4. There are 1760 yards in a mile, and Gregory's usual pace during the Boston Marathon is one mile every six minutes.

    CONCLUSION: Bob wins the Boston Marathon.

    A. The conclusion is proved by statements 1-4.
    B. The conclusion is disproved by statements 1-4.
    C. The facts are not sufficient to prove or disprove the conclusion.

21

22. FACTUAL STATEMENTS:

    1. Four brothers are named Earl, John, Gary, and Pete.
    2. Earl and Pete are unmarried.
    3. John is shorter than the youngest of the four.
    4. The oldest brother is married, and is also the tallest.

    CONCLUSION: Gary is the oldest brother.

    A. The conclusion is proved by statements 1-4.
    B. The conclusion is disproved by statements 1-4.
    C. The facts are not sufficient to prove or disprove the conclusion.

22

23. FACTUAL STATEMENTS:

    1. Brigade X is ten miles from the demilitarized zone.
    2. If General Woundwort gives the order, Brigade X will advance to the demilitarized zone, but not quickly enough to reach the zone before the conflict begins.
    3. Brigade Y, five miles behind Brigade X, will not advance unless General Woundwort gives the order.
    4. Brigade Y advances.

    CONCLUSION: Brigade X reaches the demilitarized zone before the conflict begins.

A. The conclusion is proved by statements 1-4.
B. The conclusion is disproved by statements 1-4.
C. The facts are not sufficient to prove or disprove the conclusion.

24. FACTUAL STATEMENTS:
24._____

1. Jerry has decided to take a cab from Fullerton to Elverton.
2. Chubby Cab charges $5 plus $3 a mile.
3. Orange Cab charges $7.50 but gives free mileage for the first 5 miles.
4. After the first 5 miles, Orange Cab charges $2.50 a mile.

CONCLUSION: Orange Cab is the cheaper fare from Fullerton to Elverton.

A. The conclusion is proved by statements 1-4.
B. The conclusion is disproved by statements 1-4.
C. The facts are not sufficient to prove or disprove the conclusion.

25. FACTUAL STATEMENTS:
25._____

1. Dan is never in class when his friend Lucy is absent.
2. Lucy is never absent unless her mother is sick.
3. If Lucy is in class, Sergio is in class also
4. Sergio is never in class when Dalton is absent.

CONCLUSION: If Lucy is absent, Dalton may be in class.

A. The conclusion is proved by statements 1-4.
B. The conclusion is disproved by statements 1-4.
C. The facts are not sufficient to prove or disprove the conclusion.

KEY (CORRECT ANSWERS)

1.	C		11.	E
2.	B		12.	B
3.	B		13.	D
4.	C		14.	E
5.	A		15.	A
6.	A		16.	E
7.	B		17.	C
8.	C		18.	B
9.	C		19.	A
10.	B		20.	C

21.	C
22.	A
23.	B
24.	A
25.	B

SOLUTIONS TO PROBLEMS

1) (C) Statement 1 only tells us that some employees who work in the Testing Department are statisticians. This means that we need to allow the possibility that at least one person in this department is not a statistician. Thus, if a person works in the Testing Department, we cannot conclude whether or not this individual is a statistician.

2) (B) If Hank had six coins, then the total of Gails collection and Lawrence's collection would be four. Thus, if Gail gave all her coins to Lawrence, Lawrence would only have four coins. Thus, it would be impossible for Lawrence to have more coins than Hank.

3) (B) Statement 1 tells us that nobody loves everybody. If everybody loved Janet, then Statement 3 would imply that Ken loves everybody. This would contradict statement 1. The conclusion is disproved.

4) (C) Although most of the Torres family lives in East Los Angeles, we can assume that some members of this family do not live in East Los Angeles. Thus, we cannot prove or disprove that Joe, who is a member of the Torres family, lives in East Los Angeles.

5) (A) Since Dr. Johnson is on the 4th floor, either (a) Dr. Kane is on the 5th floor and Dr. Conlon is on the 3rd floor, or (b) Dr. Kane is on the 3rd floor and Dr. Conlon is on the 5th floor. If option (b) were correct, then since Dr. Assad would be on the 1st floor, it would be impossible for Dr. Steen's office to be between Dr. Conlon and Dr. Assad's office. Therefore, Dr. Kane's office must be on the 5th floor. The order of the doctors' offices, from 5th floor down to the 1st floor is: Dr. Kane, Dr. Johnson, Dr. Conlon, Dr. Steen, Dr. Assad.

6) (A) Ray does not satisfy the requirement of holding his breath for two minutes under water, since he can only hold his breath for one minute in that setting. But if he tunnels through a snowbank with just a T-shirt and shorts, he will satisfy the eligibility requirement. Note that the eligibility requirement contains the key word "or." So only one of the two clauses separated by "or" need to be fulfilled.

7) (B) Statement 2 says that four sharps is equivalent to one tinplot. This means that a tinplot is worth more than a sharp. The conclusion is disproved. We note that the order of these items, from most valuable to least valuable are: tinplot, sharp, mark, plunk.

8) (C) We can only conclude that gibbons and lemurs are fed lettuce and bananas. We can neither prove or disprove that these animals are types of monkeys.

9) (C) We know that all Salishan Indians live east of the Continental Divide. But some nonmembers of this tribe of Indians may also live east of the Continental Divide. Since none of the members of the Blackfoot tribe belong to the Salishan Indian tribe, we cannot draw any conclusion about the location of the Blackfoot tribe with respect to the Continental Divide.

18) (B) Since the pepper is second from the left and the nutmeg is between the sage and the pepper, the positions 2, 3, and 4 (from the left) are pepper, nutmeg, sage. By statement 2, the basil must be in position 5, which implies that the parsley is in position 1. Therefore, the basil, not the sage is farthest to the right. The conclusion disproved.

19) (A) Statement 2 assures us that if switch C is ON, then Gear X is rotating in a counterclockwise direction. The conclusion is proved.

20) (C) Based on Statement 4, followed by Statement 2, we conclude that Ganz and Rourke will file their reports on time. Statement 3 reveals that if Terence and Jackson attend the security meeting, they will fail to file their reports on time. We have no further information if Terence and Jackson attended the security meeting, so we are not able to either confirm or deny that their reports were filed on time. This implies that we cannot know for certain that Lane will leave for his meeting in Toronto.

21) (C) Although Bob is in second place behind Gregory, we cannot deduce how far behind Gregory he is running. At Gregory's current pace, he will cover four miles in 24 minutes. If Bob were only 100 yards behind Gregory, he would catch up to Gregory in one minute. But if Bob were very far behind Gregory, for example 5 miles, this is the equivalent of $(5)(1760) = 8800$ yards. Then Bob would need $8800/100 = 88$ minutes to catch up to Gregory. Thus, the given facts are not sufficient to draw a conclusion.

22) (A) Statement 2 tells us that neither Earl nor Pete could be the oldest; also, either John or Gary is married. Statement 4 reveals that the oldest brother is both married and the tallest. By statement 3, John cannot be the tallest. Since John is not the tallest, he is not the oldest. Thus, the oldest brother must be Gary. The conclusion is proved.

23) (B) By statements 3 and 4, General Woundwort must have given the order to advance. Statement 2 then tells us that Brigade X will advance to the demilitarized zone, but not soon enough before the conflict begins. Thus, the conclusion is disproved.

24) (A) If the distance is 5 miles or less, then the cost for the Orange Cab is only $7.50, whereas the cost for the Chubby Cab is $5 + 3x$, where x represents the number of miles traveled. For 1 to 5 miles, the cost of the Chubby Cab is between $8 and $20. This means that for a distance of 5 miles, the Orange Cab costs $7.50, whereas the Chubby Cab costs $20. After 5 miles, the cost per mile of the Chubby Cab exceeds the cost per mile of the Orange Cab. Thus, regardless of the actual distance between Fullerton and Elverton, the cost for the Orange Cab will be cheaper than that of the Chubby Cab.

25) (B) It looks like "Dalton" should be replaced by "Dan in the conclusion. Then by statement 1, if Lucy is absent, Dan is never in class. Thus, the conclusion is disproved.

READING COMPREHENSION
UNDERSTANDING AND INTERPRETING WRITTEN MATERIAL
COMMENTARY

The ability to read, understand, and interpret written materials texts, publications, newspapers, orders, directions, expositions, legal passages is a skill basic to a functioning democracy and to an efficient business or viable government.

That is why almost all examinations – for beginning, middle, and senior levels – test reading comprehension, directly or indirectly.

The reading test measures how well you understand what you read. This is how it is done: You read a paragraph and several statements based on a question. From the statements, you choose the *one* statement, or answer, that is *BEST* supported by, or *BEST* matches, what is said in the paragraph.

SAMPLE QUESTIONS

DIRECTIONS: Each question has five suggested answers, lettered A, B, C, D, and E. Decide which one is the *BEST* answer. *PRINT THE LETTER OF THE CORRECT ANSWER IN THE SPACE AT THE RIGHT.*

1. The prevention of accidents makes it necessary not only that safety devices be used to guard exposed machinery but also that mechanics be instructed in safety rules which they must follow for their own protection and that the light in the plant be adequate.
   The paragraph BEST supports the statement that industrial accidents

   A. are always avoidable
   B. may be due to ignorance
   C. usually result from inadequate machinery
   D. cannot be entirely overcome
   E. result in damage to machinery

ANALYSIS
Remember what you have to do -
   First   -   Read the paragraph.
   Second -   Decide what the paragraph means.
   Third   -   Read the five suggested answers.
   Fourth -   Select the one answer which *BEST* matches what the paragraph says or is *BEST* supported by something in the paragraph. (Sometimes you may have to read the paragraph again in order to be sure which suggested answer is best.)

This paragraph is talking about three steps that should be taken to prevent industrial accidents:
   1. use safety devices on machines
   2. instruct mechanics in safety rules
   3. provide adequate lighting

SELECTION

With this in mind, let's look at each suggested answer. Each one starts with "Industrial accidents ..."

SUGGESTED ANSWER A.
Industrial accidents (A) are always avoidable.
(The paragraph talks about how to avoid accidents but does not say that accidents are always avoidable.)

SUGGESTED ANSWER B.
Industrial accidents (B) may be due to ignorance.
(One of the steps given in the paragraph to prevent accidents is to instruct mechanics on safety rules. This suggests that lack of knowledge or ignorance of safety rules causes accidents. This suggested answer sounds like a good possibility for being the right answer.)

SUGGESTED ANSWER C.
Industrial accidents (C) usually result from inadequate machinery.
(The paragraph does suggest that exposed machines cause accidents, but it doesn't say that it is the usual cause of accidents. The word *usually* makes this a wrong answer.)

SUGGESTED ANSWER D.
Industrial accidents (D) cannot be entirely overcome.
(You may know from your own experience that this is a true statement. But that is not what the paragraph is talking about. Therefore, it is NOT the correct answer.)

SUGGESTED ANSWER E.
Industrial accidents (E) result in damage to machinery.
(This is a statement that may or may not be true, but, in any case, it is NOT covered by the paragraph.)

———

Looking back, you see that the one suggested answer of the five given that *BEST* matches what the paragraph says is

Industrial accidents (B) may be due to ignorance.
The *CORRECT* answer then is B.
Be sure you read *ALL* the possible answers before you make your choice. You may think that none of the five answers is really good, but choose the *BEST* one of the five.

———

2. Probably few people realize, as they drive on a concrete road, that steel is used to keep the surface flat in spite of the weight of the busses and trucks. Steel bars, deeply embedded in the concrete, provide sinews to take the stresses so that the stresses cannot crack the slab or make it wavy.
The paragraph BEST supports the statement that a concrete road

A. is expensive to build
B. usually cracks under heavy weights
C. looks like any other road
D. is used only for heavy traffic
E. is reinforced with other material

ANALYSIS

This paragraph is commenting on the fact that -
1. few people realize, as they drive on a concrete road, that steel is deeply embedded
2. steel keeps the surface flat
3. steel bars enable the road to take the stresses without cracking or becoming wavy

SELECTION

Now read and think about the possible answers:
A. A concrete road is expensive to build.
(Maybe so but that is not what the paragraph is about.)
B. A concrete road usually cracks under heavy weights.
(The paragraph talks about using steel bars to prevent heavy weights from cracking concrete roads. It says nothing about how usual it is for the roads to crack. The word *usually* makes this suggested answer wrong.)
C. A concrete road looks like any other road.
(This may or may not be true. The important thing to note is that it has nothing to do with what the paragraph is about.)
D. A concrete road is used only for heavy traffic.
(This answer at least has something to do with the paragraph–concrete roads are used with heavy traffic but it does not say "used only.")
E. A concrete road is reinforced with other material.
(This choice seems to be the correct one on two counts: *First*, the paragraph does suggest that concrete roads are made stronger by embedding steel bars in them. This is another way of saying "concrete roads are reinforced with steel bars." *Second*, by the process of elimination, the other four choices are ruled out as correct answers simply because they do not apply.)
You can be sure that not all the reading questions will be so easy as these.

SUGGESTIONS FOR ANSWERING READING QUESTIONS

1. Read the paragraph carefully. Then read each suggested answer carefully. Read every word, because often one word can make the difference between a right and a wrong answer.
2. Choose that answer which is supported in the paragraph itself. Do not choose an answer which is a correct statement unless it is based on information in the paragraph.
3. Even though a suggested answer has many of the words used in the paragraph, it may still be wrong.
4. Look out for words – such as *always, never, entirely, or only*–which tend to make a suggested answer wrong.

5. Answer first those questions which you can answer most easily. Then work on the other questions.
6. If you can't figure out the answer to the question, guess.

———————

READING COMPREHENSION
UNDERSTANDING AND INTERPRETING WRITTEN MATERIAL
EXAMINATION SECTION
TEST 1

DIRECTIONS: Each question or incomplete statement is followed by several suggested answers or completions. Select the one that BEST answers the question or completes the statement. *PRINT THE LETTER OF THE CORRECT ANSWER IN THE SPACE AT THE RIGHT.*

Questions 1-3.

DIRECTIONS: Answer Questions 1 through 3 *SOLELY* on the basis of the following statement:
The final step in an accident investigation is the making out of the police report. In the case of a traffic accident, the officer should go right from the scene to his office to write up the report. However, if a person was injured in the accident and taken to a hospital, the officer should visit him there before going to his office to prepare his report. This personal visit to the injured person does not mean that the office must make a physical examination; but he should make an effort to obtain a statement from the injured person or persons. If this is not possible, information should be obtained from the attending physician as to the extent of the injury. In any event, without fail, the name of the physician should be secured and the report should state the name of the physician and the fact that he told the officer that, at a certain stated time on a certain stated date, the injuries were of such and such a nature. If the injured person dies before the officer arrives at the hospital, it may be necessary to take the responsible person into custody at once.

1. When a person has been injured in a traffic accident, the one of the following actions which it is necessry for a police officer to take in connection with the accident report is to

    A. prepare the police report immediately after the accident, and then go to the hospital to speak to the victim
    B. do his utmost to verify the victim's story prior to preparing the official police report of the incident
    C. be sure to include the victim's statement in the police report in every case
    D. try to get the victim's version of the accident prior to preparing the police report

1._____

2. When one of the persons injured in a motor vehicle accident dies, the above paragraph provides that the police officer

    A. must immediately take the responsible person into custody, if the injured person is already dead when the officer appears at the scene of the accident
    B. must either arrest the responsible person or get a statement from him, if the injured person dies after arrival at the hospital
    C. may have to immediately arrest the responsible person, if the injured person dies in the hospital prior to the officer's arrival there
    D. may refrain from arresting the responsible person, but only if the responsible person is also seriously injured

2._____

3. When someone has been injured in a collision between two automobiles and is given medical treatment shortly thereafter by a physician, the *one* of the following actions which the police officer *MUST* take with regard to the physician is to

    A. obtain his name and his diagnosis of the injuries, regardless of the place where treatment was given
    B. obtain his approval of the portion of the police report relating to the injured person and the treatment given him prior to and after his arrival at the hospital
    C. obtain his name, his opinion of the extent of the person's injuries, and his signed statement of the treatment he gave the injured person
    D. set a certain stated time on a certain stated date for interviewing him, unless he is an attending physician in a hospital

3.____

Questions 4-7.

DIRECTIONS: Answer Questions 4 through 7 *SOLELY* on the basis of the following statement:

Because of the importance of preserving physical evidence, the patrolman should not enter a scene of a crime if it can be examined visually from one position and if no other pressing duty requires his presence there. However, there are some responsibilities that take precedence over preservation of evidence. Some examples are: rescue work, disarming dangerous persons, quelling a disturbance. However, the patrolman should learn how to accomplish these more vital tasks, while at the same time preserving as much evidence as possible. If he finds it necessary to enter upon the scene, he should quickly study the place of entry to learn if any evidence will suffer by his contact; then he should determine the routes to be used in walking to the spot where his presence is required. Every place where a foot will fall or where a hand or other part of his body will touch, should be examined with the eye. Objects should not be touched or moved unless there is a definite and compelling reason. For identification of most items of physical evidence at the initial investigation, it is seldom necessary to touch or move them.

4. The *one* of the following titles which is the *MOST* appropriate for the above paragraph is:

    A. Determining the Priority of Tasks at the Scene of a Crime
    B. The Principal Reasons for Preserving Evidence at the Scene of a Crime
    C. Precuations to Take at the Scene of a Crime
    D. Evidence to be Examined at the Scene of a Crime

4.____

5. When a patrolman feels that it is essential for him to enter the immediate area where a crime has been committed, he *should*

    A. quickly but carefully glance around to determine whether his entering the area will damage any evidence present
    B. remove all objects of evidence from his predetermined route in order to avoid stepping on them
    C. carefully replace any object immediately if it is moved or touched by his hands or any other part of his body
    D. use only the usual place of entry to the scene in order to avoid disturbing any possible clues left on rear doors and windows by the criminal

5.____

6. The one of the following which is the *LEAST* urgent duty of a police officer who has just reported to the scene of a crime is to   6.____

   A. disarm the hysterical victim of the crime who is wildly waving a loaded gun in all directions
   B. give first aid to a possible suspect who has been injured while attempting to leave the scene of the crime
   C. prevent observers from attacking and injuring the persons suspected of having committed the crime
   D. preserve from damage or destruction any evidence necessary for the proper prosecution of the case against the criminals

7. A police officer has just reported to the scene of a crime in response to a phone call. The *BEST* of the following actions for him to take with respect to objects of physical evidence present at the scene is to   7.____

   A. make no attempt to enter the crime scene if his entry will disturb any vital physical evidence
   B. map out the shortest straight path to follow in walking to the spot where the most physical evidence may be found
   C. move such objects of physical evidence as are necessary to enable him to assist the wounded victim of the crime
   D. quickly examine all objects of physical evidence in order to determine which objects may be touched and which may not

Questions 8-11.

DIRECTIONS: Answer Questions 8 through 11 *SOLELY* on the basis of the following statement:

After examining a document and comparing the characters with specimens of other handwritings, the laboratory technician may conclude that a certain individual definitely did write the questioned document. This opinion could be based on a large number of similar, as well as a small number of dissimilar but explainable, characteristics. On the other hand, if the laboratory technician concludes that the person in question did not write the questioned document, such an opinion could be based on the large number of characteristics which are dissimilar, or even on a small number which are dissimilar provided that these are of overriding significance, and despite the presence of explainable similarities. The laboratory expert is not always able to give a positive opinion. He may state that a certain individual probably did or did not write the questioned document. Such an opinion is usually the result of insufficient material, either in the questioned document or in the specimens submitted for comparison. Finally, the expert may be unable to come to any conclusion at all because of insufficient material submitted for comparison or because of improper specimens.

8. The one of the following which is the *MOST* appropriate title for the above statement is: 8.____

   A. Similar and Dissimilar Characteristics in Handwriting
   B. The Limitations of Handwriting Analysis in Identifying the Writer
   C. The Positive Identification of Suspects Through Their Handwriting
   D. The Inability to Identify an Individual Through His Handwriting

9. When a handwriting expert compares the handwriting on two separate documents and   9.____
   decides that they were written by the same person, his conclusions are *generally* based
   on the fact that

   A. a large number of characteristics in both documents are dissimilar but the few sim-
      ilar characteristics are more important
   B. all the characteristics are alike in both documents
   C. similar characteristics need to be explained as to the cause for their similarity
   D. most of the characteristics in both documents are alike and their few differences
      are readily explainable

10. If a fingerprint technician carefully examines a handwritten threatening letter and com-   10.____
    pares it with specimens of handwriting made by a suspect, he would be *most likely* to
    decide that the suspect did *NOT* write the threatening letter when the handwriting speci-
    mens and the letter have

    A. a small number of dissimilarities
    B. a small number of dissimilar but explainable characteristics
    C. important dissimilarities despite the fact that these may be few
    D. some similar characteristics that are easily imitated or disguised

11. There are instances when even a trained handwriting expert cannot decide definitely   11.____
    whether or not a certain document and a set of handwriting specimens were written by
    the same person. This inability to make a positive decision *generally* arises in situations
    where

    A. only one document of considerable length is available for comparison with a suffi-
       cient supply of handwriting specimens
    B. the limited nature of the handwriting specimens submitted restricts their compara-
       bility with the questioned document
    C. the dissimilarities are not explainable
    D. the document submitted for comparison does not include all the characteristics
       included in the handwriting specimens

Questions 12-14.

DIRECTIONS: Answer Questions 12 through 14 *SOLELY* on the basis of the following state-
              ment:
      In cases of drunken driving, or of disorderly conduct while intoxicated, too many times
some person who had been completely under the influence of alcoholic liquor at the time of
his arrest has walked out of court without any conviction just because an officer failed to
make the proper observation. Many of the larger cities and counties make use of various scientific methods to determine the degree of intoxication of a person, such as breath, urine, and
blood tests. Many of the smaller cities, however, do not have the facilities to make these various tests, and must, therefore, rely on the observation tests given at the scene. These consist, among other things, of noticing how the subject walked, talked, and acted. One test that
is usually given at night is the eye reaction to light, which the officer gives by shining his flashlight into the eyes of the subject. The manner in which the pupils of the eyes react to the light
helps to determine the sobriety of a person. If he is intoxicated, the pupils of his eyes are
dilated more at night than the eyes of a sober person. Also, when a light is flashed into the
eyes of a sober person, his pupils contract instantly, but in the case of a person under the
influence of liquor, the pupils contract very slowly.

12. Many persons who have been arrested on a charge of driving while completely intoxicated have been acquitted by a judge because the arresting officer had *neglected* to

    A. bring the driver to court while he was still under the influence of alcohol
    B. make the required scientific tests to fully substantiate his careful personal observations of the driver's intoxicated condition
    C. submit to the court any test results showing the driver's condition or degree of drunkenness
    D. watch the driver closely for some pertinent facts which would support the officer's suspicions of the driver's intoxicated condition

12.____

13. When a person is arrested for acting in a disorderly and apparently intoxicated manner in public, the kind of test which would fit in *BEST* with the thought of the above statement is:

    A. In many smaller cities, a close watch on his behavior and of his reactions to various blood and body tests
    B. In many smaller cities, having him walk a straight line
    C. In most larger counties, a close watch of the speed of his reactions to the flashlight test
    D. In most cities of all sizes, the application of the latest scientific techniques in the analysis of his breath

13.____

14. When a person suspected of driving a motor vehicle while intoxicated is being examined to determine whether or not he actually is intoxicated, one of the methods used is to shine the light of a flashlight into his eyes. When this method is used, the *normal* result is that the pupils of the suspect's eyes will

    A. expand instantly if he is fully intoxicated, and remain unchanged if he is completely sober
    B. expand very slowly if he has had only a small amount of alcohol, and very rapidly if he has had a considerable amount of alcohol
    C. grow smaller at once if he is sober, and grow smaller more slowly if he is intoxicated
    D. grow smaller very slowly if he is fully sober, and grow smaller instantaneously if he is fully intoxicated

14.____

Questions 15-17.

DIRECTIONS: Answer Questions 15 through 17 *SOLELY* on the basis of the following statement:

Where an officer has personal knowledge of facts, sufficient to constitute reasonable grounds to believe that a person has committed or is committing a felony, he may arrest him, and, after having lawfully placed him under arrest, may search and take into his possession any incriminating evidence. The right of an officer to make an arrest and search is not limited to cases where the officer has personal knowledge of the commission of a felony, because he may act upon information conveyed to him by third persons which he believes to be reliable. Where an officer, charged with the duty of enforcing the law, receives information from apparently reliable sources, which would induce in the mind of the prudent person a belief that a felony was being or had been committed, he may make an arrest and search the person of a defendant, but he is not justified in acting on anonymous information alone.

15. When a felony has been committed, an officer would be acting *MOST* properly if he arrested a man   15.___

    A. when he, the officer, has a police report that the man is suspected of having been involved in several minor offenses
    B. when he, the officer, has received information from a usually reliable source that the man was involved in the crime
    C. only when he, the officer, has personal knowledge that the man has committed the felony
    D. when he, the officer, knows for a fact that the man has associated in the past with several persons who had been seen near the scene of the felony

16. An officer would be acting *MOST* properly if he searched a suspect for incriminating evidence   16.___

    A. *when* he has received detailed information concerning the fact that the suspect is going to commit a felony
    B. *only* after having lawfully arrested the suspect and charged him with having committed a felony
    C. *when* he has just received an anonymous tip that the suspect had just committed a felony and is in illegal possession of stolen goods
    D. *in order to* find in his possession legally admissible evidence on the basis of which the officer could then proceed to arrest the suspect for having committed a felony

17. A police officer has received information from an informant that a crime has been committed. The informant has also named two persons who he says committed the crime. The officer's decision to *both* arrest and search the two suspects would be: 17.___

    A. *Correct,* if it would not be unreasonable to assume that the crime committed is a felony, and if the informant has been trustworthy in the past
    B. *Incorrect,* if the informant has no proof but his own wdrd to offer that a felony has been committed, although he has always been trustworthy in the past
    C. *Correct,* if it would be logical and prudent to assume that the information is accurate regardless of whether the offense committed is a felony or a less serious crime
    D. *Incorrect,* even if the informant produces objective and seemingly convincing proof that a felony has been committed, but has a reputation of occasional past unreliability

Questions 18-20.

DIRECTIONS: Answer Questions 18 through 20 *SOLELY* on the basis of the following statement:

If there are many persons at the scene of a hit-and-run accident, it would be a waste of time to question all of them; the witness needed is the one who can best describe the missing auto. Usually the person most qualified to do this is a youth of fifteen or sixteen years of age. He is more likely to be able to tell the make and year of a car than most other persons. A woman may be a good witness as to how the accident occurred, but usually will be unable to tell the make of the car. As soon as any information with regard to the missing car or its description is obtained, the officer should call or radio headquarters and have the information put on the air. This should be done without waiting for further details, for time is an important factor. If a good description of the wanted car is obtained, then the next task is to get a description of the driver. In this hunt, it is found that a woman is often a more accurate witness than a man. Usually she will be able to state the color of clothes worn by the driver. If the wanted driver is a woman, another woman will often be able to tell the color and sometimes even the material of the clothing worn.

18. A hit-and-run accident has occurred and a police officer is attempting to obtain information from persons who had witnessed the incident. It would generally be *BEST* for him to question a

    A. boy in his late teens, when the officer is seeking an accurate description of the age, coloring, and physical build of the driver of the car
    B. man, when the officer is seeking an accurate description of the driver of the car and the color and material of his coat, suit, and hat
    C. woman, when the officer is seeking an accurate description of the driver of the car
    D. young teenage girl, when the officer is seeking an accurate description of the style and color of the clothes worn by the driver of the car

18._____

19. Time is an important factor when an attempt is being made to apprehend the guilty driver in a hit-and-run accident. However, the *EARLIEST* moment when the police should broadcast a radio announcement of the crime is *when* a(n)

    A. description of the missing car or any facts concerning it have been obtained
    B. tentative identification of the driver of the missing car has been made
    C. detailed description of the missing car and its occupants has been obtained
    D. eyewitness account has been obtained of the accident, including the identity of the victim, the extent of injuries, and the make and license number of the car

19._____

20. The time when it would be *MOST* desirable to get a description of the driver of the hit-and-run car is

    A. *after* getting a description of the car itself
    B. *before* transmitting information concerning the car to headquarters for broadcasting
    C. *as soon as* the officer arrives at the scene of the accident
    D. *as soon as* the victim of the accident has been given needed medical assistance

20._____

KEY (CORRECT ANSWERS)

1.	D	11.	B
2.	C	12.	D
3.	A	13.	B
4.	C	14.	C
5.	A	15.	B
6.	D	16.	B
7.	C	17.	A
8.	B	18.	C
9.	D	19.	A
10.	C	20.	A

TEST 2

Questions 1-4.

DIRECTIONS: Answer Questions 1 through 4 *SOLELY* on the basis of the following state-
              ment:

Automobile tire tracks found at the scene of a crime constitute an important link in the
chain of physical evidence. In many cases, these are the only clues available. In some areas,
unpaved ground adjoins the highway or paved streets. A suspect will often park his car off the
paved portion of the street when committing a crime, sometimes leaving excellent tire tracks.
Comparison of the tire track impressions with the tires is possible only when the vehicle has
been found. However, the intial problem facing the police is the task of determining what kind
of car probably made the impressions found at the scene of the crime. If the make, model,and
year of the car which made the impressions can be determined, it is obvsious that the task of
elimination is greatly lessened.

1. The one of the following which is the *MOST* appropriate title for the above paragraph is: 1._____

    A. The Use of Automobiles in the Commission of Crimes
    B. The Use of Tire Tracks in Police Work
    C. The Capture of Criminals by Scientific Police Work
    D. The Positive Identification of Criminals Through Their Cars

2. When searching for clear signs left by the car used in the commission of a crime, the   2._____
    MOST likely place for the police to look would be on the

    A. highway adjoining unpaved streets
    B. highway adjacent to paved street
    C. paved street adjacent to the highway
    D. unpaved ground adjacent to a highway

3. Automobile tire tracks found at the scene of a crime are of *value* as evidence in that they   3._____
    are

    A. generally sufficient to trap and convict a suspect
    B. the most important link in the chain of physical evidence
    C. often the only evidence at hand
    D. circumstantial rather than direct

4. The *PRIMARY* reason for the police to try to find out which make, model, and year of car   4._____
    was involved in the commission of a crime, is to

    A. compare the tire tracks left at the scene of the crime with the type of tires used on
        cars of that make
    B. determine if the mud on the tires of the suspected car matches the mud in the
        unpaved road near the scene of the crime
    C. reduce to a large extent the amount of work involved in determining the particular
        car used in the commission of a crime
    D. alert the police patrol forces to question the occupants of all automobiles of this
        type

Questions 5-8.

DIRECTIONS: Answer Questions 5 through 8 *SOLELY* on the basis of the following statement:

When stopping vehicles on highways to check for suspects or fugitives, the police use an automobile roadblock whenever possible. This consists of three cars placed in prearranged positions. Car number one is parked across the left lane of the roadway with the front diagonally facing toward the center line. Car number two is parked across the right lane, with the front of the vehicle also toward the center line, in a position perpendicular to car number one and approximately twenty feet to the rear. Continuing another twenty feet to the rear along the highway, car number three is parked in an identical manner to car number one. The width of the highway determines the angle or position in which the autos should be placed. In addition to the regular roadblock signs and the use of flares at night only, there is an officer located at both the entrance and exit to direct and control traffic from both directions. This type of roadblock forces all approaching autos to reduce speed and zigzag around the police cars. Officers standing behind the parked cars can most safely and carefully view all passing motorists. Once a suspect is inside the block it becomes extremely difficult to crash out.

5. Of the following, the *MOST* appropropriate title for this statement is: 5.____

   A. The Construction of an Escape-Proof Roadblock
   B. Regulation of Automobile Traffic Through a Police Roadblock
   C. Safety Precautions Necessary in Making an Automobile Roadblock
   D. Structure of a Roadblock to Detain Suspects or Fugitives

6. When setting up a three-car roadblock, the *relative* positions of the cars should be *such that* 6.____

   A. the front of car number one is placed diagonally to the center line and faces car number three
   B. car number three is placed parallel to the center line and its front faces the right side of the road
   C. car number two is placed about 20 feet from car number one and its front faces the left side of the road
   D. car number three is parallel to and about 20 feet away from car number one

7. Officers can observe occupants of all cars passing through the roadblock with *GREATEST* safety when 7.____

   A. warning flares are lighted to illuminate the area sufficiently at night
   B. warning signs are put up at each end of the roadblock
   C. they are stationed at both the exit and the entrance of the roadblock
   D. they take up positions behind cars in the roadblock

8. The type of automobile roadblock described in the above paragraph is *of value* in police work because 8.____

   A. a suspect is unable to escape its confines by using force
   B. it is frequently used to capture suspects with no danger to the police
   C. it requires only two officers to set up and operate
   D. vehicular traffic within its confines is controled as to speed and direction

Questions 9-11.

DIRECTIONS: Answer Questions 9 through 11 *SOLELY* on the basis of the following statement:

A problem facing the police department in one area of the city was to try to reduce the
number of bicycle thefts which had been increasing at an alarming rate in the past three or
four years. A new program was adopted to get at the root of the problem. Tags were printed,
reminding youngsters that bicycles left unlocked can be easily stolen. The police concen-
trated on such places as theaters, a municipal swimming pool, an athletic field, and the local
high school, and tied tags on all bicycles which were not locked. The majority of bicycle thefts
took place at the swimming pool. In 2006, during the first two weeks the pool was open, an
average of 10 bicycles was stolen there daily. During the same two-week period, 30 bicycles
a week were stolen at the athletic field, 15 at the high school, and 11 at all theaters combined.
In 2007, after tagging the unlocked bicycles, it was found that 20 bicycles a week were stolen
at the pool and 5 at the high school. It was felt that the police tags had helped the most,
although the school officials had helped to a great extent in this program by distributing "lock-
ing" notices to parents and children, and the use of the loudspeaker at the pool urging children to lock their bicycles had also been very helpful.

9.   The one of the following which had the *GREATEST* effect in the campaign to reduce   9.____
     bicycle stealing was the

     A.   distribution of "locking" notices by the school officials
     B.   locking of all bicycles left in public places
     C.   police tagging of bicycles left unlocked by youngsters
     D.   use of the loudspeaker at the swimming pool

10.   The tagging program was instituted by the police department *CHIEFLY* to   10.____

      A.   determine the areas where most bicycle thieves operated
      B.   instill in youngsters the importance of punishing bicycle thieves
      C.   lessen the rising rate of bicycle thefts
      D.   recover as many as possible of the stolen bicycles

11.   The figures showing the number of bicycle thefts in the various areas surveyed indicate   11.____
      that in 2006

      A.   almost as many thefts occurred at the swimming pool as at all the theaters com-
           bined
      B.   fewer thefts occurred at the athletic field than at both the high school and all the-
           aters combined
      C.   more than half the thefts occurred at the swimming pool
      D.   twice as many thefts occurred at the high school as at the athletic field

Questions 12-13.

DIRECTIONS: Answer Questions 12 and 13 *SOLELY* on the bais of the following statement:
       A survey has shown that crime prevention work is most successful if the officers are
assigned on rotating shifts to provide for around-the-clock coverage. An officer may work
days for a time and then be switched to nights. The prime object of the night work is to enable
the officer to spot conditions inviting burglars. Complete lack of, or faulty locations of, night
lights and other conditions that may invite burglars, which might go unnoticed during daylight

hours, can be located and corrected more readily through night work. Night work also enables the officer to check local hangouts of juveniles, such as bus and railway depots, certain cafes or pool halls, the local roller rink, and the building where a juvenile dance is held every Friday night. Detectives also join patrolmen cruising in radio patrol cars to check on juveniles loitering late at night and to spot-check local bars for juveniles.

12. The *MOST* important purpose of assigning officers to night shifts is to make it possible for them to

    A. correct conditions which may not be readily noticed during the day
    B. discover the location of, and replace, missing and faulty night lights
    C. locate criminal hangouts
    D. notice things at night which cannot be noticed during the daytime

12.____

13. The type of shifting of officers which *BEST* prevents crime is to have

    A. day-shift officers rotated to night work
    B. rotating shifts provide sufficient officers for coverage 24 hours daily
    C. an officer work around the clock on a 24-hour basis as police needs arise
    D. rotating shifts to give the officers varied experience

13.____

Questions 14-15.

DIRECTIONS: Answer Questions 14 and 15 *SOLELY* on the basis of the following statement:
    Proper firearms training is one phase of law enforcement which cannot be ignored. No part of the training of a police officer is more important or more valuable. The officer's life and often the lives of his fellow officers depend directly upon his skill with the weapon he is carrying. Proficiency with the revolver is not attained exclusively by the volume of ammunition used and the number of hours spent on the firing line. Supervised practice and the use of training aids and techniques help make the shooter. It is essential to have a good firing range where new officers are trained and older personnel practice in scheduled firearms sessions. The fundamental points to be stressed are grip, stance, breathing, sight alignment and trigger squeeze. Coordination of thought, vision, and motion must be achieved before the officer gains confidence in his shooting ability. Attaining this ability will make the student a better officer and enhance his value to the force.

14. A police officer will gain confidence in his shooting ability *only after* he has

    A. spent the required number of hours on the firing line
    B. been given sufficient supervised practice
    C. learned the five fundamental points
    D. learned to coordinate revolver movement with his sight and thought

14.____

15. Proper training in the use of firearms is one aspect of law enforcement which must be given serious consideration *CHIEFLY* because it is the

    A. most useful and essential single factor in the training of a police officer
    B. one phase of police officer training which stresses mental and physical coordination
    C. costliest aspect of police officer training, involving considerable expense for the ammunition used in target practice
    D. most difficult part of police officer training, involving the expenditure of many hours on the firing line

15.____

Questions 16-20.

DIRECTIONS: Answer Questions 16 through 20 *SOLELY* on the basis of the following statement:

Lifting consists of transferring a print that has been dusted with powder to a transfer medium in order to preserve the print. Chemically developed prints cannot be lifted. Proper lifting of fingerprints is difficult and should be undertaken only when other means of recording the print are neither available nor suitable. Lifting should not be attempted from a porous surface. There are two types of commercial lifting tape which, are good transfer mediums: rubber adhesive lift, one side of which is gummed and covered with thin, transparent celluloid; and transparent lifting tape, made of cellophane, one side of which is gummed. A package of acetate covers, frosted on one side and used to cover and protect the lifted print, accompanies each roll. If commercial tape is not available, transparent scotch tape may be used. The investigator should remove the celluloid or acetate cover from the lifting tape; smooth the tape, gummy side down, firmly and evenly over the entire print; gently peel the tape off the surface; replace the cover; and attach pertinent identifying data to the tape. All parts of the print should come in contact with the tape; air pockets should be avoided. The print will adhere to the lifting tape. The cover permits the print to be viewed and protects it from damage. Transparent lifting tape does not reverse the print. If a rubber adhesive lift is utilized, the print is reversed. Before a direct comparison can be made, the lifted print must be photographed, the negative reversed, and a positive made.

16.   An investigator wishing to preserve a record of fingerprints on a highly porous surface should

    16._____

    A.   develop them chemically before attempting to lift them
    B.   lift them with scotch tape only when no other means of recording the prints are available
    C.   employ some method other than lifting
    D.   dust them with powder before attempting to lift them with rubber adhesive lift

17.   Disregarding all other considerations, the *SIMPLEST* process to use in lifting a fingerprint from a window pane is *that* involving the use of

    17._____

    A.   rubber adhesive lift, because it gives a positive print in one step
    B.   dusting powder and a camera, because the photograph is less likely to break than the window pane
    C.   a chemical process, because it both develops and preserves the print at the same time
    D.   transparent lifting tape, because it does not reverse the print

18.   When a piece of commercial lifting tape is being used by an investigator wishing to lift a clear fingerprint from a smoothly-finished metal safe-door, he *should*

    18._____

    A.   prevent the ends of the tape from getting stuck to the metal surface because of the danger of forming air-pockets and thus damaging the print
    B.   make certain that the tape covers all parts of the print and no air-pockets are formed
    C.   carefully roll the tape over the most significant parts of the print only to avoid forming air-pockets
    D.   be especially cautious not to destroy the air-pockets since this would tend to blur the print

19. When fingerprints lifted from an object found at the scene of a crime are to be compared with the fingerprints of a suspect, the lifted print

    A. can be compared directly only if a rubber adhesive lift was used
    B. cannot be compared directly if transparent scotch tape was used
    C. can be compared directly if transparent scotch tape was used
    D. must be photographed first and a positive made if any commercial lifting tape was used

19.____

20. When a rubber adhesive lift is to be used to lift a fingerprint, the one of the following which must be gently peeled off *FIRST* is the

    A. acetate cover   B. celluloid strip
    C. dusted surface   D. tape off the print surface

20.____

KEY (CORRECT ANSWERS)

1.	B		11.	C
2.	D		12.	A
3.	C		13.	B
4.	C		14.	D
5.	D		15.	A
6.	C		16.	C
7.	D		17.	D
8.	D		18.	B
9.	C		19.	C
10.	C		20.	B

READING COMPREHENSION
UNDERSTANDING AND INTERPRETING WRITTEN MATERIAL
EXAMINATION SECTION
TEST 1

DIRECTIONS: Each question or incomplete statement is followed by several suggested answers or completions. Select the one that BEST answers the question or completes the statement. *PRINT THE LETTER OF THE CORRECT ANSWER IN THE SPACE AT THE RIGHT.*

Questions 1-3.

DIRECTIONS: Questions 1 through 3 are to be answered SOLELY on the basis of the following passage.

When police officers search for a stolen car, they first check for the color of the car, then for make, model, year, body damage, and finally license number. The first five can be detected from almost any angle, while the recognition of the license number is often not immediately apparent. The serial number and motor number, though less likely to be changed than the easily substituted license number, cannot be observed in initial detection of the stolen car.

1. According to the above passage, the one of the following features which is LEAST   1.____
readily observed in checking for a stolen car in moving traffic is

    A. license number   B. serial number   C. model
    D. make   E. color

2. The feature of a car that cannot be determined from most angles of observation is the   2.____

    A. make   B. model   C. year
    D. license number   E. color

3. Of the following, the feature of a stolen car that is MOST likely to be altered by a car thief   3.____
shortly after the car is stolen is the

    A. license number   B. motor number   C. color
    D. model   E. minor body damage

Questions 4-5.

DIRECTIONS: Questions 4 and 5 are to be answered SOLELY on the basis of the following passage.

The racketeer is primarily concerned with business affairs, legitimate or otherwise, and preferably those which are close to the margin of legitimacy. He gets his best opportunities from business organizations which meet the need of large sections of the public for goods or services which are defined as illegitimate by the same public, such as prostitution, gambling, illicit drugs or liquor. In contrast to the thief, the racketeer and the establishments he controls deliver goods and services for money received.

4. From the above paragraph, it can be *deduced* that suppression of racketeers is *DIFFI-CULT* because

    A. victims of racketeers are not guilty of violating the law
    B. racketeers are generally engaged in fully legitimate enterprises
    C. many people want services which are not obtainable through legitimate sources
    D. the racketeers are well organized
    E. laws prohibiting gambling and prostitution are unenforceable

4.____

5. According to the above paragraph, racketeering, unlike theft, involves

    A. objects of value
    B. payment for goods received
    C. organized gangs
    D. public approval
    E. unlawful activities

5.____

Questions 6-8.

DIRECTIONS: Answer Questions 6 to 8 *SOLELY* on the basis of the following statement:

A number of crimes, such as robbery, assault, rape, certain forms of theft and burglary, are high visibility crimes in that it is apparent to all concerned that they are cirminal acts prior to or at the time they are committed. In contrast to these, check forgeries, especially those committed by first offenders, have low visibility. There is little in the criminal act or in the inter-action between the check passer and the person cashing the check to identify it as a crime. Closely related to this special quality of the forgery crime is the fact that, while it is formally defined and treated as a felonious or "infamous" crime, it is informally held by the legally untrained public to be a relatively harmless form of crime.

6. According to the above paragraph, crimes of "high visibility"

    A. are immediately recognized as crimes by the victims
    B. take place in public view
    C. always involve violence or the threat of violence
    D. usually are committed after dark
    E. can be observed from a distance

6.____

7. According to the above paragraph,

    A. the public regards check forgery as a minor crime
    B. the law regards check forgery as a minor crime
    C. the law distinguishes between check forgery and other forgery
    D. it is easier to spot inexperienced check forgers than other criminals
    E. it is more difficult to identify check forgers than other criminals

7.____

8. As used in this paragraph, an "infamous" crime is

    A. a crime attracting great attention from the public
    B. more serious than a felony
    C. less serious than a felony
    D. more or less serious than a felony, depending upon the surrounding circumstances
    E. the same as a felony

8.____

Questions 9-11.

DIRECTIONS: Answer Questions 9 to 11 *SOLELY* on the basis of the following statement:

Criminal science is largely the science of identification. Progress in this field has been marked and sometimes very spectacular because new techniques, instruments and facts flow continuously from the scientists. But the crime laboratories are undermanned, trade secrets still prevail, and inaccurate conclusions are often the result. However, modern gadgets cannot substitute for the skilled intelligent investigator; he must be their master.

9. According to this paragraph, criminal science   9.____

    A. excludes the field of investigation
    B. is primarily interested in establishing identity
    C. is based on the equipment used in crime laboratories
    D. uses techniques different from those used in other sciences
    E. is essentially secret in nature

10. Advances in criminal science have been, according to the above paragraph,   10.____

    A. extremely limited   B. slow but steady
    C. unusually reliable   D. outstanding
    E. infrequently worthwhile

11. A problem that has *NOT* been overcome *completely* in crime work is, according to the   11.____
     above paragraph,

    A. unskilled investigators
    B. the expense of new equipment and techniques
    C. an insufficient number of personnel in crime laboratories
    D. inaccurate equipment used in laboratories
    E. conclusions of the public about the value of this field

Questions 12-14.

DIRECTIONS: Answer Questions 12 to 14 *SOLELY* on the basis of the following statement:

The New York City Police Department will accept for investigation no report of a person missing from his residence if such residence is located outside of New York City. The person reporting same will be advised to report such fact to the police department of the locality where the missing person lives, which will, if necessary, communicate officially with the New York City Police Department. However, a report will be accepted of a person who is missing from a temporary residence in New York City, but the person making the report will be instructed to make a report also to the police department of the locality where the missing person lives.

12. According to the above paragraph, a report to the New York City Police Department of a   12.____
     missing person whose permanent residence is outside of New York City will

    A. *always be* investigated provided that a report is also made to his local police
        authorities
    B. *never be* investigated unless requested officially by his local police authorities

4 (#1)

C. *be* investigated in cases of temporary New York City residence, but a report should always be made to his local police authorities
D. *be* investigated if the person making the report is a New York City resident
E. *always be* investigated and a report will be made to the local police authorities by the New York City Police Department

13. Of the following, the *most likely* reason for the procedure described in the above paragraph is that   13.____

A. non-residents are not entitled to free police services from New York City
B. local police authorities would resent interference in their jurisdiction
C. local police authorities sometimes try to unload their problems on the New York City police
D. local police authorities may be better able to conduct an investigation
E. few persons are erroneously reported as missing

14. Mr. Smith, who lives in Jersey City, and Mr. Jones, who lives in Newark, arrange to meet   14.____
in New York City, but Mr. Jones doesn't keep the appointment. Mr. Smith telephones Mr. Jones several times the next day and gets no answer. Mr. Smith believes that something has happened to Mr. Jones.
According to the above paragraph, Mr. Smith should apply to the police authorities of

A. Jersey City
B. Newark
C. Newark and New York City
D. Jersey City and New York City
E. Newark, Jersey City, and New York City

Questions 15-17.

DIRECTIONS: Answer Questions 15 to 17 *SOLELY* on the basis of the following statement:

Some early psychologists believed that the basic characteristic of the criminal type was inferiority of intelligence, if not outright feeble-mindedness. They were misled by the fact that they had measurements for all kinds of criminals but, until World War I gave them a draft-army sample, they had no information on a comparable group of non-criminal adults. As soon as acceptable measurements could be taken of criminals and a comparable group of non-criminals, concern with feeblemindedness or with low intelligence as a type took on less and less significance in research in criminology.

15. According to the above paragraph, some early psychologists were in error because they   15.____
didn't

A. distinguish among the various types of criminals
B. devise a suitable method of measuring intelligence
C. measure the intelligence of non-criminals as a basis for comparison
D. distinguish between feeblemindedness and inferiority of intelligence
E. clearly define the term "intelligence"

230

16. The above paragraph *implies* that studies of the intelligence of criminals and non-crimi-   16.____
nals

    A. are useless because it is impossible to obtain comparable groups
    B. are not meaningful because only the less intelligent criminals are detected
    C. indicate that criminals are more intelligent than non-criminals
    D. indicate that criminals are less intelligent than non-criminals
    E. do not indicate that there are any differences between the two groups

17. According to the above paragraph, studies of the World War I draft gave psychologists   17.____
vital information concerning

    A. adaptability to army life of criminals and non-criminals
    B. criminal tendencies among draftees
    C. the intelligence scores of large numbers of men
    D. differences between intelligence scores of draftees and volunteers
    E. the behavior of men under abnormal conditions

Questions 18-20.

DIRECTIONS: Answer Questions 18 to 20 *SOLELY* on the basis of the following statement:

The use of a roadblock is simply an adaptation to police practice of the military concept of encirclement. Successful operation of a roadblock plan depends almost entirely on the amount of advance study and planning given to such operations. A thorough and detailed examination of the roads and terrain under the jurisdiction of a given police agency should be made with the locations of the roadblocks pinpointed in advance. The first principle to be borne in mind in the location of each roadblock is the time element. Its location must be at a point beyond which the fugitive could not have possibly traveled in the time elapsed from the commission of the crime to the arrival of the officers at the roadblock.

18. According to the above paragraph,   18.____

    A. military operations have made extensive use of roadblocks
    B. the military concept of encirclement is an adaptation of police use of roadblocks
    C. the technique of encirclement has been widely used by military forces
    D. a roadblock is generally more effective than encirclement
    E. police use of roadblocks is based on the idea of military encirclement

19. According to the above paragraph,   19.____

    A. the factor of time is the sole consideration in the location of a roadblock
    B. the maximum speed possible in the method of escape is of major importance in roadblock location
    C. the time of arrival of officers at the site of a proposed roadblock is of little importance
    D. if the method of escape is not known it should be assumed that the escape is by automobile
    E. a roadblock should be sited as close to the scene of the crime as the terrain will permit

20. According to the above paragraph,   20._____

    A. advance study and planning are of minor importance in the success of roadblock operations

    B. a thorough and detailed examination of all roads within a radius of fifty miles should precede the determination of a roadblock location

    C. consideration of terrain features are important in planning the location of road-blocks

    D. the pinpointing of roadblocks should be performed before any advance study is made

    E. a roadblock operation can seldom be successfully undertaken by a single police agency

---

KEY (CORRECT ANSWERS)

1.	D		11.	C
2.	B		12.	C
3.	A		13.	D
4.	C		14.	B
5.	B		15.	C
6.	A		16.	E
7.	A		17.	C
8.	E		18.	E
9.	B		19.	B
10.	D		20.	C

TEST 2

Questions 1-3.

DIRECTIONS: Answer Questions 1 to 3 *SOLELY* on the basis of the following statement:

All members of the police force must recognize that the people, through their representatives, hire and pay the police and that, as in any other employment, there must exist a proper employer-employee relationship. The police officer must understand that the essence of a correct police attitude is a willingness to serve, but at the same time he should distinguish between service and servility, and between courtesy and softness. He must be firm but also courteous, avoiding even an appearance of rudeness. He should develop a position that is friendly and unbiased, pleasant and sympathetic, in his relations with the general public, but firm and impersonal on occasions calling for regulation and control. A police officer should understand that his primary purpose is to prevent violations, not to arrest people. He should recognize the line of demarcation between a police function and passing judgment which is a court function. On the other side, a public that cooperates with the police, that supports them in their efforts and that observes laws and regulations may be said to have a desirable attitude.

1. In accordance with this paragraph, the *proper* attitude for a police officer to take is to   1.____

    A. be pleasant and sympathetic at all times
    B. be friendly, firm and impartial
    C. be stern and severe in meting out justice to all
    D. avoid being rude, except in those cases where the public is uncooperative

2. Assume that an officer is assigned by his superior officer to a busy traffic intersection and   2.____
    is warned to be on the lookout for motorists who skip the light or who are speeding.
    According to this paragraph, it would be *proper* for the officer in this assignment to

    A. give a summons to every motorist whose car was crossing when the light changed
    B. hide behind a truck and wait for drivers who violate traffic laws
    C. select at random motorists who seem to be impatient and lecture them sternly on
        traffic safety
    D. stand on post in order to deter violations and give offenders a summons or a warning as required

3. According to this paragraph, a police officer must realize that the *PRIMARY* purpose of   3.____
    police work is to

    A. provide proper police service in a courteous manner
    B. decide whether those who violate the law should be punished
    C. arrest those who violate laws
    D. establish a proper employer-employee relationship

Questions 4-5.

DIRECTIONS: Answer Questions 4 and 5 *SOLELY* on the basis of the following statement:

If a motor vehicle fails to pass inspection, the owner will be given a rejection notice by the inspection station. Repairs must be made within ten days after this notice is issued. It is not necessary to have the required adjustment or repairs made at the station where the inspection occurred. The vehicle may be taken to any other garage. Re-inspection after repairs may be made at any official inspection station, not necessarily the same station which made the initial inspection. The registration of any motor vehicle for which an inspection sticker has not been obtained as required, or which is not repaired and inspected within ten days after inspection indicates defects, is subject to suspension. A vehicle cannot be used on public highways while its registration is under suspension.

4. According to the above paragraph, the owner of a car which does not pass inspection *must*

    A. have repairs made at the same station which rejected his car
    B. take the car to another station and have it re-inspected
    C. have repairs made anywhere and then have the car re-inspected
    D. not use the car on a public highway until the necessary repairs have been made

4.____

5. According to the above paragraph, the one of the following which may be cause for suspension of the registration of a vehicle is that

    A. an inspection sticker was issued before the rejection notice had been in force for ten days
    B. it was not re-inspected by the station that rejected it originally
    C. it was not re-inspected either by the station that rejected it originally or by the garage which made the repairs
    D. it has not had defective parts repaired within ten days after inspection

5.____

Questions 6-10.

DIRECTIONS: Answer Questions 6 to 10 *SOLELY* on the basis of the following statement:

If we are to study crime in its widest social setting, we will find a variety of conduct which, although criminal in the legal sense, is not offensive to the moral conscience of a considerable number of persons. Traffic violations, for example, do not brand the offender as guilty of moral offense. In fact, the recipient of a traffic ticket is usually simply the subject of some good natured joking by his friends. Although there may be indignation among certain groups of citizens against gambling and liquor law violations, these activities are often tolerated, if not openly supported, by the more numerous residents of the community. Indeed, certain social and service clubs regularly conduct gambling games and lotteries for the purpose of raising funds. Some communities regard violations involving the sale of liquor with little concern in order to profit from increased license fees and taxes paid by dealers. The thousand and one forms of political graft and corruption which infest our urban centers only occasionally arouse public condemnation and official action.

6. According to the above paragraph, *all* types of illegal conduct are 6.____

    A. condemned by all elements of the community
    B. considered a moral offense, although some are tolerated by a few citizens
    C. violations of the law, but some are acceptable to certain elements of the community
    D. found in a social setting which is not punishable by law

7. According to the above paragraph, traffic violations are *generally* considered by society as 7.____

    A. crimes requiring the maximum penalty set by the law
    B. more serious than violations of the liquor laws
    C. offenses against the morals of the community
    D. relatively minor offenses requiring minimum punishment

8. According to the above paragraph, a lottery conducted for the purpose of raising funds for a church 8.____

    A. is considered a serious violation of law
    B. may be tolerated by a community which has laws against gambling
    C. may be conducted under special laws demanded by the more numerous residents of a community
    D. arouses indignation in most communities

9. On the basis of the above paragraph, the *most likely* reaction in the community to a police raid on a gambling casino would be 9.____

    A. more an attitude of indifference than interest in the raid
    B. general approval of the raid
    C. condemnation of the raid by most people
    D. demand for further action, since this raid is not sufficient to end gambling activities

10. The one of the following which *BEST* describes the central thought of this paragraph and would be *MOST* suitable as a title for it is: 10.____

    A. Crime and the Police
    B. Public Condemnation of Graft and Corruption
    C. Gambling Is Not Always a Vicious Business
    D. Public Attitude toward Law Violations

Questions 11-13.

DIRECTIONS: Answer Questions 11-13 *SOLELY* on the basis of the following statement:

The law enforcement agency is one of the most important agencies in the field of juvenile delinquency prevention. This is so, not because of the social work connected with this problem, however, for this is not a police matter, but because the officers are usually the first to come in contact with the delinquent. The manner of arrest and detention makes a deep impression upon him and affects his lifelong attitude toward society and the law. The juvenile court is perhaps the most important agency in this work. Contrary to the general opinion, however, it is not primarily concerned with putting children into correctional schools. The main purpose of the juvenile court is to save the child and to develop his emotional make-up, in order that he can grow up to be a decent and well-balanced citizen. The system of probation is the means whereby the court seeks to accomplish these goals.

11. According to this paragraph, police work is an *important* part of a program to prevent juvenile delinquency because

    11.____

    A. social work is no longer considered important in juvenile delinquency prevention
    B. police officers are the first to have contact with the delinquent
    C. police officers jail the offender in order to be able to change his attitude toward society and the law
    D. it is the first step in placing the delinquent in jail

12. According to this paragraph, the *CHIEF* purpose of the juvenile court is to

    12.____

    A. punish the child for his offense
    B. select a suitable correctional school for the delinquent
    C. use available means to help the delinquent become a better citizen
    D. provide psychiatric care for the delinquent

13. According to this paragraph, the juvenile court directs the development of delinquents under its care *CHIEFLY* by

    13.____

    A. placing the child under probation
    B. sending the child to a correctional school
    C. keeping the delinquent in prison
    D. returning the child to his home

Questions 14-17.

DIRECTIONS: Answer Questions 14 to 17 *SOLELY* on the basis of the following statement:

    When a vehicle has been disabled in the tunnel, the office on patrol in this zone should press the *emergency truck* light button. In the fast lane, red lights will go on throughout the tunnel; in the slow lane, amber lights will go on throughout the tunnel. The yellow zone light will go on at each signal control station throughout the tunnel and will flash the number of the zone in which the stoppage has occurred. A red flashing pilot light will appear only at the signal control station at which the *emergency truck* button was pressed. The emergency garage will receive an audible and visual signal indicating the signal control station at which the *emergency truck* button was pressed. The garage officer shall acknowledge receipt of the signal by pressing the acknowledgment button. This will cause the pilot light at the operated signal control station in the tunnel to cease flashing and to remain steady. It is an answer to the officer at the operated signal control station that the emergency truck is responding to the call.

14. According to this paragraph, when the *emergency truck* light button is pressed

    14.____

    A. amber lights will go on in every lane throughout the tunnel
    B. emergency signal lights will go on only in the lane in which the disabled vehicle happens to be
    C. red lights will go on in the fast lane throughout the tunnel
    D. pilot lights at all signal control stations will turn amber

15. According to this paragraph, the number of the zone in which the stoppage has occurred is flashed   15.____

    A. immediately after all the lights in the tunnel turn red
    B. by the yellow zone light at each signal control station
    C. by the emergency truck at the point of stoppage
    D. by the emergency garage

16. According to this paragraph, an officer near the disabled vehicle will know that the emergency tow truck is coming when   16.____

    A. the pilot light at the operated signal control station appears and flashes red
    B. an audible signal is heard in the tunnel
    C. the zone light at the operated signal control station turns red
    D. the pilot light at the operated signal control station becomes steady

17. Under the system described in the above paragraph, it would be *correct* to come to the conclusion that   17.____

    A. officers at all signal control stations are expected to acknowledge that they have received the stoppage signal
    B. officers at all signal control stations will know where the stoppage has occurred
    C. all traffic in both lanes of that side of the tunnel in which the stoppage has occurred must stop until the emergency truck has arrived
    D. there are two emergency garages, each able to respond to stoppages in traffic going in one particular direction

Questions 18-20.

DIRECTIONS: Answer Questions 18 to 20 *SOLELY* on the basis of the following statement:

In cases of accident it is most important for an officer to obtain the name, age, residence, occupation and a full description of the person injured, names and addresses of witnesses. He shall also obtain a statement of the attendant circumstances. He shall carefully note contributory conditions, if any, such as broken pavement, excavation, lights not burning, snow and ice on the roadway, etc. He shall enter all the facts in his memorandum book and on Form NY-17 or Form NY-18, and promptly transmit the original of the form to his superior officer and the duplicate to headquarters.

An officer shall render reasonable assistance to sick or injured persons. If the circumstances appear to require the services of a physician, he shall summon a physician by telephoning the superior officer on duty and notifying him of the apparent nature of the illness or accident and the location where the physician will be required. He may summon other officers to assist if circumstances warrant.

In case of an accident or where a person is sick on city property, an officer shall obtain the information necessary to fill out card Form NY-18 and record this in his memorandum book and promptly telephone the facts to his superior officer. He shall deliver the original card at the expiration of his tour to his superior officer and transmit the duplicate to headquarters.

18. According to this statement, the *MOST* important consideration in any report on a case of accident or injury is to 18.____

 A. obtain all the facts
 B. telephone his superior officer at once
 C. obtain a statement of the attendant circumstances
 D. determine ownership of the property on which the accident occurred

19. According to this statement, in the case of an accident on city property, the officer should *always* 19.____

 A. summon a physician before filling out any forms or making any entries in his memorandum book
 B. give his superior officer on duty a prompt report by telephone
 C. immediately bring the original of Form NY-18 to his superior officer on duty
 D. call at least one other officer to the scene to witness conditions

20. If the procedures stated were followed for all accidents in the city, an impartial survey of accidents occurring during any period of time in this city may be *most easily* made by 20.____

 A. asking a typical officer to show you his memorandum book
 B. having a superior officer investigate whether contributory conditions mentioned by witnesses actually exist
 C. checking all the records of all superior officers
 D. checking the duplicate card files at headquarters

KEY (CORRECT ANSWERS)

1.	B	11.	B
2.	D	12.	C
3.	A	13.	A
4.	C	14.	C
5.	D	15.	B
6.	C	16.	D
7.	D	17.	B
8.	B	18.	A
9.	A	19.	B
10.	D	20.	D

TEST 3

DIRECTIONS: The following questions are intended to test your ability to read with comprehension and to understand and interpret written materials, particularly legal passages. Each question has several suggested answers. *PRINT THE LETTER OF THE CORRECT ANSWER IN THE SPACE AT THE RIGHT.*

Questions 1-3.

DIRECTIONS: Answer Questions 1 to 3 *SOLELY* on the basis of the following statement:

Modern police science may be said to have three phases. The first phase embraces the identification of living and dead persons. The second embraces the field work carried out by specially-trained detectives at the scene of the crime. The third embraces methods used in the police laboratory to examine and analyze clues and traces discovered in the course of the investigation. While modern police science has had a striking influence on detective work and will surely further enhance its effectiveness, the time-honored methods and practical detective work will always be important. The time-honored methods, that is, knowledge of methods used by criminals, patience, tact, industry, thoroughness, and imagination, will always be requisites for successful detective work.

1. According to the above statement, we may expect modern police science to   1.____

   A. help detective work more and more
   B. become more and more scientific
   C. depend less and less on the time-honored methods
   D. bring together the many different approaches to detective work
   E. play a less important role in detective work

2. According to the above statement, a knowledge of the procedures used by criminals is   2.____

   A. solely an element of the modern police science approach to detective work
   B. related to the identification of persons
   C. not related to detective field work
   D. related to methods used in the police laboratory
   E. an element of the traditional approach to detective work

3. Modern police science and practical detective work, according to the above statement,   3.____

   A. when used together, can only lead to confusion
   B. are based on distinctly different theories of detective work
   C. have had strikingly different influences on detective work
   D. should both be used for successful detective work
   E. lead usually to similar results

Questions 4-7.

DIRECTIONS: Answer Questions 4 to 7 *SOLELY* on the basis of the following statement:

A member of the force shall render reasonable aid to a sick or injured person. He shall summon an ambulance, if necessary, by telephoning the communications bureau of the county, who shall notify the precinct concerned. If possible, he shall wait in full view of the arriving ambulance and take necessary action to direct the responding doctor or attendant to the patient, without delay. If the ambulance does not arrive in twenty minutes, he shall send in a second call. However, if the sick person is in his or her own home, a member of the force, before summoning an ambulance, will ascertain whether such person is willing to be taken to a hospital for treatment.

4. According to the above statement, if a police officer wants to get an ambulance for a sick   4.____
person, he should telephone

    A. the precinct concerned
    B. only if the sick person is in his home
    C. the nearest hospital
    D. only if the sick person is not in his home
    E. the county communications bureau

5. According to the above statement, if a police officer telephones for an ambulance and   5.____
none arrives within twenty minutes, he should

    A. ask the injured person whether he is willing to be taken to a hospital
    B. call the county communications bureau
    C. call the precinct concerned
    D. attempt to give the injured person such assistance as he may need
    E. call the nearest hospital

6. A police officer is called to help a woman who has fallen in her own home and has appar-   6.____
ently broken her leg. According to the above statement, he should

    A. ask her whether she wants to go to a hospital
    B. try to set her leg if it is necessary
    C. call for an ambulance at once
    D. attempt to get a doctor as quickly as possible
    E. not attempt to help the woman in any way before competent medical aid arrives

7. A man falls from a window into the backyard of an apartment house. Assume that you   7.____
are a police officer and that you are called to assist this man.
According to the above statement, after you have called for an ambulance and comforted the injured man as much as you can, you should

    A. wait in front of the house for the ambulance
    B. ask the injured man if he wishes to go to the hospital for treatment
    C. remain with the injured man until the ambulance arrives
    D. send a bystander to direct the nearest doctor to the patient
    E. not ask the man to explain how the accident happened

Questions 8-10.

DIRECTIONS: Answer Questions 8 to 10 *SOLELY* on the basis of the following statement.

What is required is a program that will protect our citizens and their property from criminal and antisocial acts, will effectively restrain and reform juvenile delinquents, and will prevent the further development of antisocial behavior. Discipline and punishment of offenders must necessarily play an important part in any such program. Serious offenders cannot be mollycoddled merely because they are under twenty-one. Restraint and punishment necessarily follow serious antisocial acts. But punishment, if it is to be effective, must be a planned part of a more comprehensive program of treating delinquency.

8. The one of the following goals NOT included among those listed above is to   8._____

    A. stop young people from defacing public property
    B. keep homes from being broken into
    C. develop an intra-city boys' baseball league
    D. change juvenile delinquents into useful citizens
    E. prevent young people from developing antisocial behavior patterns

9. According to the above statement, punishment is   9._____

    A. not satisfactory in any program dealing with juvenile delinquents
    B. the most effective means by which young vandals and hooligans can be reformed
    C. not used sufficiently when dealing with serious offenders who are under twenty-one
    D. of value in reducing juvenile delinquency only if it is part of a complete program
    E. most effective when it does not relate to specific antisocial acts

10. With respect to serious offenders who are under twenty-one, the above statement suggests that they   10._____

    A. be mollycoddled
    B. be dealt with as part of a comprehensive program to punish mature criminals
    C. should be punished
    D. be prevented, by brute force if necessary, from performing antisocial acts
    E. be treated as delinquent children who require more love than punishment

KEY (CORRECT ANSWERS)

1.	A		6.	A
2.	E		7.	A
3.	D		8.	C
4.	E		9.	D
5.	B		10.	C

READING COMPREHENSION
UNDERSTANDING AND INTERPRETING WRITTEN MATERIAL
EXAMINATION SECTION
TEST 1

DIRECTIONS: Each question or incomplete statement is followed by several suggested answers or completions. Select the one that BEST answers the question or completes the statement. *PRINT THE LETTER OF THE CORRECT ANSWER IN THE SPACE AT THE RIGHT.*

Questions 1-6.

DIRECTIONS: Questions 1 through 6 are to be answered SOLELY on the basis of the following passage.

Delinquency and crime and reactions to them are social products and are socially defined. Society as a whole, not individuals, creates and defines rules, pejoratively labels those who break rules, and prescribes ways for reacting to the labeled person. Moreover, at times the societal process of defining, labeling, and reacting may not affect behavior but at other times it is influential in determining both who shall enter the correctional process and what its outcome will be

What's more, the labeling process is often a means of isolating offenders from, rather than integrating them in, effective participation in such major societal institutions as schools, businesses, unions, and political, community, and fraternal organizations. These institutions are the major access routes to a successful, non-delinquent career. Those who are in power in them are the gatekeepers of society and, if offenders and correctional programs are isolated from them, then the personal wishes and characteristics of offenders will have little bearing on whether correctional programs succeed or fail.

1. According to the above passage, the MAJOR determinant of whether an offender will succeed in society is his   1._____

    A. self-confidence and general intelligence
    B. degree of participation in the major societal institutions
    C. attitude toward the entire criminal justice system
    D. overall criminal record

2. The above passage suggests that the isolation of offenders from certain groups within society through the labeling process is   2._____

    A. intentional   B. unlawful
    C. beneficial   D. irreversible

3. Of the following, the MOST appropriate title for the passage is   3._____

    A. METHODS OF REFORMING THE ATTITUDES OF SOCIETY
    B. UNJUST JUSTICE
    C. DELINQUENCY AND CRIME
    D. SOCIETY'S REJECTION OF OFFENDERS

4.   According to the passage, delinquency and crime are created by the   4._____

   A.   characteristics of offenders
   B.   correctional process itself
   C.   operations of society
   D.   gatekeepers of major institutions

5.   Of the following suggested methods of helping offenders adjust to society, the one which   5._____
   the passage would be LEAST likely to favor would be to

   A.   establish cooperative relations between correctional programs in cooperation with
        influential members of society
   B.   keep the public informed of current developments in the corrections field by con-
        tributing information to local newspapers
   C.   create an organizational structure within correctional institutions which, wherever
        practicable, resembles life in society
   D.   encourage offenders to maintain close ties with other offenders with whom they
        become friendly while incarcerated

6.   According to the passage, the rehabilitation of the offender is MOST likely to be deter-   6._____
   mined by

   A.   the individual inmate himself
   B.   dynamic reformation programs
   C.   society as a whole
   D.   the specific correctional institution

Questions 7-10.

DIRECTIONS: Questions 7 through 10 are to be answered SOLELY on the basis of the follow-
              ing paragraph.

   Urban crime rates are generally higher than those prevailing in rural areas. This apparent
preponderance of urban crime has been observed by many criminologists both here and
abroad and, although the factual basis for their conclusion that more crime occurs in urban
areas does not lend itself to close measurement, there seems to be sufficient reason to
accept it at face value. But there is an increasing body of evidence accumulating in the United
States indicative that a profound change in these relationships may be in progress. For murder and rape, the rural crime rate of this country now equals the urban rate. As to all homi-
cides, it exceeds the urban crime rate of the New England, Middle Atlantic, and North Central
states, and shows such impressive advances for aggravated assault and robbery as to
greatly reduce the former disparity. Such changes raise the question whether rural crimes,
reacting to new means of transport and consequent interchange of population, which are
urban influences, may not now be in the process of attaining urban crime levels. Certain it is
that crimes against the person have for centuries been relatively more numerous in rural
areas than crimes against property. Hence, the new trend is in a sense an extension of a condition of long standing.

7.   According to the above passage, the statement that crime rates are generally higher in   7._____
   urban areas than in rural areas

A. has not been definitely established although there is strong evidence to support such a view

B. is justified but does not necessarily indicate that more crime is actually committed in urban areas

C. has been definitely established despite some contrary evidence submitted by criminologists

D. is not justified since the facts gathered by many criminologists do not lend themselves to close measurement

8. Concerning the present relationship between rural and urban crime rates, it would be MOST correct to state, according to the above passage, that for　　8.＿＿＿

A. aggravated assault and robbery, the urban rate remained stationary while the rural rate increased

B. murder and rape, the rural rate equals the urban rate in the Middle Atlantic states

C. aggravated assault and robbery, the rural rate was formerly lower than the urban rate

D. murder and rape, the urban rate is less than the rural rate in the North Central states

9. The development of new means of transport, according to the above passage,　　9.＿＿＿

A. may or may not be an urban influence but it definitely contributed to a rise in rural crime levels

B. is an urban influence and may or may not contribute to a rise in rural crime levels

C. may or may not be an urban influence and may or may not contribute to a rise in rural crime levels

D. is an urban influence and has definitely contributed to a rise in rural crime levels

10. The new trend is BEST defined, according to the above passage, as a tendency for crimes against　　10.＿＿＿

A. the person to be more numerous in rural areas than they have been in the past in urban areas

B. property to be less numerous in urban areas than they are in rural areas

C. the person to be more numerous in rural areas than they have been in the past in rural areas

D. property to be more numerous in urban areas than they have been in the past in urban areas

Questions 11-15.

DIRECTIONS: Questions 11 through 15 are to be answered SOLELY on the basis of the following paragraph.

If we are to study crime in its widest social setting, we will find a variety of conduct which, although criminal in the legal sense, is not offensive to the moral conscience of a considerable number of persons. Traffic violations, for example, do not brand the offender as guilty of moral offense. In fact, the recipient of a traffic ticket is usually simply the subject of some good-natured joking by his friends. Although there may be indignation among certain groups of citizens against gambling and liquor law violations, these activities are often tolerated, if not openly supported, by the more numerous residents of the community. Indeed, certain social and service clubs regularly conduct gambling games and lotteries for the purpose of raising funds. Some communities regard violations involving the sale of liquor with little concern in order to profit from increased license fees and taxes paid by dealers. The thousand and one forms of political graft and corruption which infest our urban centers only occasionally arouse public condemnation and official action.

11. According to the above paragraph, all types of illegal conduct are   11._____

    A. condemned by all elements of the community
    B. considered a moral offense, although some are tolerated by a few citizens
    C. violations of the law, but some are acceptable to certain elements of the community
    D. found in a social setting which is not punishable by law

12. According to the above paragraph, traffic violations are GENERALLY considered by society as   12._____

    A. crimes requiring the maximum penalty set by the law
    B. more serious than violations of the liquor laws
    C. offenses against the morals of the community
    D. relatively minor offenses requiring minimum punishment

13. According to the above paragraph, a lottery conducted for the purpose of raising funds for a church   13._____

    A. is considered a serious violation of law
    B. may be tolerated by a community which has laws against gambling
    C. may be conducted under special laws demanded by the more numerous residents of a community
    D. arouses indignation in most communities

14. On the basis of the paragraph, the MOST likely reaction in the community to a police raid on a gambling casino would be   14._____

    A. more an attitude of indifference than interest in the raid
    B. general approval of the raid
    C. condemnation of the raid by most people
    D. demand for further action, since this raid is not sufficient to end gambling activities

15. The one of the following which BEST describes the central thought of this paragraph and would be MOST suitable as a title for it is   15._____

    A. CRIME AND THE POLICE
    B. PUBLIC CONDEMNATION OF GRAFT AND CORRUPTION
    C. GAMBLING IS NOT ALWAYS A VICIOUS BUSINESS
    D. PUBLIC ATTITUDE TOWARD LAW VIOLATIONS

Questions 16-18.

DIRECTIONS: Questions 16 through 18 are to be answered SOLELY on the basis of the following paragraphs.

The rise of urban-industrial society has complicated the social arrangements needed to regulate contacts between people. As a consequence, there has been an unprecedented increase in the volume of laws and regulations designed to control individual conduct and to govern the relationship of the individual to others. In a century there has been an eight-fold increase in the crimes for which one may be prosecuted.

For these offenses, the courts have the ultimate responsibility for redressing wrongs and convicting the guilty. The body of legal precepts gives the impression of an abstract and even-handed dispensation of justice. Actually, the personnel of the agencies applying these precepts are faced with the difficulties of fitting abstract principles to highly variable situations emerging from the dynamics of everyday life. It is inevitable that discrepancies should exist between precept and practice.

The legal institutions serve as a framework for the social order by their slowness to respond to the caprices of transitory fad. This valuable contribution exacts a price in terms of the inflexibility of legal institutions in responding to new circumstances. This possibility is promoted by the changes in values and norms of the dynamic larger culture of which the legal precepts are a part.

16. According to the above passage, the increase in the number of laws and regulations during the twentieth century can be attributed to the   16._____

    A. complexity of modern industrial society
    B. increased seriousness of offenses committed
    C. growth of individualism
    D. anonymity of urban living

17. According to the above passage, which of the following presents a problem to the staff of legal agencies?   17._____

    A. The need to eliminate the discrepancy between precept and practice
    B. The necessity to apply abstract legal precepts to rapidly changing conditions
    C. The responsibility for reducing the number of abstract legal principles
    D. The responsibility for understanding offenses in terms of the real life situations from which they emerge

18. According to the above passage, it can be concluded that legal institutions affect social institutions by   18._____

    A. preventing change
    B. keeping pace with its norms and values
    C. changing its norms and values
    D. providing stability

Questions 19-21.

DIRECTIONS: Questions 19 through 21 are to be answered SOLELY on the basis of the following paragraph.

This research lends additional emphasis to the contention that crime, as reported and recorded in the United States, is largely a function of social and cultural factors rather than biological, psychological, or entirely chance of factors. In the absence of significant biological variations or significant differences in basic mental processes on a regional or sectional basis, all other things being equal, one would expect a rather even crime rate from state to state. Since vast differences in crime rates on a sectional basis are found to persist over a period of time, one may hypothesize that subcultural variations of a regional or sectional nature are responsible for these regional or sectional patterns of crime. Even if this hypothesis cannot be accepted due to underreporting of crime, the least that the data may be said to demonstrate is a distinctly sectional variation in reporting and recording practices, indicating great disparities in sectional reactions to various types of human, or more specifically, criminal behavior.

19. According to the above paragraph, sectional crime rates   19.____

   A. are not affected significantly by entirely chance factors in the absence of psycho-
      logical factors
   B. can be affected by biological variations or differences in basic mental processes
   C. vary little with significant biological factors in the population
   D. vary significantly in the absence of variable social and cultural factors

20. According to the above paragraph, great differences in the crime pattern and incidence in   20.____
    different sections of the United States may be said to be, assuming adequate reporting,

   A. a function of sectional variations in reporting and recording practices
   B. based on the specificity of some types of criminal behavior and the lack of a pat-
      tern in others
   C. based primarily on differences in the extent of urbanization of the population
   D. the result of regional cultural variations that are persistent over a period of time

21. According to the above paragraph, the statement that is MOST acceptable concerning   21.____
    the interpretation of crime data distribution by states or regions is that

   A. a more or less even crime rate from state to state indicates absence of significant
      biological variations
   B. consistent patterns of crime incidence are solely attributable to similar cultural and
      social factors
   C. failure to report crime that has occurred is indicative of differences in reaction to
      different types of crimes committed
   D. uniform reporting practices tend to eliminate sectional disparities in causality of
      crime

Questions 22-26.

DIRECTIONS: Questions 22 through 26 are to be answered SOLELY on the basis of the fol-
              lowing paragraph.

Criminals were once considered sinners who chose to offend against the laws of God and man. They were severely punished for their crimes. Modern criminologists regard society itself as in large part responsible for the crimes committed against it. Poverty, poor living conditions, and inadequate education are all causes of crime. Crime is fundamentally the result of society's failure to provide a decent life for all the people. It is especially common in times when values are changing, as after a war, or in countries where people of different backgrounds and values are thrown together, as in the United States. Crimes, generally speaking, are fewer in countries where there is a settled way of life and a traditional respect for law.

22. This passage deals with

   A. criminals
   B. society
   C. the reasons for crime
   D. crime in the United States

22.____

23. The MAIN idea of this passage is that

   A. crime is common when values are changing
   B. crime is the result of poverty
   C. traditional respect for law prevents a crime
   D. society is largely responsible for crime

23.____

24. According to the passage, which is NOT a cause of crime?

   A. Poverty
   C. Ethnic mixing
   B. Wickedness
   D. Unsettled way of life

24.____

25. Crime is MOST common in

   A. periods of instability
   C. wartime
   B. the United States
   D. suburbs

25.____

26. To prevent crime, the author implies that society should

   A. provide stiffer penalties for criminals
   B. provide a decent way of life for everyone
   C. segregate the poor
   D. give broader powers to the police

26.____

Questions 27-30.

DIRECTIONS: Questions 27 through 30 are to be answered SOLELY on the basis of the following passage.

Perpetrators of crimes are often described by witnesses or victims in terms of salient facial features. The Bertillon System of identification which preceded the widespread use of fingerprints was based on body measurements. Recently, there have been developments in the quantification of procedures used in the classification and comparison of facial characteristics. Devices are now available which enable a trained operator, with the aid of a witness, to form a composite picture of a suspect's face and to translate that composite into a numerical code. Further developments in this area are possible, using computers to develop efficient sequences of questions so that witnesses may quickly arrive at the proper description.

Recent studies of voice analysis and synthesis, originally motivated by problems of efficient telephone transmission, have led to the development of the audio-frequency profile or *voice print.* Each voice print may be sufficiently unique to permit development of a classification system that will make possible positive identification of the source of a voice print. This method of identification, using an expert to identify the voice patterns, has been introduced in more than 40 cases by 15 different police departments. As with all identification systems that rely on experts to perform the identification, controlled laboratory tests are needed to establish with care the relative frequency of errors of omission and commission made by experts.

27. The MOST appropriate title for the above passage is   27.____

    A. TECHNOLOGY IN MODERN INVESTIGATIVE DETECTION
    B. IDENTIFICATION BY PHYSICAL FEATURES
    C. VERIFICATION OF IDENTIFICATIONS BY EXPERTS
    D. THE USE OF ELECTRONIC IDENTIFICATION TECHNIQUES

28. According to the above passage, computers may be used in conjunction with which of   28.____
the following identification techniques?

    A. Fingerprints   B. Bertillon System
    C. Voice prints   D. Composite Facial Pictures

29. According to the above passage, the ability to identify individuals based on facial charac- 29.____
teristics has improved as a result of

    A. an increase in the number of facial types which can be shown to witnesses
    B. information which is derived from other body measurements
    C. coded classification and comparison techniques
    D. greater reliance upon experts to make the identifications

30. According to the above passage, it is CORRECT to state that audio-frequency profiles or   30.____
voice prints

    A. have been decisive in many prosecutions
    B. reduce the number of errors made by experts
    C. developed as a result of problems in telephonic communications
    D. are unlikely to result in positive identifications

KEY (CORRECT ANSWERS)

1.	B		16.	A
2.	A		17.	B
3.	D		18.	D
4.	C		19.	D
5.	D		20.	D
6.	C		21.	C
7.	B		22.	C
8.	C		23.	A
9.	D		24.	B
10.	C		25.	A
11.	C		26.	B
12.	D		27.	B
13.	B		28.	D
14.	A		29.	C
15.	D		30.	C

TEST 2

DIRECTIONS: Each question or incomplete statement is followed by several suggested answers or completions. Select the one that BEST answers the question or completes the statement. *PRINT THE LETTER OF THE CORRECT ANSWER IN THE SPACE AT THE RIGHT.*

Questions 1-7.

DIRECTIONS: Questions 1 through 7 are to be answered SOLELY on the basis of the following rules. These rules are not intended to be an exact copy of the rules of any institution.

SECTION OF RULES

All members of the department shall treat as confidential the official business of the department. An employee shall under no circumstances impart information to anyone relating to the official business of the department, except when she is a witness under oath in a court of law. When answering a department telephone, an employee shall give the name of the institution to which she is attached, her rank, and full name. Officers shall not give the name of any bondsman or attorney to inmates. The head of the institution shall be notified immediately when an inmate requests an officer for the name of a bondsman or attorney. All inmates awaiting trial shall be advised that they are entitled to one free twenty-five cent telephone call- within the city. All other telephone calls must be paid for by the inmate. Officers assigned to the examination of parcels or letters for inmates shall do so with utmost care. Failure to discover contraband shall be presumptive evidence of negligence. When an officer is assigned to accompany an inmate to court, to the District Attorney's office, or elsewhere, she must handcuff the inmate and must, under no circumstances, visit any places except such as are designated in the document calling for the inmate's presence.

1. Assume that Mary Jones is assigned to the House of Detention as a Correction Officer with shield number 781.
   When she answers the institution's phone, she should say

   A. House of Detention, Officer Mary Jones
   B. House of Detention, Officer Mary Jones, shield number 781
   C. Officer Mary Jones, shield number 781
   D. This is the House of Detention, Officer Jones speaking

   1._____

2. An inmate awaiting trial asks for permission to make a telephone call to New Jersey. She should be

   A. allowed to make the call if she has not made any other free calls
   B. permitted to make the call at her own expense
   C. told that only local telephone calls are permitted
   D. told that she will have to pay all charges over twenty-five cents

   2._____

3. An inmate awaiting trial asks you for the name of a lawyer who will not charge a large fee, as she does not have much money.
   You should

   3._____

A. bring her request to the attention of the head of the institution
B. remind her that under the rules inmates are forbidden to ask an officer for the name of an attorney
C. tell her that you don't know any lawyers who charge low fees
D. tell her the state will furnish a lawyer without charge

4. A supervisor has an inmate whose case received a great deal of publicity in the newspapers. One day a reporter comes to the supervisor's home to interview him about this prisoner.
   The supervisor should

   A. give him only such information as has already appeared in the daily press
   B. give him only such information which is not considered confidential
   C. tell him that he is prohibited by the rules from discussing the case with him
   D. tell him that an interview will be granted if he can produce a letter from the Commissioner giving him permission for the interview

4.____

5. An officer is assigned to deliver a prisoner to the hospital prison ward in accordance with a court order. He is given a department car and chauffeur for this purpose. Before he leaves, the Superintendent of the prison also gives him some important official papers requiring the Commissioner's immediate attention for delivery to Central Office. On the way to the hospital, he will pass Central Office.
   He should stop at Central Office

   A. and send the chauffeur in with the papers while he waits in the car with the prisoner
   B. on his way back from the hospital, after he has delivered his prisoner
   C. to deliver the papers, leaving the handcuffed prisoner in the car in charge of the chauffeur
   D. to deliver the papers, taking the handcuffed prisoner with him

5.____

6. According to the rules, if an article of contraband is successfully smuggled into the prison in a package for an inmate, it is

   A. possible that the contraband may have been extremely well concealed
   B. possible that the employee who inspected the package did not realize that the article in question constituted contraband
   C. probable that the employee who inspected the package was careless
   D. sufficient cause to make the employee who inspected the package subject to dismissal

6.____

7. According to the rules,

   A. an employee may testify about official business in court
   B. only a competent court or the District Attorney can order a prisoner to be produced
   C. sentenced inmates are not allowed to make telephone calls out of the institution
   D. while packages for inmates are censored, their personal mail is not

7.____

Questions 8-11.

DIRECTIONS: Questions 8 through 11 are to be answered on the basis of the following passage.

Female criminality is very much under-reported, especially if one considers offenses such as shoplifting, thefts by prostitutes, offenses against children, and homicide. There are even certain offenses such as homosexuality and exhibitionism that go practically unprosecuted if committed by women. Female offenders are really protected by men, even by victims, who are usually disinclined to complain to authorities. Since women play much less active roles in society than men do, one must be prepared for the fact that women are often the instigators of crimes committed by men and, as instigators, they are hard to detect. There are several crimes that are ordinarily highly detectable in men but have very low detectability in women. Her roles as homemaker, mother, nurse, wife, and so forth, permit the female to commit a crime and yet screen that crime from public view - for example, slowly poisoning her husband or treating her children abusively. In addition, law enforcement officers, judges, and juries are much more lenient toward women than toward men. Such considerations lead to the conclusion that criminality of women is *largely masked criminality*. Consequently, official statistics and records of criminality should be expected to under-report female offenses. The true measure of female crime must be sought from unofficial sources. The masked character of female crime and its gross under-reporting are consistent with the official view that the female is a very low risk for crime.

8. What has the writer inferred about the incidence of female offenses? 8._____

    A. It gives an adequate representation of the number of crimes committed by men but instigated by women.
    B. It is not to be considered an important area of criminality.
    C. It is understated because the classic female role makes her less visible to social scrutiny.
    D. In every crime the incidence of male offenses is more difficult to detect than that of women.

9. Judges are inclined to be lenient toward female offenders because 9._____

    A. the role of the woman in society has stereotyped her as maternal and non-hostile
    B. the majority of their crimes does not physically harm others
    C. they commit crimes which are difficult to detect
    D. official statistics report them as less likely to commit crimes

10. Of the following, the title MOST suitable for this passage is 10._____

    A. MALE CRIMINALITY
    B. THE PETTY OFFENDER
    C. THE FEMALE MURDERER
    D. EXPOSING FEMALE CRIMINALITY

11. According to the passage, which of the following crimes is LEAST likely to be prosecuted against a woman? 11._____

    A. Child abuse   B. Exhibitionism
    C. Homicide   D. Prostitution

Questions 12-16.

DIRECTIONS: Questions 12 through 16 are to be answered SOLELY on the basis of the following paragraph. Each of the questions consists of two statements. Read the paragraph carefully, and then mark your answer

      A - if both statements are correct according to the information given in the paragraph

      B - if both statements are incorrect according to the information given in the paragraph

      C - if one statement is correct and one is incorrect according to the information given in the paragraph

      D - if the correctness or incorrectness of one or both of the statements cannot be determined from the information given in the paragraph.

The twentieth century has opened to women many pursuits from which they were formerly excluded and thus has given them new opportunities for crime. Can we assume that as a result of this development female crime will change its nature and become like masculine crime through losing its masked character? In periods of pronounced social stress, such as war, in which women assume many roles otherwise open only to men, experience indicates that crimes of women against property increase. Can we assume, further, that simultaneously the amount of undiscovered female crime decreases? Further study contradicts the validity of this assumption. Their new roles have become wage earners and household heads, but they have not stopped being the homemakers, the rearers of children, the nurses, or the shoppers. With the burden of their social functions increased, their opportunities for crime have not undergone a process of substitution so much as a process of increase.

12.   I. As women assumed increased social burdens, there was a marked change in the character of their opportunities for crime.   12.____
     II. Although the crimes committed by women have increased, they are still fewer in number than those committed by men.

13.   I. Male crime is less masked in character than female crime.   13.____
     II. The opportunities of women to commit crimes have increased in the last fifty years.

14.   I. In wartime, when they have increased employment opportunities, women commit fewer crimes against property.   14.____
     II. When the social equality of women increases, the number of undetected crimes which they commit decreases.

15.   I. In the period between 1900 and 1968, women did not gain many new opportunities for employment.   15.____
     II. In a family unit, the role of the shopper is traditionally that of the wife rather than that of the husband.

16.   I. The crime rate increases in periods of social stress, such as war.   16.____
     II. Because women have not wanted to be limited to their traditional roles of homemaker and rearer of children, they have sought social equality with men.

Questions 17-18.

DIRECTIONS: Questions 17 and 18 are to be answered SOLELY on the basis of the following passage.

The public has become increasingly aware that rehabilitation that great battle cry of prison reform is one of the great myths of 20th century penology. The hard truth is that punishment and retribution are the primary, if not the only, functions served by most correctional institutions. Courts can provide enlightened rule-making to assist prison reform and ombudsmen can give prisoners a forum to consider their complaints but the results would be limited. The corrections system will never run with any real efficiency until: (a) prisoners want to be reformed; (b) prison administrators want to help them reform; (c) courts want to help both toward a system of reform; and (d) they all define reform in the same way. If this is not done, the criminal justice system will continue to operate on the model of concentric layers of coercion, a grossly inefficient model.

17. According to the above passage, all of the following will be required in order to improve the corrections system EXCEPT   17._____

   A. commitment to reform by prison administrators
   B. development by penal experts of criteria for meaningful rehabilitation
   C. acceptance by prisoners of the need for their cooperation
   D. assistance by the courts in providing a system where reform is possible

18. According to the above selection, meaningful prison reform is MOST likely to result from   18._____

   A. the appointment of ombudsmen to replace the courts in ruling on prisoners' complaints
   B. coordination by sociologists of efforts to improve prison conditions
   C. a realization by society that rehabilitation of prisoners is no longer a realistic objective
   D. the joint efforts of those directly concerned and a common understanding of the goals to be achieved

Questions 19-25.

DIRECTIONS: Each of Questions 19 through 25 begins with a statement. Your answer to each of these questions MUST be based only upon this statement and not on any other information you may have.

19. At any given moment, the number of people coming out of prisons in the United States is substantially as great as the number entering them.
   Of the following, the MOST reasonable assumption on the basis of the preceding statement is that   19._____

   A. most prisoners in the United States prisons are recidivists
   B. the crime rate in this country is decreasing
   C. the crime rate in this country is increasing
   D. the prison population of this country is constant

20. The indeterminate sentence usually sets a lower limit for the time to be served, and an upper limit. In some cases, there is a maximum limit, but no minimum; in some, a minimum but no maximum; and in others, neither a maximum nor a minimum, the time to be served being determined by the prisoner's conduct and other considerations.
In the preceding statement, the one of the following which is NOT given as a characteristic of the indeterminate sentence is that

    A. sometimes the maximum time which must be served is not set at the time of sentence
    B. sometimes the minimum time which must be served is not set at the time of sentence
    C. the exact length of time to be served is fixed at the time of sentence
    D. the length of time to be served may vary with the prisoner's behavior

20._____

21. Overcrowding in a prison makes segregation of prisoners more difficult, complicates the maintenance of order and discipline, and endangers health and morals.
Of the following, the MOST reasonable assumption based on the preceding statement is that

    A. if prisoners are allowed to associate too freely their health and morals will be endangered
    B. in a prison that is not overcrowded there will not be any problems of order and discipline
    C. it is undesirable for the inmate population to exceed unduly the intended capacity of a prison
    D. segregation of prisoners is carried on mainly for the purpose of better prison administration

21._____

22. Most non-professional shoplifters are women of comfortable means who could buy the things they steal.
Of the following, the MOST valid conclusion which can be drawn from the preceding statement is that

    A. some well-to-do women are shoplifters
    B. most professional shoplifters are men
    C. few women practice shoplifting as a profession
    D. most shoplifters suffer from a mental ailment rather than from a moral deficiency

22._____

23. Since accomplices and instigators are harder to detect and successfully prosecute than overt perpetrators, most women offenders therefore escape punishment.
Of the following, the MOST valid conclusion which can be drawn from the preceding statement is that

    A. judges deal more leniently with female than with male offenders
    B. men who are accomplices or instigators of crimes are easier to detect and prosecute than women
    C. successful prosecution of women offenders depends to a large extent on their successful detection
    D. women are more often accomplices in, rather than actual perpetrators of, criminal acts

23._____

24. Through the juvenile court, the recognition of social responsibility in the delinquent acts   24.____
of an individual has been established.
The MOST accurate of the following statements on the basis of the preceding statement is that

   A. delinquent behavior is an evidence of an individual's social irresponsibility
   B. some individuals are responsible for their delinquent acts
   C. the juvenile court is evidence of society's willingness to assume some blame for
      the anti-social behavior of its younger members
   D. the juvenile court takes into consideration the age, social background, and offense
      of the individual before deciding upon his punishment

25. The way to win more offenders to lasting good behavior is to provide treatment to each   25.____
offender based on an understanding of the causes of his actions and of his emotional
needs in the light of modern insight into human nature. Of the following, the MOST valid
inference which can be drawn from the preceding statement is that

   A. few offenders are reformed today because they are not led to an understanding of
      the causes of their criminal actions
   B. individualized attention is required to achieve reform in criminals
   C. penologists have a better understanding of the causes of criminal behavior
      because of recent developments in the study of human nature
   D. unsolved emotional conflicts frequently result in criminal acts

KEY (CORRECT ANSWERS)

1. A		11. B	
2. B		12. D	
3. A		13. A	
4. C		14. B	
5. B		15. C	
6. C		16. D	
7. A		17. B	
8. C		18. D	
9. A		19. D	
10. D		20. C	

21. C
22. A
23. D
24. C
25. B

POLICE SCIENCE NOTES

BASIC CONCEPTS OF LAW AND ARREST

Man has been puzzling over the appropriateness of community controls throughout his recorded history and undoubtedly before that. What he has been trying to decide are the answers to: "Who is/are going to run the show." "Under what restrictions must authority operate?" and "What acts by community members shall be required or prohibited?" Basic to an understanding of the complexity of answers to these questions is an awareness of the variety of systems and laws under which various societies have lived and are living. At some time some community has lived under laws directly opposite to those under which we now control ourselves, and their requirements were "right" for that time and place. In fact, we can bring to mind examples of changes which have occurred in our own United States of America during its existence—even within our own lifetime. The requirements placed upon the members of any community by its government consist of laws which filter out by prevailing over others in the market place of ideas and which are manifested by their issuance through formal governmental organizations.

Every police officer should be aware of the fact that there is no law which has not been enacted in response to and for the purpose of correcting a problem which has become significant by the degree to which some members of the community have acted in opposition to the common belief. In short, where there is no meaningful opposition to the feelings of the majority there is no law in support of those beliefs. For example, cannibalism is not prohibited in the United States because opposition to it is so pervasive that it is reasonable to say that only the mentally ill have engaged in that gruesome activity.

Individuals and communities require guidelines defining acceptable conduct and reciprocal duties and responsibilities in order to attain feelings of tranquility, a sense of well being, and a belief that conformance to group requirements will result in the society's respect for and supply of individual needs in response. Basic to any society, primitive or modern, is the necessity for compliance with authority, the necessity for disciplined behavior, and the necessity for community tranquility. Each individual must relinquish his right to act entirely for his own self-interest in return for the agreement of others not to deprive him unduly of his right to personal freedom or to impinge upon his reciprocal rights under the law. Every requirement of law acts to some degree to reduce individual freedom of action, but reasonable restrictions on absolute freedom are essential to community living and to protect individuals against others. As the danger to any community belief increases so will the group response grow in severity to reduce that threat, especially when the common belief is basic and widely accepted without reservation.

Police officers are faced with daily frustration caused by their inability to understand clearly that the freedom-loving citizens of our Nation have learned from past experiences (some of which initiated our Nation's birth) that absolute authority demands rigid compliance with even the smallest and relatively unimportant requirement and results in stultifying repression of personal freedom. The ultimately efficient government can only be one in which power is so centralized that it is dictatorial and undemocratic. Therefore, laws have developed which restrict the police to that level of efficiency which is acceptable to the citizens and which permits the greatest possible individual freedom. Again, there is no law where there is no problem. Therefore, there should be little serious doubt that one of the highest duties of a police officer is to know and follow the law because it has been developed in answer to previously existing actions which were conducted in opposition to the beliefs of the people. Officials who are responsible for law enforcement must personify lawfulness as they interact with offenders. A peace officer is endowed with awesome power over life and property, and he must not only restrict his actions to those the law but also restrain himself personally to be considered a thoughtful, objective, police professional.

It is important that every police officer understands the basics of the checks and balances system under which we govern ourselves. Our forefathers so constructed our governmental system that none of the three branches of our government, the legislative, the executive, and the judicial, could become so strong that it would be able to dominate the people completely. The basic objective of this system is to prevent one or a few people from absolute control and overwhelming power. In its operation, the checks and balances system prevents domination by providing stumbling blocks in the paths of requirements which do not meet with the approval of the great majority of the citizens. Without considerable support, legislatures will not pass laws, the executive branch will not actively enforce them, and the courts will overturn them. However, those requirements which are backed by the great majority of the people are enacted by legislatures, enforced with great universality and vigor by the executive branch, and upheld by the courts.

The individual professional police officer understands the checks and balances system and acts within the law because of this knowledge. At the operational level, even though a patrol officer is aware of a problem he does not attempt to "enforce the law" when the legislature has not passed a statute dealing with it. He neither strains to fit the facts of an incident into another statute nor makes an arrest for an unrelated offense in order to harrass the "law breaker." At the executive level, the professional police administrator or agency head allocates the resources of his department according to

priorities so that enforcement of important offenses is emphasized. The accompanying spinoff is naturally the deemphasis of enforcement against those offenses which are determined to be of lesser importance. The term which applies to this assignment of priorities is *selective enforcement*.

Professional Demeanor

The appropriateness of the reasons for and the manner by which members of a community are deprived of their liberty is one of the most difficult problems to be solved by members of a society and its lawmakers. An arrest or detention is a matter of preventing the free movement of a person. In most cases what is more important to the person subject to this deprivation of liberty is the manner in which an arrest or detention is effected. There is a great difference between simply following the directions of another without the free will to do any other thing one might wish to do and that loss *plus* being searched, handcuffed, placed in obvious incarceration, and even being stripped of all clothing and dignity for the purpose of maximizing security. In fact, most people will understand the necessity of appropriate loss of liberty, but what makes them seriously upset is the public spectacle and loss of face which it can entail when improperly conducted, especially when the arresting officer shows personal antagonism toward the prisoner.

The professional officer balances the importance of each factor involved in an arrest situation. Although safety to himself, his fellow officers and the general public is very important, he is well aware that it is not always the most important factor. In fact, he knows that some persons will submit to an arrest quietly unless demeaning security precautions are utilized or personal antagonism is manifested by the arresting officer.[2]

[2]The use of psychological games, "loaded" words, gestures, and "body language" indicate one's true feelings. The sum or totality of these messages constitutes non-verbal communication, which is often the major influencing factor upon the feelings which exist between individuals who are experiencing personal interaction.

Unfortunately, the unprofessional officer often considers security and safety to be uppermost and controlling in nearly every case and is personally offended by lawbreakers. When these conditions prevail, arrested and detained persons are often subjected to such overwhelming threats to their psychological well being (or face) that they find it necessary to fight back against those who are creating the threat. In some cases their loss of face or distress is so great that they physically attack any person who obstructs their liberty and are willing to kill to escape rather than to suffer the public humiliation of detention or arrest. Therefore, the professional officer effects his detentions and arrests with circumspection and avoids excessive psychological distress to those being restricted. By making the arrest as easy as possible on the offender, the arresting officer also makes it as easy as possible on himself and his coworkers. The professional exerts his will over those whom he is arresting by the use of reasoning rather than his club. The officer who is involved in fights significantly more often than his coworkers, however, soon becomes well known and is avoided as a partner.

Persons usually react in three general ways to a police officer who is enforcing the law or is about to make an arrest. They may submit to his directions or the arrest without resistance. Such persons follow the directions of the officer because they believe that the officer is correct in what he is doing or they simply bow to the inevitable. The professional, skilled police officer will so conduct himself that the great majority of persons will react to his directions in this way.

Other persons may feel gravely threatened by the officer's actions and believe it necessary to attack, either verbally or physically, or flee. Whatever their action may be, it is an attempt to reduce the real or imagined threat to their physical or mental well being. Although the attack will usually be directed at the source of the threat, the officer, it may be against another person-an "innocent" third party. This is still an attempt to reduce their feelings of frustration, however, but the target will be an object or person who cannot "fight back." We have all witnessed examples of distressed persons who kick their cats, shout at their children, or drive their automobiles recklessly when frustrated. In fact, many times officers find themselves to be the "cat" whom it is necessary for the person to "kick" to compensate for a frustrating experience which occurred prior to the officer's arrival on the scene. The professional officer, because of his self confidence, is never threatened by verbal "cat kicking." He is able to control these excited persons through the use of his calm, professional, competent manner so that they soon begin to accept his directions. This same technique is usually effective with those offenders who are inclined towards physical attack. The experienced professional officer knows with reasonable accuracy those who cannot be dissuaded and with reasonable force acts to protect himself and others from physical attack.

The professional officer asks himself questions such as these: "This person is attacking me verbally, therefore, he (NOT I) is greatly threatened by somethingam I the threat, or is it something else?" "Is this attack going to be all talk, or will it turn into a physical attack?" "What can I do to reduce his feeling of distress?" The unprofessional reacts out of his own fear of the verbal attack, retaliates in kind, and the situation rapidly escalates into physical combat or the bringing of inappropriate charges out of spite. Invariably the result of retaliatory action by an officer who attacks to save his own face, no matter how poorly the offender may have acted to initiate the incident, is the salvation of the offender's conscience. This is because the offender will be able to say to himself that the officer attacked him, therefore, no matter what the offender has done, the officer has become the "bad guy" who is subject to all the blame-the "offensive cat," if you will.

The third reaction is that of ignoring or remaining unaffected by the threat. Persons who manifest this type of reaction are those who are secure, unconcerned, and believe that they truly are not endangered by the threat. They are convinced that those who are acting aggressively towards them cannot in fact harm them in any basic way. In every day language, this type of individual is called a person with "self confidence." It is this type of confidence that the professional police officer exhibits. It is a quiet confidence, as opposed to the blatant, pushy, aggressive, officious manner of those who are unsure of themselves and who try to make up for it with bluster, which is immediately recognizable as a lack of confidence.

Self confidence is the kind of attitude which makes it possible to exert one's will upon others while encountering the least resistance from them. The officer who exhibits this confidence brings the belief into the minds of those he is controlling that: "This officer will not ask anything of me which is not only lawful but also reasonable and necessary, and if I refuse to act in response to his requests, I will be not only unlawful but also unreasonable and appear foolish to others." On the other hand, if it is the person who is to be arrested who exhibits the self confidence, that person is the one who has the greatest chance of defeating the officer and taking over control of the situation. The officer who allows himself to be manipulated is in for a very uncomfortable experience. The danger to the officer is rarely that of physical attack, rather he will feel greatly threatened psychologically. He may begin to believe that he is appearing foolish and damaged in his self image (loss of face; receiving severe blows to his ego, etc.). Unless he retains his self control, he may well commit a rash or illegal act which can easily result in disciplinary action or a civil suit naming him and his department as defendants. But the experienced professional officer never loses during these encounters because:

He never presses or demands more than is absolutely necessary

Even though the law may empower him to do
more
He always acts within the law

And utilized it to accomplish its basic purpose,
not just technical requirements which were designed to accomplish some other objective.

His actions assure that his opponent becomes aware that:
What the officer requires is within the law
The full extent of the available powers are never utilized without full reason
The officer never acts out of personal vengeance

Professional Discretion

ONLY ROOKIES TRY TO ENFORCE ALL THE LAWS ALL THE TIME, AND ONLY ROOKIES CONFINE THEIR ENFORCEMENT ACTIVITY ALMOST EXCLUSIVELY TO AN ARREST. The experienced professional officer has learned that enforcement of some laws is best accomplished by simply being present and visible. Other laws can be enforced by a warning or an educationally oriented conversion with actual or potential offenders. There are certain laws which do require that offenders be processed through the criminal justice system by either a summons or physical arrest. In most jurisdictions, with rare exceptions, no officer is in fact required to arrest for an offense except when ordered to do so by a magistrate, either by the judge in person or under his written order in the form of a warrant.[3]

Criminal Law

A crime or an offense is an act or omission forbidden by law, prosecuted by the governmental officials of the jurisdiction, and punishable upon conviction. The statutes which define what acts or omissions are crimes or offenses must clearly state the

---

3 Administrative orders which require a particular type of enforcement action for specific offenses or offenders must be followed, however.

kind of conduct which is prohibited or required and designate the punishment which is to be applied to those adjudged guilty.

Each statute which defines a crime is constructed of elements or criteria which the prosecution must prove before a defendant may be found guilty of the charge. The words used in statutes each have very special and particular meaning under law, and an officer must be careful to be aware of these legal terms because definitions in law sometimes differ from the meanings they convey when used in informal or daily conversation. For example, larceny or theft involves the *taking* of the *personal property of another.* Each of the underlined words is an element of the offense, and they are not the only elements. The "thief has not taken if he has not gained possession, it is not personal property if it is an attachment to a house, and it is not another's if the thief is a part owner or the property has been abandoned. Furthermore, even if he does commit all those acts, he has not committed theft unless he intended to steal. For example, the acts were committed under his reasonable belief that the property was his. Also, no matter how fervent was his intention to steal, there cannot be a conviction where the item "stolen" was not subject to ownership which is protected by law, for example an illegal lottery ticket.

Detentions

Police officers are empowered to make detentions and arrests under appropriate restrictions. A detention is a temporary restriction of one's liberty during which the detaining person is permitted to make a short investigation for the purpose of determining whether or not the person detained is subject to arrest for an offense.[4] The authority and restrictions upon it which apply to this power of an officer are delineated by either court decisions or statutes, dependant upon the law which prevails within a particular

jurisdiction. This type of detention is generally referred to as "stop and frisk."[5] These three little words, however, have become the subject of thousands of pages of court decisions and statutes. This manual must cover the subject with just a few words, and readers should bear in mind that jurisdictions differ in what is permissible. Each officer should become well versed in the law on this subject as it is applied in his jurisdiction.

The stop and detention of a person is generally authorized when an officer has reasonable grounds for *suspecting* that the individual whom he intends to detain:

Has committed a crime
Is committing a crime
Ia about to commit a crime

Note that the facts on which the officer bases his stop and detention are less than those necessary for him to effect an arrest, and it is essential to his authority that the person to be detained must be suspected of criminal activity. An arrest requires that the officer has reasonable grounds for *believing* that the person has committed or is committing a crime, but a detention requires the officer to have reasonable grounds for *suspecting* involvement in criminal activity. Because the officer is possessed of information short of that required to make an arrest, he may not use deadly force to stop or detain the person.[6]

An important factor in the laws dealing with detentions is that of the duration which will be permitted. In jurisdictions where the courts have delineated the law on this subject, case law permits officers to detain persons a reasonable time. The duration permitted is determined by the relative

---

4 Detention is also used to describe the incarceration of an individual in a jail or other facility after being charged with an offense.

5 The officer's authority to stop and his right to frisk are separate and distinct. In fact, in the majority of cases the officer will not have the right to frisk the person detained.

6 Of course, if the person resists by the use of deadly force the officer may respond with deadly force in self defense.

importance of permitting the officer time necessary to ascertain whether or not the person has committed a crime and the loss of freedom suffered by the person detained. Each case is decided on its own facts. Where statutes control, legislatures either permit a reasonable time, similar to court holdings, or specifically limit the duration, varying from ten minutes to two hours. Under both case law and statutes, however, an officer in every jurisdiction is required to release the person immediately after he has determined that the person has not committed a crime. Where the duration is limited to a specified time period, when the time limit has expired the officer must either arrest the person for a crime or immediately release him, even though with more time to investigate the officer might have been able to develop sufficient information to effect an arrest.

Another critical difference among the various jurisdictions is the right of the officer to transport the person detained during the course of the investigation. In some jurisdictions the officer is not permitted to remove the person from the place at which the detention was initiated. In areas where it is permitted, the transportation must be conducted only when it is reasonably necessary for the purpose of investigating the possible criminal involvement of the person detained, and unless the investigation results in the person's arrest he should be returned to the place from which he was removed. The officer may ask any pertinent question of the person detained, for example his name, an explanation of what he is doing or where he is going, the ownership of any property in his possession, etc., but the officer must constantly remain aware that the person detained is under *no* obligation to answer *any* question. The detained individual may remain absolutely silent during the whole period of detention, is under no obligation to produce any identification or other property for the officer's inspection, and the officer

has no right to take *anything* from the person except a weapon.[7]

Frisks

The frisk is a very limited search which may be conducted by an officer who has detained a person. It may be performed only when the officer:

Knows that the person has a weapon in his immediate possession

Reasonably suspects that the person has a weapon in his immediate possession.

Note that the frisk is for weapons only, and that the officer must be able to state the facts which caused the development of his belief that the person possessed a weapon. The frisk:

Must be only for the purpose of locating the weapon

Must be initially restricted to touching or grasping only the *outer* clothing of the individual

May be continued inside the outer clothing, pockets, etc., only after the officer has felt something which reasonably causes him to believe that a weapon is contained within.

If the officer finds a weapon he may remove it from the person's possession. If the possession of the weapon on the part of the person constitutes a crime the officer may arrest for that offense and retain the weapon as evidence. If the person is not

---

7 Refusal to identify oneself or being passively uncooperative makes the investigation more difficult and in some jurisdictions will extend the permitted duration of the detention, but the person commits no offense.

Exceptions would be circumstances under which the person detained is performing some activity or possesses something which is subject to licensing. For example, driving an auto-mobile, in which case the officer has the right to demand the person's driver's license and vehicle registration. Refusal to product these items upon demand is a crime which subjects the person to arrest, but prior to effecting the arrest the officer has no right to search for or take these items.

arrested the officer shall return the weapon at the end of the detention.[8]

Arrests

An arrest is the deprivation of one's liberty by another for the purpose of initiating the arrested person's processing through the justice system, usually the criminal justice system. An arrest must be made in compliance with the restrictions which surround such an action. Otherwise it is considered a false arrest and will cause the loss of the admissibility of any resulting evidence and possible loss of a conviction. The arresting officer may also possibly be subject to a suit for civil damages and be charged with a crime. An "arrest"" which is made without the intention of processing the party into or through the justice system would be kidnapping within the statutes of most jurisdictions. Arrests can be made either under the authority of an arrest warrant or with out a warrant, and the arresting person can be either a police officer or a person.[9]

An arrest involves the following elements:

---

[8]If the person has a right to possess the weapon generally but committed the offense by the facts existing at the time, for example carrying a handgun concealed without a permit, the officer may return the weapon if the person ceases to commit the offense. Under the aforementioned facts, if the person continues on his way while carrying the handgun openly. However, if the weapon is contraband, i.e., he is prohibited from possessing the weapon under any circumstances, the officer should retain the weapon for the purpose of turning it in to the police department for eventual destruction. Examples of contraband weapons are switchblades, brass knuckles, sling shot, sword canes, machineguns, explosive and gas grenades, etc.

[9] An arrest made by a person is usually called a "citizen's arrest," but it is not required that the person be a citizen of the United States of America. There is no age requirement to be met by the person; juveniles and even children may effect an arrest. Police officers have no immunity from arrest, although they need not give up their weapons except to another officer.

1. The arresting party "intends" to take the arrested person into custody. Although in most cases the arresting party's actual intention is to take the person into custody, and the best way to express this is by stating words such as, "You are under arrest for...," courts determine the intention from all the defend himself from false arrest liability by simply claiming that he had no intention to arrest.

2. The arresting party acts under the belief that he has legal authority. If the arresting party is correct in his belief the arrest is valid, but if he actually does not have the authority it is an illegal arrest. Examples of lack of authority would be arrests made under a void or nonexistent warrant, even though the officer had been informed that there was a warrant, and arresting for a misdemeanor not committed in his presence, if this is not permitted in his jurisdiction.

3. The arresting party gains custody and control of the arrested person. An arrest is not complete until the arrested person comes within the custody and control of the arresting party, and this state exists when either the person submits or his resistance is overcome. It is not necessary that the person be touched or that any force be applied if he understands that he is in the power of the arresting person and submits to control; that his liberty is restrained is sufficient. On the other hand, if the officer's words "You are under arrest for .. ." are immediately followed by the suspect's running away there has been no arrest. In fact, unless the flight includes some physical contact or the application of force between the suspect and the

arresting party, the flight does not constitute resisting arrest.[10]

An arrest warrant is an order of a court directing police officers to arrest and bring before the court the person named in the warrant.[11] If it is practicable an officer should obtain a warrant before making an arrest. The basic purpose served by the warrant process is to protect persons from unjustified arrests and prosecutions. The warrant is one of the manifestations of the checks and balances system in that a member of the judicial branch
passes upon the legitimacy of actions intended by the executive branch. Given the same circumstances or facts known to an officer, if he arrests after obtaining a warrant the courts will in all probability sustain the arrest, but if he arrests without one his action will be much more closely scrutinized for probable cause.

Following are common requirements for a valid arrest warrant:

1. Probable cause.

The magistrate issuing the warrant must make an impartial judgment on the basis of the evidence presented that probable cause exists that a crime has been committed by the person to be arrested. Probable cause is more than mere suspicion on the part of the officer requesting the warrant, but he is not required to present proof beyond a reasonable doubt of the person"s guilt. Information supplied by informants may be used, even if their identity is not disclosed, but officers must be able to state facts which indicate the probable reliability of such information which they have not acquired through their own observation.

2. Affidavit supported by oath or affirmation. Some person must swear to his belief in the truth of the statements contained in the affidavit.

3. Person particularly described.

The description must be such that the officer serving the warrant is supplied with information sufficient for him to believe with reasonable certainty that the person whom he is about to arrest is the person described. Ordinarily the warrant includes the name of the person, but sometimes this is not known. In such cases a physical description, occupation or place of employment, residence address or other information may be utilized to particularly describe the person.

4. Nature of the offense.

Although the language need not describe the offense with the same detail as in an indictment or information, it must be sufficient to inform the person of the subject of the accusation.

5. Officers designated.

The warrant may direct an individual officer or a class of officers to arrest the person. For example, the warrant may be addressed to all police officers in the state.

6. Issued in the name of the jurisdiction.

Warrants must be issued either in the name of the state under which the issuing magistrate's authority exists or in the name of the United States when issued by a federal official.

7. Signed by the issuing official.

Only an official authorized by law may sign a warrant, and he must be a neutral and impartial person, a magistrate or judicial officer.

Requirements to be followed in serving a warrant:

1. Person serving warrant must be named in it. Either the officer or person serving the warrant must be specifically named in the warrant or he must be within the class of persons designated.

2. Must be served within the jurisdiction.

A warrant issued in one state may not be served in another unless the second state has authorized this service by statute. An officer in the second state may arrest if he has knowledge of the warrant's issuance, however, his knowledge constituting the rea-

---

[10] Flight in a motor vehicle is a crime in most jurisdictions, however, because of the extreme hazards involved in such actions.

[11] Most warrants are directed only to police officers. A private person can arrest under the authority of a warrant only if he is specifically named in it.

sonable grounds for his belief that a felony has been committed by the person.

3. Officer make known his purpose.

Unless the information will imperil the arrest or the person flees or resists before the officer can convey his intention, the officer must inform the person of his intention to arrest and the cause for it.

4. Show the warrant or inform person it exists. Under common law the officer must possess the warrant and show it to the person if he demands it, but most modern codes have relaxed this requirement under the needs of today's society. However, the officer's belief in the existence of the warrant must be reasonable, and it shall be shown to the person as soon as practicable if he so requests.

Arrests can be made without a warrant by both officers and private persons. The authority of a police officer is more extensive, but not as much so as most people believe.

1. Both an officer and a private person can arrest for a felony committed in their presence and for a felony which has actually been committed but not in their presence.[12]

2. An officer can arrest for a felony which he reasonably believes has been committed by the individual to be arrested, even though the crime has not been committed, but a private person may not. Stated in another way, the officer is protected if he makes a reasonable mistake, but the private person is not.

3. In all jurisdictions an officer can arrest for a misdemeanor which is committed in his presence, but in some jurisdictions a private person may not.

4. In some jurisdictions an officer may arrest for a misdemeanor not committed in his presence when he has reasonable cause to believe that it has been committed by the suspect, but a private person may not do so in any jurisdiction.

The Constitution, statutes, and court decisions refer to the necessity of the "reasonable cause" and "probable cause" which must exist before the authority to arrest arises. This degree of proof, evidence, or information to be possessed by the officer who intends an arrest must be more than good faith suspicion (enough to effect a detention for investigation), but it need not be proof beyond a reasonable doubt of the person's guilt. The reasonable cause is determined as of the time the arrest is effected. Evidence acquired after the arrest may not be utilized to validate a preceding arrest. In fact, if the arrest is not based on probable cause that evidence will be excluded no matter how condemning and conclusive it might have been in proving the defendant's guilt.

The standards by which an officer's reasonable cause to arrest is ascertained is determined individually for each case. That is, the information in his possession and its relationship to the development of probable cause in his mind (as opposed to a reasonable man test) in the light of his personal experience and the circumstances of the case before the court will all be considered by the court in arriving at its holding that there was or was not probable cause to arrest. Actions which do not attract the attention of untrained or inexperienced persons or officers may convince the experienced and trained officer that a particular offense is being committed. This experience may include not only the activity but also the person performing it. An officer who knows of the past criminal record of a suspect may consider that history along with other facts in developing reasonable cause, but the officer may not arrest on only the basis of one's previous criminal record.

12 An offense may be a felony in one jurisdiction and a misdemeanor in another. Generally a crime punishable by either death or imprisonment in a state prison is a felony, and most states do not provide for imprisonment in their state prisons for terms of less than one year. The laws in each jurisdiction should be consulted, and if the statute declares that the offense is a felony or punishment is death or imprisonment in the state prison the offense is a felony.

10

The following are sources which can develop reasonable cause to arrest for the officer:

1. Complaints from victims and information from witnesses.

Statements and information received which indicate that a crime has been committed and which provide evidence by which the offender can be ascertained by developing reasonable cause to arrest. An officer must bear in mind that if the crime complained of is less than a felony no arrest will be valid unless a warrant is first issued, unless their jurisdiction is one in which officers are permitted to arrest for misdemeanors on reasonable cause. But if the jurisdiction is one in which private persons can arrest for misdemeanors, the victim or a witness can make the arrest and turn the prisoner over to the officer.

2. Information from an informant.

The reliability of the informant is an important factor. An officer should maintain records on the cases in which the particular informant's information has proven to be accurate, and whenever possible the officer should make further investigation to determine that the information is correct prior to making his arrest without a warrant.

3. Observation of the officer.

When the officer witnesses the actual commission of the crime there is reasonable grounds to arrest without serious question. But when his observations lead him to a reasonable suspicion only, then he must first detain until his investigation leads to reasonable cause to arrest. When all the circumstances lead the officer to the reasonable belief that a felony has been committed he may arrest under his reasonable belief in any jurisdiction, but for a misdemeanor only if his jurisdiction permits that type of arrest. An officer can always obtain a warrant and effect the arrest later for the misdemeanor.

4. Physical evidence.

Fingerprints, identification dropped at the scene of the crime, footprints leading from the scene of the crime to the place of apprehension, and other physical evidence closely tying the suspect to the crime would be sufficient to give rise to reasonable cause to arrest.

5. Information received from the officer's department or from another agency.

Information received over the police radio, at briefings, or from wanted circulars or lists may form the basis for reasonable cause, however, persons initiating these messages must have reasonable cause for doing so.

CITATION/SUMMONS PROCESS

The processing of offenders into the justice system is ordinarily begun when he is contacted by the police. At this point the person may be "physically" arrested and taken to jail or other place of detention to await his appearance before the court. Very few defendants want to spend time in jail, and the purpose of such incarceration is only to assure the appearance of the defendant before the magistrate.[13] Originally, under our criminal law, incarceration to await court appearance was the only process utilized no matter what the degree of the offense. Beginning with the widespread use of the automobile and the numerous offenses committed by motorists, spurred by the growth of more liberal feelings toward offenders by both the general community and persons involved in the administration of justice, and because of the great savings in time and money which the method causes, written notification to an offender of the charge to be made and the time and place to appear before a magistrate has now become prevalent. Commonly called "a ticket," the citation or summons process is now not only used universally for traffic code offenses but has expanded to include many other types as well, such as theft, assault,

---

[13] Although the only purpose under law is to assure appearance in court, jailing is often utilized to serve other purposes. For example, detention of persons likely to harm themselves or others, detention to prevent obvious offenders from committing further crimes, and detention to provide additional time in which to conduct an investigation. In practice this is usually accomplished by setting bail too high for the defendant to meet.

battery, a variety of regulatory statutes, and other misdemeanor offenses. Whenever possible or permitted an officer should use this process.

The "ticket" procedure can proceed in three ways, an arrest followed by release, a detention followed by release, or the delivery of a notice of charges to be filed to the person charged. Although definitions differ somewhat, the citation process is that which involves an arrest by an officer followed by the offender's signing on the citation that he promises to appear in court at the time indicated, at which time he is given a copy of the citation and released from arrest. The defendant's signature and promise is his "bail". Should he fail to appear he commits an offense which is separate from that of the original charge. The offender may refuse to sign the citation, but if he chooses to exert this right the officer is required to incarcerate him.

In jurisdictions in which the summons process is utilized, the offender is detained (not arrested) for a period necessary for the officer to determine the defendant's identity and write the summons, a copy is given to the person (he is not required to take it), and he is then released from detention. The suspect is not required to sign the summons, he commits no offense if he does not appear, and upon his non-appearance the court simply issues a warrant of arrest for the charge made.[14]

The notice process involves leaving a written notice to be discovered by the person to be charged or otherwise delivering such notice, for example by mail. The vast majority of cases in which this process is used involves parking offenses, but it can also be utilized for many other offenses. Whether the person receives the notice or not, the charge is filed before the court, and if the defendant does not appear as directed in the notice an arrest warrant will be issued by the court. Each officer must be aware of the law concerning these processes in his area because in many jurisdictions numerous offenses have been required by statutes and departmental regulations to be so handled. Therefore, an officer who incarcerates a person who is entitled under law or departmental regulation to be offered a citation or summons will be subject to prosecution, civil suit, and/or disciplinary action.

___

14 Of course, the defendant who deliberately fails to appear cannot reasonably expect the judge to be pleased, but he can reasonably expect little consideration from the court if its finding on the charge is "guilty."

POLICE SCIENCE NOTES

FORCE, SEARCH, AND SEIZURE

Use of Force

The right to use force against another varies according to the reasonable and apparent necessity that it be applied. The most important factors considered in the determination of how much force may be used by an officer are the following:

1. Is the force used or contemplated essential, or could the actor reasonably foresee that less force would be sufficient?

2. Does the crime to be prevented or the arrest to be attempted involve a felony or misdemeanor?

3. Does the act or crime to be prevented by force endanger property rights or human life and limb, and to what extent?

4. What are the responsibilities under law between the actor and what or whom he is attempting to protect with force?

5. Do departmental regulations restrict officers to less force than that permitted by statutes and court decisions?

When necessary, a police officer is permitted to use force in the performance of his duty to accomplish the following objectives:

1. To preserve the peace, prevent commission of offenses, or prevent suicide or self-inflicted injury.

2. To make *lawful* arrests and searches, to overcome resistance to such arrests and searches, and to prevent escapes from custody.

3. To defend himself or another against unlawful violence to his person or property.

4. To interrupt an intrusion on or interference with the lawful possession of property.

Lawful force is an aggressive act committed by a police officer in the performance of his duty when it is necessary to accomplish any of the objectives listed above. Deadly force is that which under the prevailing circumstances is capable of or intended to cause death or great bodily injury. Although lawful, or necessary, force is ti *minimum* amount sufficient to achieve a legitimate poh objective, this does not mean that an officer is permitted to escalate the force he uses without limit until the police objective is accomplished. For example, it would be illegal and immoral for an officer to use deadly force to prevent a person from unlawfully interfering with or even destroying anothers personal property such as an automobile, even if under the circumstances, shooting the person would be the only way the destruction could be stopped.

Deadly force may be used to prevent a felony which threatens the life or safety of a person. However, when the felony does not involve such danger, the tendency of the law among jurisdictions to prohibit such extreme measures is steadily growing. Even in those jurisdictions in which the statutes and court cases continue to permit deadly force to be used to prevent felonies in which life is not endangered police departments are prohibiting it through their policies and regulations.

Once a crime has been committed the chief law enforcement interest is the apprehension of the offender. Although laws vary, deadly force may generally be used to effect the arrest of a dangerous criminal who is endangering or has threatened human life, but this amount of force may not be used on a thief no matter how much he stole. No jurisdiction punishes theft with the death penalty, so no officer should apply "capital punishment" to a thief.[1]

---

[1] It is still permissible in some jurisdictions to apply deadly force when necessary to effect the arrest of any felon, and some jurisdictions have even enacted such laws recently. See Florida Statutes 776.05, 051, 1975, Nevada Revised Statutes 200.140, 1975.

In no jurisdiction is deadly force permitted to effect an arrest for a misdemeanor. If the subject resists, the officer may escalate the amount of his force until it becomes deadly if this is necessary to protect himself from death or great bodily injury, and the officer is not required to retreat. However, the use of deadly force is not justified to apprehend a misdemeanant even though he is in flight and there is no other way to capture him.

The right of self-defense is based on the necessity of permitting a person who is attacked to take reasonable steps to prevent harm to himself. This right permits him to use any reasonable force to prevent threatened harm, offensive bodily contact or confinement. Since it is a defense to a charge or accusation of use of force, the burden is on the actor to show the facts which caused him to use force and that it was reasonable.

The privilege to act to defend oneself arises not only when the danger is real but even when the danger does not in fact exist, providing that the belief in the presence and degree of danger is reasonable. For example, if after a long, high speed, wild and reckless attempt on the part of a motorist to escape an officer the offender stops, leaps from his car and whips his hand inside his jacket, it would be reasonable for the officer to believe that he was about to be fired upon. It would be lawful use of deadly force for the officer to draw and fire his sidearm at the offender even if, in fact, the motorist was unarmed and reaching for only his wallet and driver license. The belief that he is threatened, however, must be that which a reasonable man would have under the circumstances. The person defending himself is not required to restrain himself with outstanding bravery, but on the other hand the reasonable man standard does not permit an abject coward to attack when there is no reasonable ground for his belief that he is in danger.

If force is continued after an attacker is disarmed, defeated, helpless, or the danger has passed, it is unlawful. No matter how gross the provocation had been on the part of the original attacker, there is no right to continue the use of force for revenge or punishment.

No officer should possess or use any weapon or incapacitating device which is neither issued nor approved by his department, including the ammunition in his firearm. Naturally, issued or approved weapons which have been materially altered to increase the force which they may apply should also not be possessed or used.

Under normal circumstances only the methods or weapons listed below should be used to apply force. It is the officers responsibility to first exhaust every reasonable means of employing lesser force before escalating to a more severe application of force. The following methods are listed in ascending order from the least severe to the most drastic:

1. Physical strength and skill.
2. Approved noxious substance, mace, gas, etc.
3. Approved baton, sap, or blackjack.
4. Approved sidearm or other firearm loaded with approved ammunition.

Weapons should never be brandished or displayed as a threat unless their use under the circumstances would be reasonable and lawful.

Only those security devices or measures issued or approved by the department should be used to restrain those in custory, and the devices and measures should be used reasonably and only for the purpose of preventing:

1. Escape
2. Destruction of evidence
3. Attack
4. Self-inflicted injury
5. Commission of an offense

An officer who, out of anger or for the purpose of inflicting punishment or pain, cinches handcuffs too tightly, places a person in s straight jacket, strips a prisoner naked, puts an offender into a padded cell, incarcerates an offender with others who may attack him, or continues security measures when they are no longer reasonably necessary is acting unlawfully and reprehensibly.[2] It is the responsibility of the courts to punish, not the police.

The decision of an officer to use handcuffs or not is a difficult one. Opinions on this subject vary among experienced, professional officers. Where departmental regulations have been issued which state the circumstances under which handcuffs shall, may or must not be utilized they should be followed. However, because of the difficulty involved in covering all the possible situations in a regulation, they have not been written for officers guidance in many agencies. The officer must then utilize his professional discretion.

The officer who decides whether or not to use handcuffs on the basis of his answer to, "If I were this prisoner, would I realize or could I be lead to understand that handcuffs are reasonable and necessary?" will arrive at the appropriate conclusion. An officer who states that "I handcuff everybody I arrest," does not, it is to be hoped, really do so. It is obviously ridiculous to handcuff "little oP ladies" and small children without exception. On the other hand, the officer who fails to restrain dangerous felons, persons in a state of rage, or others who can be reasonably expected to do any of the acts which security measures are designed to prevent certainly should be handcuffed.

An officer who fails to use his cuffs when it is appropriate endangers himself, his coworkers, the prisoner and others.[3]

---

[2] An officer who deliberately deprives a person of his constitutional rights violates 18 U.S.C. 242, a federal criminal statute. Intentional unnecessary violence has been held to deprive a prisoner of the right to due process before punishment. United States v. Stokes, 506 F.2d 771, 1975.

[3] Officers have been killed and injured by children of astonishingly tender ages. The ability to accurately determine from the circumstances, including nonverbal communications and body language, the inclinations of persons contacted is an important skill to be developed by every officer.

Persons who are restrained by security devices are helpless, and officers must remain constantly aware of the possibility that such prisoners may be injured or suffer needlessly if precautions are not utilized. Therefore, secured persons must not be left unattended unnecessarily or otherwise subjected to needless danger or discomfort. The variety of possible situations to be avoided are too numerous to mention, but two must be. Prisoners should never be handcuffed to a vehicle which is used to transport them. If the vehicle is involved in an accident they cannot be removed from it if the officer is incapacitated or otherwise incapable of releasing them. It is appropriate to restrain handcuffed prisoners with safety belts because anybody can release the belts. However, if the person is handcuffed to the vehicle, only an officer can provide the key to the cuffs. Prisoners who indicate that they need to relieve themselves must be permitted to do so as soon as possible. The officer who refuses to permit his prisoner to use toilet facilities or to aid the nauseated person who must vomit is inflicting cruel and unusual punishment upon him.

Search and Seizure*

The most important factor relating to the law of search and seizure, and what each officer should seriously consider before he begins any search for or collection of evidence, is that WHENEVER POSSIBLE A SEARCH WARRANT SHOULD BE OBTAINED BEFORE SEARCHING FOR OR SEIZING EVIDENCE.

Both State and federal constitutions guarantee to everybody protection against unreasonable searches and seizures. This protection extends to their person, houses, papers and other property. No search warrant may be issued without probable cause, supported by oath or affirmation, and every warrant must

---

*For a thorough discussion of current issues in search and seizure law see Israel, *Legislative Regulation of Searches and Seizures: The Michigan Proposals,* 73 Mich. L. Rev. 222 (1975).

particularly describe the place to be searched and the persons or things to be seized.[4]

The protection given by the Fourth Amendment arose from the unpleasant experiences suffered by colonial Americans when searches by English soldiers were conducted under the authority of "writs of assistance" or "general warrants" These writs and warrants were issued with little restraint, without probable cause, and empowered authorities to conduct searches virtually any place on the mere suspicion that goods subject to seizure might be discovered.

The words of the Fourth Amendment must be interpreted by the courts so that the meaning of the law can be applied to the fact situations of each case presented. Thousands of cases have defined "person" "houses" "probable cause" "search" and other words which appear in the Amendment.

Although persons subjected to unlawful searches and seizures have recourse to civil actions against officials who violate their rights,[5] the most common procedure by which they protect themselves is through the application of the exclusionary evidence rule. The exclusionary rule is simply that evidence

obtained by unreasonable searches and seizures will not be admitted upon trial, usually upon objection raised by the defendant at a pre-trial "suppression hearing." The rule is not provided for in the Constitution, rather it was developed by the courts as their solution to the means by which the provision of the Amendment would be enforced not adopt it. Today, however, it is universally applied in both federal and state courts because of the holding of the Supreme Court of the United Stated in the case of Mapp v. Ohio in 1961.[6] The purpose to be fulfilled by the rule is that officers will be deterred from illegally searching for or seizing evidence when they know that it cannot be used against the defendant to prove his guilt.7

Search Warrants

A search warrant is an order written in the name of the State, signed by a judicial officer in the proper exercise of his authority, directing a sheriff, constable, or other officer to search a specified place for evidence, stolen property or other "fruits" of a crime, or contraband, and to bring the articles enumerated before the court if they are discovered.

The following are criteria or requirements which must be met before a valid search warrant may be issued:

1. *Probable Cause*

If the facts in the affidavit are sufficient to lead a reasonable and prudent man to believe that a crime has been committed and that the articles described can be found at the place specified, then issuance of a search warrant is justified.[8] Information received by an officer from an undisclosed

[4]The Fourth Amendment to the Constitution reads: "The right of the people to be secure in their persons, houses, papers, and effects against unreasonable searches and seizures, shall not be violated, and no Warrants shall issue, but upon probable cause, supported by Oath or affirmation, and particularly describing the place to be searched, and the persons or things to be seized." The protection provided is both to the person, restricting arrests and detentions, and to his property, restricting searches for and seizures of things.

[5]42 U.S.C. 1983 allows a civil suit for damages when a person acting under color of state law deprives another person of "any rights, privileges, or immunities secured by the Constitution and laws." See *Monroe* v. *Pope,* 365 U.S. 167, 1961.

[6]*Mapp v. Ohio,* 367 U.S. 643 (1961). The federal courts have operated under the exclusionary rule since *Weeks* v. *United States,* 232 U.S. 383 (1914).

[7] Other common law courts, such as the English, have not adopted the exclusionary rule.

[8]For an often quoted discussion of probable cause see *Brinegar v. United States,* 338 U.S. 160, 1949.

informant may be used as the basis for a search warrant, but the applicant for the warrant must be able to give the judicial officer substantial reasons to support the probable validity of the information which has been provided. The underlying circumstances upon which the applicant bases his belief must be specified by him. It is not sufficient to merely state, even with fervor, the police officers belief. The facts of which he is aware which led to the development of that belief must also be stated.[9]

2. *Oath or Affirmation*

If this requirement is not fulfilled, the evidence obtained will not be admitted. The presumption that the magistrate had sworn the applicant is rebuttable by the defendant, and if no oath was administered the warrant is invalid and the evidence will be lost (excluded).

3. *Particular Description of Place and Things*

Whatever the wording to describe the place to be searched, the objective to be served is that the officers who are commanded to conduct the search will not, if they follow the description included in the warrant, search the wrong premises and disturb the rights of the innocent. If the warrant does not identify the property to be seized, it will not justify any seizure of that property. Contraband such as prohibited arms, explosive devices, and gambling equipment will ordinarily not be required to be as specifically described as stolen goods, since contraband is S3izable by any officer lawfully observing it. When warrants are obtained for contraband the best description possible under the circumstances should always be attempted.

4. *Issuing Official*

The purpose served by requiring warrants is to assure that the innocent will not be disturbed by uncontrolled and unreasonable actions of officials of the executive branch of government. Therefore, the impartial and objective consideration by the judiciary of the probable cause and the reasonableness of the contemplated action is interposed as a restraint. Attempts to bypass this objective, even to accomplish other well founded purposes such as the efficient issuance of warrants, have generally been found unconstitutional by the courts.[10]

5. *Property Subject to Seizure*

Under early law, only stolen property could be seized under a search warrant. However, types of articles subject to seizure have been greatly expanded. Limitations still exist in some states such as requiring that only stolen or embezzled property (fruits of the crime), articles used to commit the crime (instrumentalities), or articles which are prohibited or controlled by statutes (contraband) may be seized. Such restrictions prevent officers from taking objects which are important as evidence, such as shoes worn by a suspect which could be compared with footprints found at the scene, but which fail to meet the definition of statutory restrictions. The United States Supreme Court in *Warden v. Hoyden* held in 1967,[11] that statutes which permitted search warrants to issue for "mere evidence" are constitutional. It is up to those states which still follow the old rule to change their statutes or court decisions to permit seizure of evidence, but they are not

[9] The so-called Spinnelli-Aguilar rule was formulated in *Spinelli v. United States,* 394 U.S. 410, 1969, and *Aquilar v. Texas,* 378 U.S. 108, 1964.

[10] Efficiencies are clearly possible within this requirement. California and Arizona allow officers to secure search warrants by phonw, making it possible in some areas to get 65% of all warrants in under one hour and most of the rest within two hours. Miller, "Telephonic Search Warrants: The San Diego Experience," 9 *The Prosecutor* 385, 1974.

[11] 387 U.S. 294, 1967.

required to do so.

Only those items specified in the warrant may be seized. If other property is seized it must be under authority other than that provided by the warrant.

6. *Execution Only By Those Ordered*

A search warrant may only be executed by those commanded by it to act, but the person designated may be specifically by either name or class (peace officers, for example). The person designated may be assisted by others, however.[12]

7. *Time Limit*

A search warrant must be executed within a reasonable time or it will fail to meet constitutional requirements. The amount of time which is reasonable varies, of course, according to the circumstances of each case. Most jurisdictions have by statute limited the time in which a search warrant may be executed, and the permissible period varies from a number of hours to more than a week. Some jurisdictions require special judicial authorization for warrants to be served at night.

8. *Prior Notice, Demand, and Forcible Entry*

If the local law allows and the warrant is for the seizure of items which can be destroyed quickly or if officers are aware of facts which reasonably lead them to believe notice to occupants would lead to danger of attack, entry may usually be effected without notice. Otherwise they are first required to notify persons within the premises of their identity and right to enter and make a demand that they be permitted to enter. Reasonable and necessary force may be used to effect entry when officers must act quickly to avoid evidence destruction or

attack, or if they are denied entry after notice has been given and their demand had been refused. Force may also be used to enter unoccupied premises or when the denial is passive, for example, when occupants remain silent and do not open the door.

Warrantless Searches and Seizures

Three factors have influenced and caused the development of those laws under which warrantless searches are permitted. They are permitted and lawful:
1. By consent
2. When necessity or emergency require immediate action
3. Where no right to protection exists

Consent Searches

A general principle of law is that one can waive any right or privilege to which he is entitled. However, because rights and privileges have arisen from previously experienced problems, courts observe very carefully the evidence presented in support of contentions that a defendant consented to a search.

Consent must be voluntary, the prosecution has the burden of proving consent clearly, and some sort of positive action by the person waiving must be shown.[13] For example, unless the person positively states his consent or makes some clearly understood gesture, the consent will not be held to be voluntary.

The search cannot extend beyond that granted by the terms of the consent in either area or time. That is, consent to search a room will not permit other rooms or the whole house to be searched, and the person may stop the search at any time simply by revoking his consent.[14]

---

[12] Nonfederal officers should always be assisted by federal officers when serving a search warrant based on probable cause for a search relating to a strictly federal crime. United States v. Townsend, 394 F.Supp. 736, 1975

[13] See *Schneckloth v. Bustamonte,* 412 U.S. 218, 1973.

[14] Some states hold otherwise, that once given, consent cannot be withdrawn, but the trend of cases is that searches must stop immediately upon any revocation.

7

The person consenting must have the capacity to do so. A person who has the right to possess premises or things may give consent, but others may not. For example, the occupant of a hotel room may consent to its search but not the management;[15] a parent can consent to a search of a minor childs room but not that of an adult child if the room is exclusively that childs, although permission to search areas used in common by the family is valid; a minor childs consent is unlikely to be held valid, but an adult child can consent to a search of at least jointly used areas; a spouse can consent if the premises are occupied by both spouses; and a person caring for the personal property of another may permit search of it.[16]

Immediate Action Required

The most prevalent situations under which this exception is granted are searches made incident to a lawful arrest. Necessity is the motivating factor in permitting these searches. The two purposes served are to protect the arresting officer from attack and to prevent the person from access to things which would facilitate his escape, and to assure that evidence will not be destroyed by the defendant.[17]

Should any of the following criteria not be met the evidence discovered will be excluded:

1. The arrest must be lawful.
2. The search must be made for the purposes listed above (protection, security, evidence).

* An arrest for an unlicensed vehicle, to be followed by a citation, may not be the basis for a search for drugs as there is no relationship between the offense and the purpose of the search.

3. The arrest must not be a sham or subterfuge made only to initiate a search not based on reasonable cause.[18]

* An arrest warrant sworn out by officers (who merely suspect a burglary by the subject) charging the defendant with spitting on the sidewalk for the purpose of gaining entrance to his residence when they execute it-evidence of the burglary would be excluded.

Both the area searched and the time during which the search will be permitted are limited. Officers may make a reasonable search of areas within the persons reach or the distance through which he might be able to quickly leap in order to obtain a weapon for attack or evidence to destroy. Searching for evidence during an arrest beyond this area is no longer permitted without a search warrant.[19] The search must be made contemporaneously with the arrest. After the subject has been removed from the scene and/or confined in jail the necessity of immediate action no longer prevails, and the officer must obtain a search warrant to search the area of the arrest.[20] An arrestees person may be immediately fully searched, as opposed to a mere pat-down for weapons, incident to an arrest for which he is actually being taken into custody, or the search may be delayed until booking.[21]

[18] Of course, if an officer can point to facts which, in the light of his experience, lead to the reasonable inference that the person whom he has stopped for a traffic offense is armed, he may search for the weapon to protect himself, *Terry v. Ohio*, 392 U.S. 88, 1968; but if he merely suspects that the person may be armed and *then* stops the person for a traffic violation as an excuse to search, the weapon will not be admissible.

[19]*Chimel v. California*, 395 U.S. 752, 1969, overruled the older rule allowing broader searches found in *Harris v. United States*, 331 U.S. 145, 1947, and *United States v. Rabinowitz*, 339 U.S. 56, 1960.

[20] United States v. Davis, 423 F.2d 974, 1970.

[21] United States v. Robinson, 414 U.S. 218, 1973, and Gustafson v. Florida, 414 U.S. 260, 1973. New York, California and Hawaiis State supreme courts have limited this recent expansion of police search freedom, however.

[15]*Stoner v. California*, 376 U.S. 483, 1964.
[16]*Frazier v. Cupp*, 394 U.S. 731, 1969.
[17]*Chimel v. California*, 395 U.S. 752, 1969. Note that the same limitations on what types of articled (fruits of the crime, etc.) may be seized under a search warrant also apply in warrantless searches according to the law in the particular jurisdiction.

8

Once in jail, an arrestee or his property room effects may be researched without a warrant where the searches are not unreasonably made, i.e., harassment searches.[22]

The right of officers to search a car beyond the reach of the subject being arrested, for example in the closed trunk or even the locked glove compartment, would have to be based on grounds other than the arrest itself, i.e., on probable cause to search those areas, on consent, or "plain sight," or on a valid inventory.

When probable cause exists and the evidence is contained within a moving (or about to be moved) vehicle, officers may search.[23] There is a significant difference in the necessity for immediate action between searches of buildings and searches of vehicles which may speedily be moved out of the jurisdiction before a search warrant can be obtained. An occupied car on a highway is movable, and the persons within it are alerted to the presence of officers. The evidence may never again be located if courts were to require officers to obtain a warrant to search under these circumstances. To conduct a warrantless search of a "moving" vehicle, the officer should have that amount of information which would cause a court to readily issue a search warrant if there were time to procure one. The officer may make the search without first arresting the person. The search will be upheld under the vehicle exception if the essential requirements of probable cause are shown to have existed prior to the search.[24]

Where No Right to Protection Exists

Seizures of evidence without a search is not a violation of the Fourth Amendment

when officers are lawfully present and the article seized is seen by them. Courts do not require officers to leave obvious evidence to be destroyed, but officers must not be trespassers at the time the evidence is observed. Furthermore, if an officer is a trespasser when he does see evidence, he cannot then procure a search warrant on the basis of the information he acquired as a trespasser.[25]

The protection offered by constitutional provisions are to protect persons against the acts of government officers, not private parties. Therefore, if a private person obtains evidence through unlawful entrance or burglary the evidence may be used against the criminal defendant. Of course, if an officer initiated the private persons action or participated in it, the evidence would be excluded. Searches and seizures are unlawful when they unreasonably intrude into areas where the person can reasonably expect privacy, but not outside those areas. Open fields, public streets and other places of similar description are outside the restrictions of the Fourth Amendment.[26]

Inventories of vehicles which come into the hands of the police through impounding procedures are permitted. The inventory made of the vehicle is for the purpose of making an inventory of its contents to protect the owner rather than a search for evidence of an offense. The officers intrusion is only justifiable if it is a good faith attempt to protect the property in the car. In effect, the evidence is discovered "accidentally" while the officer is doing what he has a right to do and where he has legitimate cause to be.[27]

[22]United States v. Edwards, U.S. , 1974. Several states have more limited rules.

[23] Texas v. White, U.S. ,1975.

[24]Carrol v. United States, 267 U.S. 132, 1925; Chambers v. Maroney, 399 U.S. 42, 1970. If the car should more properly be considered to be a part of a household, for instance it is parked in a persons driveway, and there is no danger that it will be moved, a warrant is necessary. Coolidge v. New Hampshire, 403 U.S. 443, 1971.

[25]The "plain view" doctrine was discussed in Coolidge v. New Hampshire, 403 U.S. 443, 1971.

[26]The reasonable expectation of privacy analysis, discussed at length in Katz v. United States, 389 U.S. 347, 1967, greatly limits some uses of the "plain view" doctrine. For instance, police look in defendants window from a fire escape. They are not trespassing, but may violate the defendants reasonable expectation that no one would look in his window.

[27]Cooper v. California, 386 U.S. 58, 1967; Harris v. United States, 390 U.S. 234, 1968; Cady v. Dombrowski, 413 U.S. 1074, 1973.

278

POLICE SCIENCE NOTES

POLICIES, PROCEDURES AND REGULATIONS

Good, effective management techniques applied to any organization require that each person within the agency knows what is expected of him and what to expect of others as they carry out their functions and bring the group effort to life. Professional management is important to police departments, too. All officers and employees should be well informed as to what they are to do, how they are to do it, and the goals to be attained by both their own unit and the department as a whole.

Every person in the organization should know exactly the person who is his superior as well as those who are his subordinates.

Channels should be established through which information flows up and down and through which authority is delegated. These lines of control permit the delegation of authority, the placing of responsibility, the supervision of work, and the coordination of effort. Lines of control should be clearly defined and well understood by all members so that each may know to whom he is responsible and who, in turn, is responsible to him.

Sound and adequate enforcement policies are essential to gaining enforcement objectives and will guide police officers in putting into effect the kind of enforcement program envisioned by the administration. Clear statements of policy will help to resolve doubts in determining administrative intent. Policy development is essential to the success of any organization, and policies should be in writing so that they can be used as the basis on which the departmental operations are constructed.

Policy indicates the general course of direction of an organization, within which the activities of the personnel and units must operate. This establishment of *general* administrative guidelines relates to and complements the main objectives of the organization. For example, the policy con-

cerning the issuance of citations in traffic accident cases might take the following form: "Violations of driving regulations cause traffic accidents, and accidents may be reduced to effective traffic law enforcement. Violators should be issued citations when evidence exists to justify such action." The intent of this policy statement is to inform officers that the policy of the department is to enforce laws. Obviously, this policy is not concerned with the procedures to be followed in preparing each citation, nor does it establish any precise rules. Procedures and rules and regulations must not only follow policy, but must originate from policy.

Established policy, although allowing individual supervisors to think for themselves, limits possible mistakes within manageable bounds. Independent thinking should be encouraged because it develops administrative abilities. Potential executives can be developed only by permitting discretion and initiative on the part of the supervisors. Carefully delineated policy statements allow this latitude.

The term *Policy* is not synonymous with *Procedure,* nor do either of these terms have the same meaning as *Rules* and *Regulations.* The following definitions are offered to clarify and insure uniformity of terminology:

Policy

Policy consists of principles and values which guide the performance of a department in a particular situation. It is a statement of guiding principles which should be followed in activities which are directed toward the attainment of department objectives. Policy is formulated by analyzing objectives and determining through research those principles which will best guide the department in achieving its objectives. Policy is based upon police ethics and experience, the desires of the community and the mandate of the law.

Policy is articulated to inform the public and department employees of the principles which will be adhered to in the performance of the law enforcement function. Additionally, policy establishes operational standards to assist department employees in the necessary exercise of discretion in discharging their responsibility.

An officer in the performance of his duty is confronted with an infinite variety of complex situations which require police action. Since policy is objective rather than situation oriented, it is broad enough in scope to encompass most situations. Policy, therefore, must be stated in general terms.

Procedure

A procedure is a method of performing an operation or a manner of proceeding on a course of action. It differs from policy in that it directs action in a particular situation to perform a specific task within the guidelines of policy. Both policies and procedures are objective oriented; however, policy establishes limits of action while procedure directs response within those limits.

Rule or Regulation

A rule or regulation is a specific prohibition or requirement which is stated to prevent deviations from policy or procedure. Rules and regulations allow little deviation other than for stated exceptions.

Many departments have been studied by police management consultants, and the results of these surveys are, with few exceptions, predictable. The larger the agency the better their policies and procedures (and the greater the change that they are all in writing and periodically reviewed and changed to fit present circumstances.

Policy and procedure formulation require planning and research. The larger agencies can afford such activities but the smaller ones cannot. The larger the organization is the greater the likelihood that there

is a formalized planning and research unit with permanent staff personnel. Of the nearly 40,000 police departments in the United States, 98.9% have less than 100 personnel, and 82.2% have less than five.

There should be written directives applicable to auxiliary officers. At the very minimum these should cover such matters as eligibility for membership, application procedures, use of equipment and the wearing of the uniform, agency organization, disciplinary procedures, powers of arrest, use of force (including carrying of weapons both on and off duty), pursuit driving restrictions, and procedures for separation from the force.

Sworn officers are administered oaths before entering upon their duties. The intention is to impress upon officers that their conduct must be exemplary. Oaths of office for the police and codes of ethics are usually brief, but their every word is of the greatest import.

The departmental oath for auxiliary police may be included in the application for membership in the auxiliary police. The following oath is typical:

I hereby acknowledge my complete understanding that the standby law enforcement assignment for which I am volunteering carries with it the requirement that I will, without question, obey and execute to the best of my ability the legal orders of those designated to supervise and command my activities; that I am to complete all assigned training courses; and that my violation or disregard of the Rules and Regulations of my organization will be cause for disciplinary action or dismissal. Furthermore, I understand that any false statements intentionally made in my application disqualifies me for membership in the

_____Police Auxiliary.

Signed:_____
Date:_____19____

The community expects better and more moral behavior from the police than they do of both other governmental employees and members of the private sector. These expectations apply both on and off duty, and all officers are subjected to close scrutiny in all their statements and actions. The community demands that those who enforce group standards rigidly abide by them.

Following are basic principles guiding conduct applicable to the police:

Courtesy

Officers are expected to be courteous at all times no matter how great the provocation, even if such would cause others to lose their tempers. This is not to say that they are to be servile. Although it is true that they are servants of the public need, they are not servants of individual members of the community as officers act within their sphere of authority. It is not difficult to be courteous when one learns to be an *objective* enforcer of the law, and this means that personal prejudices and anomosities are to be repressed. Officers should be particularly attentive to persons who seek information or assistance and in each case try to put themselves in the "others shoes"- no officer should act toward persons in any manner other than what hewould reasonably expect from them under similar circumstances. It must be constantly borne in mind by policemen that many persons whom they will meet professionally will be under great stress and may act in ways that they will later regret. But the officer who acts unprofessionally will be remembered negatively. The person who provoked the officer will then blame the officer for all that transpired, and the law breaker will then have a "patsy" on which to blame his own faults.

Punctuality

Officers should be punctual in their engagements and expeditious in the performance of their duties. Again, the community expects more from them than from others.

Professional Objectivity

The professional officer is just, impartial and reasonable in his enforcement of the laws he is sworn to uphold. Objective law enforcement never includes overstepping the limits of legal authority and power, and the officer's action or inaction will never be for personal gain or in vengeance.

Protection of Public Funds

Officers are custodians of the public property entrusted to their care and shall not misuse their equipment or otherwise be wasteful of public funds.

Cooperation

Law Enforcement is a cooperative effort among the community and other governmental agencies. Full cooperation by policemen should be offered to both private and public groups so that the safety and welfare of the community will be assured.

Communication

The professional officer actively disseminates practical and useful information to others regarding matters of the public safety and welfare. He does not passively wait for others to come to him.

Exemplary Conduct

The professional officer's conduct, both public and private, is such that the public regards his as an example of fidelity, stability and morality.

Governmental Allegiance

Officers should be faithful in the allegiance to our government, loyal to the ethics of their profession, and accept as a sacred obligation their responsibility as citizens to support the Constitutions of the Nation and their State and to defend our principles of liberty. Departmental rules, violation of which subjects the member to disciplinary action, often include the following:

Respect, Language

Active lack of respect, manifested by abusive language or non-verbal communication directed toward other personnel or members of the public, is prohibited.

Disobedience

The violation of or deliberate delay in the prompt completion of activities directed to be performed by the lawful orders of any superior officer is prohibited.

Confidentiality

Divulgence of any information concerning the plans, actions, internal activities or case materials of the police department without authority is prohibited.

Intoxication

The use at any time of any intoxicating drug or material proscribed by law is prohibited, and reporting for duty while under the influence of the consumption of any intoxicant while on duty is prohibited, although the ingestion of intoxicants necessarily required by the nature of the assigned (usually undercover) duties being performed by the officer may be permitted.

Misconduct

Any breach of the peace, neglect of duty, or misconduct either within or without the jurisdiction which tends to subvert the good order, efficiency, or discipline of the department or the auxiliary force or which reflects discredit upon the department is prohibited.

Misuse of Position

Affiliation with any group which professes to represent the police department or other agency of the criminal justice system while purporting to act as a representative of the police agency, and utilizing or making reference to one's affiliation with the department to sway others for political purposes is prohibited without lawful permission of superiors of the department for professional purpose.

Wearing of Uniform and Use of Equipment

The auxiliary police will wear only prescribed or issued uniform items, utilize only prescribed or issued equipment or weapons, and maintain these items; and any officer failing to meet these requirements shall be subject to disciplinary action.

Off-Duty Weapons

Off-duty auxiliary officers shall neither carry nor utilize any weapon in contravention to the laws applicable to citizens not falling within the statutory exemptions concerning the possession or use of weapons. (Or, for those agencies which permit by regulation the carrying of off duty weapons). Off duty auxiliary officers may carry any weapon permitted by law upon prior approval by and registration with the department.

Any action by an auxiliary police officer that is illegal or contrary to departmental rules and regulations subjects that officer to disciplinary action, including separation from the force.